The Richest Girl in England:

Katherine Manners, Duchess of Buckingham

Lita-Rose Betcherman

BEV EDITIONS

The Richest Girl in England

© 2017 Lita-Rose Betcherman

All Rights Reserved.

Published by Bev Editions at Kindle.

Bev Editions

131 Bloor Street West, Suite 711

Toronto, Ontario, Canada

M5S 1S3

www.beveditions.com

ISBN: 9781549640254

PART ONE:

Buckingham

CHAPTER ONE

The girl watched the rooster strutting around the barnyard followed by a line of clucking hens. She thought that the rooster was lord of the barnyard, just as her father was lord of the castle. But her father never strutted like the rooster. He was a fine gentleman with a kind word for everyone, even the lowliest of servants. While deep in her thoughts, the girl noticed Margaret Flower, who looked after the poultry, coming into the barnyard.

Disliking this servant, she hurried behind a haystack. From her hiding place, she saw the woman go over to a pile of dung and pick up a glove that lay on top of it. She recognized the small glove as belonging to her half-brother Francis. The woman sniffed it, spat on it, stuck it in her bag, and scuttled away. Should she tell her father, the little girl wondered? She had gone to him before with tales of the strange behavior of this servant and of her mother, an ugly crone who came to the castle every day to do the charring.

These two women frightened her. But when she asked her father to send them away, he explained that it was his responsibility as the landowner to help the poor tenantry by providing employment. Besides, he said with a laugh and a kiss on Kate's forehead, Mother Flower and her daughter were harmless. Although disturbed by the glove incident, Kate was a perceptive child and understood that this was no time to bother her father and stepmother with tattle-tales. Two-year-old Francis, Lord Roos, was lying ill.

For ten days, Doctor Ridgely from Newark had been staying at the castle, bleeding the sick boy under his tongue and attaching leeches to his frail body. Packages arrived daily from the apothecary. It was all the worse because only a year before, Henry, the older of her two little brothers, had died of an undiagnosed sickness. It was like a curse upon the family, Kate overheard her parents say.

Kate's father, Francis Manners, had inherited the earldom of Rutland in 1612 on the death of his childless elder brother, Roger. After the lean years of a younger son, when his only recourse had been to marry two rich widows, his sudden inheritance of the title and the wealth that came with it had seemed like manna from heaven. Although he regretted the early death of his brother Roger, he could not help feeling fortunate. He had a kind wife who had borne him two sons, and a daughter from his first wife who was the apple of his eye. Now, two years later, one son was dead and the other at death's door. If Francis died without a male heir, by law the earldom and all the entailed land and estates would go to his younger brother George. His widow and Kate would have to leave Belvoir Castle, the Rutlands' ancestral home in Leicestershire.

Kate was a wan child. Francis feared she too was not destined for a long life. Thinking to improve her health, he insisted on her riding every day, and Lady Rutland had ordered a beautiful green velvet saddle for her. At eleven, it was time for Kate to learn to ride sidesaddle instead of astride like a boy. She now learned to hook her knee over a pommel on the saddle, enabling her to sit sideways with her riding skirt draped decorously over her legs; a second pommel wedged her knee securely. Lady Katherine was soon seen galloping sidesaddle over the hundreds of acres belonging to the castle.

When little Francis survived in spite of Dr. Ridgely's dire prognosis, the Earl attributed it to the fact that he himself had recently been received into the Catholic Church. It had been his second wife Cecily, a practicing Catholic, who had made him see that the old religion was the true one. Despite anti-Catholic laws following the plot to blow up the House of Commons in 1605, the Earl had converted to Catholicism. Belvoir Castle had a resident priest, who retired discreetly to his private quarters when visitors came to the castle, and mass was regularly observed by the family and all the servants. Young Kate was brought up a Catholic.

The other passion at Belvoir Castle was horses, and Kate assimilated this as naturally as she accepted the Catholic religion. The Rutlands had been breeding hobbyhorses at Helmsley Castle in Yorkshire for generations. Their trainers had been experimenting with cross breeding native horses

The Richest Girl in England

with imported Arabians. The Helmsley stud produced the finest racehorses in England, consistent winners at King James's new racecourse at Newmarket.

Belvoir Castle ("Beever" Castle, the locals called it) was always full of company, with the gentry from surrounding counties coming to pay court to the Earl and Countess of Rutland. Among the most assiduous in attendance were Sir Thomas Compton and his wife. Obviously a well-nourished woman herself, Lady Compton would bustle over with gifts of food from their small estate: her "hartichokes", cucumbers, veal, lambs, and rabbits enriched Belvoir's larder.

Sir Thomas was her third husband. Her first marriage to an elderly widower, Sir George Villiers of Brooksby in Leicestershire, had lifted her well above her station as a poor relation of an old established gentry family. She had brought up Sir George's two sons and produced three of her own. The eldest of her sons, John Villiers, a quiet man in his twenties, sometimes came to Belvoir to play gleek - a game of cards for three persons - with the Earl and his wife. The couple loved cards and played frequently with the Comptons. Eleven-year-old Kate was often at the card table with her elders. During the game, Lady Compton would chatter endlessly about her middle son by her first marriage to Sir George Villiers.

Young George had just returned from three years in a French academy, and his mother was unstoppable in singing his praises. Although her ravings about his handsomeness and his charm hardly disturbed the game that was played for money, when she spoke of his skillful horsemanship acquired at the French academy she caught the Earl's attention. It was an open secret that she had dispatched her son to London to secure a well-to-do wife and a place at the royal court. Her ambitions were relatively modest at this time. The intended bride was an heiress of a deceased minor official at Whitehall Palace. It is possible that, sitting at the Rutlands' card table with young Lady Katherine, she raised her ambitions for her son.

Kate was not pretty, but she was very rich. She'd inherited a fortune from her late mother, the heiress of a wealthy Wiltshire knight. Kate's inheritance had been supplemented by a legacy of 500£ from her uncle Roger, the fifth Earl of Rutland. Despite her lack of beauty, the sixth Earl knew that suitors from all over the kingdom would seek her hand. When the time came, he would have his pick of young men for her. He would have none other than a Catholic son-in-law of course, and the relatively small size of the Catholic nobility was a limiting factor.

Meanwhile, there were those other than Lady Compton who were taking an interest in George Villiers. A cabal of courtiers, with the blessing of the Archbishop of Canterbury, was seeking a good-looking young man to replace King James's current favourite, the Earl of Somerset. The direction of England's foreign affairs was at stake. Somerset and his backers, the powerful Howard family, were the leaders of the pro-Spanish faction at court. The cabal favoured alliances with the Protestant states and wished to end Somerset's influence over the king.

Although James had fathered four children with his Danish wife Queen Anne, his sexual preference was definitely for men. The extraordinarily handsome newcomer from Leicestershire could be just the man to appeal to James and supplant Somerset. The introduction took place at Belvoir Castle during the king's progress in the summer of 1614.

James, like Elizabeth before him, lessened the cost of running the royal household by sponging on the nobility. When the king went on a progress the court travelled with him, thus a royal visit entailed feeding, accommodating, and entertaining hundreds of people. A royal visit was an expensive honour. Since royal patronage was the end-all and be-all, the nobles beggared themselves building magnificent country houses to keep the monarch travelling in the style they'd accustomed him. Luckily, the Earls of Rutland could well afford it.

The welcome at Belvoir was so lavish the castle became a favourite stop for James from his first visit in 1603 on his way from Scotland to ascend the English throne. Rather tastelessly, in 1612 he came with his huge retinue barely a month after the funeral of the fifth earl and the death of the sixth Earl's heir. Now he was on his third visit. George Villiers certainly caught the King's eye at Belvoir in 1614, but a jealous Somerset kept him at a distance. George would not have noticed the host's eleven year-old daughter. There was no doubt, however, that he was mightily impressed by the splendour of Belvoir Castle.

Belvoir was the second castle of that name to be built on a summit overlooking the Vale of Belvoir. Reconstructed in the 1500s by the first Earl of Rutland, it reproduced the turrets and castellation of the original medieval castle. In its lordly eminence, it could be seen from miles around. The sixth earl had done little to the exterior beyond erecting an enormous impresa on the roofline displaying the coat-of-arms of his house. In the castle were turkey carpets, heavy oak furniture, walnut paneling, tapestries, family portraits, suits of armour, and a canopied bed Queen Elizabeth slept in on her numerous progresses through Leicestershire.

Kate had lived at Belvoir since she was nine. She knew every nook and cranny in the castle, and was very happy there. But a sorrow in her young life (not forgetting her constant sadness over her sick little brother) was that she never knew her mother. She had died of smallpox when Kate was two years old. At Belvoir, there was a painting of a young woman with golden hair in a red cloak. Kate's nurse told her it was of her mother. Kate would look up at it for long periods of time. Out of consideration for his second wife, the Earl seldom spoke of the first.

But Kate would have certainly heard that her mother, known as Lady Bevill from her first marriage, had the honour of dancing in one of Queen Anne's Twelfth Night masques - the famous Masque of Blackness of 1605 when the Queen and her ladies blackened their faces and arms to play Ethiopians. Kate was proud that her mother had been one of Queen Anne's favoured court ladies before her early death.

Perhaps because she longed for her mother, she had never taken to her father's second wife. Still, she could not have had a better stepmother. Lady Rutland was protective and kind to her, gave her gifts of beautiful jewellery, and saw that she received the conventional training for a young lady. Kate learned to dance and play the lute.

On her own she discovered history and poetry. Her father, who had travelled a great deal on the Continent and was well read, had a library with the best of current writing as well as the Latin classics in translation. Kate whiled away many an hour in the library, copying some of her reading into her notebooks. In one she copied excerpts from a history of the religious wars in France, as well as verses and prose from Sir Philip Sidney's romance, *Arcadia*.

There was a close family connection with the famous poet-soldier as the fifth Earl of Rutland had married Sir Philip's only daughter, Elizabeth, who had died shortly after him in August 1612. Instead of lying beside her husband in the Rutland crypt, she had chosen to be buried beside her father in St. Paul's Cathedral. Kate, having no playmates, tended to listen in on the adults' talk and she learned that her aunt and uncle had not been happily married. It was beyond her child's understanding that the reason was her late uncle's homosexuality.

Though the Earl and Countess tolerated minor pilfering, sometime in 1615 it was brought to their attention (perhaps by Kate) that the servant Margaret Flower was stealing great quantities of provisions from the butler's pantry. Deer pies and partridges, salmon and trout from the castle's fishponds, sugar loaves and bottles of French wine found their way into Margaret's capacious bag.

The good-hearted Lady Rutland decided regretfully that she would have to let Margaret go. She treated her most generously, giving her 40 shillings (the equivalent of a year's pay), a bolster, and a woolen mattress. Mother Flower still worked regularly at the castle, although the servants noticed the Earl's joshing manner with her ceased. Rumours drifted back from the village that the Flower women - there was another daughter named Philippa who was regarded as nothing better than a slut - were cursing the Rutlands publicly and promising revenge for Margaret's dismissal.

As she entered adolescence, Kate's health deteriorated. There were now two sickly children at Belvoir. The apothecary was kept busy sending over physic that, in truth, weakened them further. Francis, the poor child, was reportedly "most barbarously and inhumanly tortured by a strange sickness" while Kate suffered "extreme maladies and unusual fits." Gradually, Kate got better in spite of the purges and leeches that sucked her blood. By the time of the King's next visit in 1617, she was quite recovered.

King James was on his way back from a progress to Scotland, his other kingdom. The Earl of Rutland had been among the party of nobles who accompanied him, so at a hint from the King he had extended the hospitality of Belvoir Castle. James's purpose in undertaking the arduous trip was to force the episcopalian Church of England upon the Presbyterian kirk that, for its part, abominated bishops. Defraying the cost of the journey by visiting his nobles was essential, as James's profligate spending on his favourites, formerly the Earl of Somerset, but of late the Earl of Buckingham, had helped to empty his personal treasury, the Privy Purse. Who was this Buckingham? None other than Lady Compton's son George.

Knighted in 1615, he had become Master of the Horse in 1616 (a position that made him the close companion of a hunter king), Viscount and Baron in August 1616 and Earl in January 1617. The changeover in power at court had been breathtakingly swift, hastened by the fact that the Earl of Somerset and his countess had been found guilty of the murder of his former friend, Sir Thomas Overbury, and the couple now resided in the Tower of London.

Somerset's fall had brought down the Howards, the family of Lady Somerset, and a whole new power structure was forming at court around the rising favourite, the Earl of Buckingham. Kate knew all about the good fortune of Lady Compton's son. The year before, her father had received the Order of the Garter in the same ceremony as George Villiers. These honours had surprised the court because Rutland had been converted by a recusant wife and Villiers was little known and poor up to that time. Rutland had come back from Hampton Court Palace to regale his ladies with the astonishing rise of this man who, as a youth, had been a familiar of the grooms at Belvoir's stables.

Kate, now a grown-up fourteen, stood with her parents at the castle gate to greet King James when he came to Belvoir in 1617. (In 1614 she could only peek out of the nursery.) She saw a red-faced man who was neither tall nor short, neither handsome nor homely, who wore a quilted doublet and wide pleated breeches that made him look fat above his spindly legs. She knew that he was anointed by God to rule his three kingdoms – her parents had explained all that - but she thought he looked an ordinary man.

When her father presented her, James stuck out his hand for her to kiss. To her surprise it was grimy, with dirt under the fingernails. Giving her a hard look, he said to the Earl in a broad Scots burr, "She na' be bonny but I dinna doubt she is a good lass." The Rutlands had to be content with that.

If the King was disappointing, Kate was utterly dazzled by the favourite. Buckingham was the handsomest man she had ever seen. Tall, slim, with curling brown hair and brilliant blue eyes, he was clean-shaven, making which made him look younger than his twenty-five years. A close-fitting doublet of white satin with slashed sleeves enhanced his magnificent build, a short skirt and long hose that showed off a fine pair of legs.

Kate said shyly, "When I was a little girl I sometimes saw you riding in the valley below Belvoir."

"Oh, so you were the little rider who flew past me on a small roan. I thought you were a boy because you rode astride," he told her.

Seemingly taking this as an aspersion on her upbringing of her stepdaughter, Lady Rutland sniffed, "Lady Katherine was riding sidesaddle by the time she was twelve."

Buckingham raised his eyebrows at this tart remark, and looking straight at Kate he winked. She could hardly restrain herself from laughing. Just then, the King roared out, "Steenie, where are ye?" With a bow, and still smiling, he left them to hasten to the King's side. As Kate would learn, the Master of the King's Horse was kept on a tighter rein than any of the thoroughbreds he purchased for the royal stables.

"Why does King James call him Steenie?' Kate asked her father.

"It is the King's short form for Stephen," he told her. "He claims to see a resemblance between Buckingham and a painting of St. Stephen." This would have her rummaging through her father's library over the next few days, searching for a likeness of St. Stephen.

There was no more opportunity for her to talk to Buckingham as King James commanded him to be at his side every minute. He leaned on his shoulder, hugged him, and slobbered kisses on his face. When he kissed him on the mouth Kate noticed that her stepmother would turn aside and begin telling her beads, imperceptibly moving them from one cupped hand to the other while she silently mouthed Hail Marys. One court watcher would later recall that he had never seen any fond husband make so much or so great dalliance over his beautiful spouse as King James did over Buckingham.

King James lived for hunting and hawking. Belvoir had a well-stocked deer park and every day began with the hullaballoo of the baying hounds and the huntmaster's horn. A blast of the horn, and the hunters set off at a gallop. The King disdained to hold his horse's reins; footmen ran on either side in relays, trying unsuccessfully to keep pace with the horse whipped into a lather by its enthusiastic rider. The King fell off repeatedly during the hunt, her father told Kate with a hint of a twinkle in his eyes. Kate was alight with interest when her father spoke of the superb way Buckingham sat a horse. The Earl, himself no mean judge of horseflesh, said that since his appointment as Master of the Horse, Buckingham had stocked the royal stud at Tutbury with the best of the native breeds as well as imported Spanish horses. This included Buckingham's own favourite, the small-size jennets. King James never tired of proclaiming that Steenie had given him the best horses and hounds he'd ever had.

At the end of the day, the hunters would return, their faces smeared with blood. The bloodying of the hunters was a ritual. The deer, with arrows still sticking in its hide, would be cut open and the King would wade

The Richest Girl in England

in the blood. He would then dip his hands in the animal's blood and press them on the courtiers' faces. The blood was not to be wiped off until the return from the hunt.

While the men were out, Kate helped Lady Rutland oversee preparations for the evening feast. The fishpond was emptied of its trout and salmon. Gigots of mutton, sides of beef, swans, and geese by the dozen were roasting and smoking up the kitchen. A huge round of Cheshire cheese sweated on a board. The pastry chef was shaping marzipan into a throne with a glaze of real molten gold on the heraldic arms at the top. All this to be washed down with gallons of claret from Bordeaux, sherry from Spain, Rhenish wine, and beer and ale brewed on the premises.

A ticklish question was where to place the enormous saltcellars on the long board table. How many should sit above the salt with King James and the leading courtiers, and how many of the less important were to sit below the salt? One would have to be the Master of Ceremonies to get this right, sighed Lady Rutland. The estimable woman was educating Kate for the role cut out for her in life.

At the feasts, King James did not gorge himself as others were doing, but he drank white wine steadily so that at the end of each meal he was tipsy. His fondling of Buckingham increased, and so did Lady Rutland's silent praying. The courtiers were used to this royal display of affection; they had seen it with the old favourite. Once he had been made an earl, however, Somerset had not hidden his aversion to the King's embraces and had reportedly refused to share the royal bedchamber. The courtiers suspected that this had more than a little to do with his fall from grace. Buckingham on the other hand, though notoriously fond of women, did not make the same mistake. He returned the King's affection with great public show, calling himself "Your Majesty's dog."

A month after the royal visit, Lord and Lady Rutland were getting ready to attend the wedding of Buckingham's older brother, Sir John Villiers, to the daughter of Sir Edward Coke. King James had decreed that the wedding should take place at Hampton Court Palace in the presence of the royal family. Lady Rutland purchased two very expensive gilt bowls for a wedding present, and the steward hired a boat to take the Earl and Countess to Hampton Court Palace. A disappointed Kate was left at Belvoir with her little brother. Treating her as a child seemed unfair to her as the bride herself was only fifteen.

As everyone knew, Frances Coke was a sacrificial lamb to her father's ambitions. Sir Edward Coke, Lord High Justice of the King's Bench, had fallen out of favour because of his judicial assaults on King James's prerogative powers. Suspended from the bench, he knew that the only way to get back into the king's good graces was through Buckingham. Coke's estranged wife, Lady Hatton, was a very wealthy woman and, as with all wives, what she had was at her husband's command. Buckingham's mother, Lady Compton, was looking out for rich wives for her sons and Frances Coke seemed ideal for her eldest son John - the Earl of Rutland's card-playing friend.

When she and her powerful son Buckingham made an offer to Coke for his daughter, he was only too willing to accept. Unfortunately Frances, a willful young girl who had learned to get her way by playing her quarrelling parents off against each other, was repelled by her father's choice of a bridegroom and refused to marry him. Sir Edward Coke proved himself the harshest of fathers. He sent a brutal son from his first marriage to forcibly abduct her from her mother's house, and, not stopping short of physical violence, her father had her tied to a bedpost and whipped until she gave in. What the wedding guests beheld was a beautiful young girl with the good fortune to marry into the family of the new favourite while King James beamed his approval. The bride herself was the picture of misery at what should have been her shining hour.

Did Kate feel sympathy for a young girl her own age who had been forced into a loveless marriage? Probably not. In her world it was an accepted fact of life that a father chose his daughter's husband. But she was soon to hear of an aristocratic young woman who broke the rule.

The marriage of Sir James Hay to the young beauty, Lady Lucy Percy, was the culmination of a romance that had titillated the court for months. Hay was one of the Scots who had come down to England when James ascended the throne in 1603. This suave gentleman lived luxuriously on royal grants and kickbacks from his office as Master of the Wardrobe. The courtiers were agog over the affair as they had been over the forced marriage of Frances Coke to Buckingham's brother. This time it was not the bride who objected to the marriage but her father. Henry Percy, ninth Earl of Northumberland, was among the greatest landlords in England. Proud and arrogant, he claimed to trace his lineage back to the Norman Conquest.

An object lesson of the proverb that pride goeth before a fall, Northumberland had been convicted (probably wrongly) of involvement in the Gunpowder Plot to assassinate King James and had been imprisoned in the Tower of London since 1606. By bribing the Lieutenant of the Tower, he had converted a section of the Tower into his private castle where he continued to live like a great lord, lacking only his freedom. As proud as ever, he could not stomach his daughter marrying a Scot – a landless one at that - and refused to sanction the marriage. So besotted was the middle-aged Hay with the seventeen-year-old girl who, by consensus of the courtiers, was judged "the most lovely damsel in all England" that he took her without a dowry. Adding spice to the romance, for a time her father kept her with him in the Tower to stop the marriage.

King James had supported Hay's suit all along and at the extravagant wedding held at the Wardrobe (Hay's residence in Blackfriars) on November 17, 1617, he himself gave away the bride. The other guests of honour were the Earl of Buckingham and the heir apparent to the throne, Charles Prince of Wales. It can be imagined with what interest Kate followed the romantic story of Lucy Percy.

CHAPTER TWO

The Earl of Rutland had recently been appointed to the Privy Council. This body composed of the great officers of state and a selection of judges, nobles, and bishops administered the government of the realm under the King's absentee direction. James rarely presided over the Council. He disliked London and left the humdrum task of running the kingdom to his Council, making his wishes known through one or another of the councillors. Most of his time was spent hunting at Royston or Newmarket or at his favourite palace Theobalds in Hertfordshire.

In appointing councillors, King James chose men he could count on to carry out his policies. In 1617, he was seeking to arrange a marriage between his son, Prince Charles, and the youngest daughter of King Philip III of Spain. Accordingly, he made several appointments of pro-Spanish nobles of whom the Earl of Rutland was one. Like virtually all the Anglo-Catholic nobility, Rutland favoured an alliance with Spain over one with France, the other major European power. The King of Spain, who bore the honorary title of the Catholic King, was the traditional ally of the papacy and its secular arm.

The Privy Council sat at Westminster Hall along with the law courts and the Houses of Parliament - the Lords in the upper chamber, the Commons in the lower. A short distance away, accessible either by the River Thames or the King's Road, stood the palace of Whitehall, the official royal residence. The palace precinct was a hive of ministerial offices and courtiers' lodgings. To assume his new duties the Earl leased a town house not far from Westminster and Whitehall. Kate was thrilled at the prospect of spending some part of the winter in London. All the nobility converged on Whitehall Palace for the Christmas festivities presided over by the King and Queen, and her father had promised to take her to the masques and banquets. She would have the opportunity to catch glimpses of the man who filled her daydreams. Even in her wildest dreams, the most she could imagine was touching Buckingham's hand in a saraband or a courante. In anticipation, she asked for more lessons from the dancing master.

In late December the Earl and Countess of Rutland and their two children took up residence at Salisbury House in the Strand, a stately mansion of brick and timber built fifteen years earlier by Sir Robert Cecil, the first Earl of Salisbury. A lovely garden sloped down to the river, serving as the main highway. The location had the added advantage for the Countess and Kate of being adjacent to the New Exchange. It was an emporium selling luxury goods that the business-minded Salisbury had built to compete with the Royal Exchange where Cornhill and Threadneedle streets converged.

Living in a castle, Kate was not overly impressed by Whitehall Palace. Unlike Belvoir with its turkey carpets, the floors were covered with rushes to warm them in the winter. The rushes were full of movement and she was not surprised to see a mouse scurrying across the floor, pursued by one of the gigantic halberdiers in red livery who stood at attention along the walls. In this respect the King's palace was no different from the humblest London dwelling where straw strewn across the dirt floor unknowingly provided an incubator for plague-bearing rats. The palace was enormous. It accommodated over six hundred servants of the Royal Household, from the Lord Chamberlain to the necessary rat catcher. The King's private apartments filled one wing of the vast palace. Queen Anne had her own palace, Denmark House, some miles down the Thames. It was there that Kate was presented to Her Majesty.

At first sight, Queen Anne appeared to Kate as a radiant vision. In a pink and gold costume with an enormous farthingale no less than four feet wide across the hips, her bodice was open down to the pit of her stomach, partially exposing her powdered breasts. Her hair, glittering with diamonds and coloured gems, was piled high on her head and was surmounted by a circlet of false hair arranged in the shape of rays that gave her headdress the appearance of a sunflower. When the Queen beckoned to her to step

However, disaster lurked. At the buffet, the hungry guests "pounced upon the prey like so many harpies" (as reported by the Venetian ambassador) that the table collapsed with "a crash of glass platters." The contrast with the dainty masque she had just witnessed left young Kate in shock. Her father informed her that such unseemly behaviour was only too frequent at James's court.

Every day brought news of fresh honours for the favourite. On the first day of the new year, his master raised him to a marquess – the second highest rank in the peerage, right next to a duke. Then to general disbelief, the King named him Lord High Admiral, the most sought-after post in the land and one for which he had no experience whatsoever. Money to maintain his new honours was showered upon him. And if all this was not enough, King James notified the court that all patronage was to be channelled through the marquess. This made him the most powerful subject in England.

The King widened his favouritism to include Buckingham's family. His mother was created Countess of Buckingham, his elder brother John, Viscount Purbeck, and the younger brother Christopher was made a gentleman of the bedchamber. These two, along with half-brothers, were enriched by grants of patents and monopolies. The Earl of Rutland told his wife and daughter that the nobility resented the meteoric rise of the favourite. Alone with her husband, the Countess did not mince words as to how he earned it.

After the London season, Kate was unable to enjoy Belvoir as she had before. The only thing she seemed to enjoy was riding, and the Countess ordered Weber the tailor to make her a fine riding coat in red velvet. The Earl could not understand his new moody Kate. He suggested taking her to visit the stables at Helmsley Castle in Yorkshire, something she had always begged for, but she did not want to go. Her secret hope was that one day the magnificent Buckingham would come riding towards her and they would gallop off together.

CHAPTER THREE

The family had no sooner taken up residence at Salisbury House for the 1619 winter season when they were greeted with the horrifying news that they were the victims of witchcraft.

The Earl and his younger brother, Sir George Manners, had been at the Newmarket races with the King and had returned to London with the royal party for the Christmas celebrations. At Whitehall Palace, the Earl was taken aside by an acquaintance who told him that his former servants, the Flower women, were under arrest at Lincoln jail for witchcraft that had caused the death of the Earl's son and heir and the sickness of his second son. Sending word to Lady Rutland, he and George galloped off to Lincoln, hell bent for leather.

Like all their contemporaries, the Rutlands believed in witches. The village idiot or an old woman mumbling to herself were taken to be accomplices of the Devil. They worked his evil will on them through their cats or other small animals known as their "familiars." In some cases, the intent to harm was present in the accused, who deluded themselves into believing that they possessed devilish powers to destroy their enemies. In Scotland, King James had persecuted reputed witches and written a treatise on demonology in which he drew wildly improbable conclusions. By the time of his accession to the English throne he had moderated his views somewhat, demanding that the judges dig a little deeper into the testimony of the accusers.

The Earl of Rutland had retained a lawyer by the name of Francis Jephson to prosecute the Flower sisters. With no one to defend them the trial was brief. The Earl of Rutland listened with grim satisfaction as Sir Henry Hobart intoned "guilty as charged" and sentenced the two women to be hanged. Afterwards, Sir Henry condoled with the Earl of Rutland, declaring himself amazed at the wickedness of these women who made a contract with the devil to damn their own souls. On March 11, 1619, Margaret and Philippa Flower were hanged at Lincoln.

At this same time, Queen Anne passed away following several years of ill health. Other than by her son, Prince Charles, she died as unmourned as the witches of Belvoir.

The official period of mourning for the Queen ended in April, but rumours that Buckingham had become romantically involved had Kate moping around Salisbury House, not eating, and refusing to accompany Lady Rutland to court functions. According to court gossip, Buckingham was about to be betrothed to Diana Cecil, the niece of the Earl of Salisbury from whom the Rutlands leased their London house. The Cecils were still pre-eminent among the English aristocracy although their glory days of power were behind them.

The present earl's grandfather, Lord Burghley, had been Queen Elizabeth's chief minister, and his father Robert, the first Earl of Salisbury, had followed in his footsteps, surviving the change of dynasty from the Tudors to the Stuarts to serve as King James's Lord Treasurer and Secretary of State until his death in 1612. The gossip appeared to be confirmed when Lady Diana was mistress of the feast where Buckingham was guest of honour (a well-understood pre-nuptial pairing). Still, months went by and there was no announcement of a betrothal. The Marquess of Buckingham continued to be the most eligible bachelor in the realm. Kate started attending court functions.

As it happened, events moved faster than she could ever have dreamed possible. Before long it was being whispered that Buckingham "had a mind to wed the Earl of Rutland's daughter." It would be overly cynical to assume that he was only interested in Kate's money. No doubt it played a large part, as did the satisfaction of marrying into the family his parents had bent the knee to. But to the courtiers who studied the favourite's every move, he appeared to be genuinely in love. Kate had no doubt that he reciprocated her love. He was tender and loving with her, and honest, confiding his serious hopes and fears that lay hidden from the rest of the world by his habitual levity.

Kate who had never shown much interest in her personal appearance, was having a new wardrobe made up and readily agreed to have her portrait painted by the society painter, William Larkin, who had painted Buckingham.

Over the summer of 1619, Lady Compton was pushing the match for all she was worth. It was no longer a game of cards that brought the favourite's mother to Belvoir Castle, nor did she come bearing gifts of "hartichokes" from her garden; she was there as her son's marriage broker and was demanding a dowry of 20,000£ and lands worth 4,000£ *in rents* a year. The Earl of Rutland thought this was outrageous. Moreover, not only was Buckingham not a Catholic, but he had a reputation for womanizing. Rutland was beginning to have his doubts. To add to the difficulties of concluding the match, the mother countesses had quarreled. Lady Rutland could not abide the puffed-up pride of Lady Buckingham. For a while there was a lull in the marriage negotiations. But Kate was madly in love, and was showing a sharp stubborn streak that her father had not seen before.

At this juncture, a real obstacle was raised by the King. While James approved of the match (he wanted his favourites to marry), he insisted that Buckingham's wife must attend the Church of England. If Katherine Manners would not convert, there would be no marriage. But much as Kate adored George, she could not bring herself to abandon the Catholic faith. King James blamed her Catholic stepmother for influencing her. In fact, it was her father, a convert, who stiffened her resolve to remain faithful to the religion in which she'd been raised. By the end of August, it was common knowledge at court that the match between the Marquess of Buckingham and the Earl of Rutland's daughter was broken off because she would not change her religion.

Such was her sincere Catholicism that she even resisted the King's personal appeals to change her mind. Having been brought up to believe that salvation lay only through the Catholic Church, she was troubled at the prospect of spending the after-life in purgatory or hell. To bring her around, James dispatched the Dean of Westminster, a persuasive cleric named John Williams. Apparently of the view that a lady, especially a young one, could not grapple with a theological argument, Williams made no attempt to relieve her mind to prove that the door to Heaven was open to two fellow nobles. As duels were against the law in England, the principals and their seconds had to go abroad, and Rutland had been considering a venue in France when King James got wind of the matter and put a stop to it. In the present instance, it was Prince Charles who prevented a duel, no doubt tipped off by Buckingham.

Instead of the sword, Buckingham picked up his pen. In a letter bristling with indignation, he told the Earl that his daughter "never received any blemish in her honour but that which came by your own tongue" and that "since you esteem so little of my friendship and her honour" he was breaking off the match and the Earl could bestow his daughter "elsewhere."

That he acted with the King's approval is evident. While the court was buzzing about the so-called abduction, Buckingham posted up to Hampton Court to tell his side of the story to King James before anyone else did. James expressed no opposition to his breaking off the marriage. Buckingham felt so secure in the King's affection he showed utter contempt for the Rutland who was a peer of ancient lineage. He asked James "to lay a strait charge upon my Lord of Rutland to call home his daughter again, or at least I may be secured that, in case I should marry her, I may have so much respite of time given me that of his stock I may sometimes beget one able to serve you in some mean employment."

Faced with the reality of the situation, the Earl of Rutland climbed down from his high horse, but not before pointing out to Buckingham that by breaking the marriage contract, "the fault is only your lordship's if the world talk of us both." Cut to the quick because he felt Kate showed "not a spark of affection" towards him, nevertheless for her sake he humbled himself to the favourite. "Although she deserves not so great a care from a father whom she so little esteems, yet I must preserve her honour if it were with hazard of my life," he wrote Buckingham. If he could be assured that "she is yours" and that his affection had not altered, Buckingham would find him "tractable to deal with like a loving father." It was a complete surrender. Buckingham would have his daughter and the dowry he demanded. Kate was never to know that her adored George was ready to throw her over if her father had not agreed to pay the dowry which, in their better bargaining position, mother and son raised from 4,000£ to 8,000£.

In April, Kate received communion according to the rites of the Church of England. But Buckingham in his arrogance must rub salt in the wounded heart of her father. At the St. George's feast later in the month, it was noticed that he slighted the Earl of Rutland. Yet the consensus was that he must marry the daughter as she had converted for his sake.

On the sixteenth of May 1620, Kate and George were married in a quiet ceremony at Lumley House near Tower Hill, attended only by King James and her father. In spite of all that had happened, Kate was the happiest girl in England. Her dream had come true. She was the wife of the man she adored.

CHAPTER FOUR

Kate was living her dream. Every day she was freshly enchanted with her handsome husband. Above all, never was a bride more satisfied with her new husband's lovemaking. She looked forward to an idyllic future with George.

Nevertheless she soon learned that there was a price to pay for her happiness. She realized she would never have George entirely to herself. Kate discovered immediately after her marriage that the King and the entire Villiers family came along with George. Their honeymoon was spent accompanying the King on his summer progress with George's relatives forming the inner circle around him. King James had made George's family his own. Kate was already acquainted with some of her new in-laws. There was George's sister Susan and her husband Sir William Feilding; George's elder brother Viscount Purbeck, whom she had known since childhood as John Villiers, and his unhappy wife the former Frances Coke; and George's younger brother Christopher, or Kit, for whom the Countess of Buckingham was trying to find a rich wife.

But Kate was meeting some of the family for the first time, one being George's stepfather, Sir Thomas Compton. This country gentleman was usually left by his wife to tramp the fields of Leicestershire with his dogs (in fact, she had declined to have him named an earl when she was created the Countess of Buckingham) but on this occasion he was present with his brother. The brother was newly raised to the peerage as Earl of

Northampton, thanks to Buckingham. He was anxious to increase his supporters in the House of Lords.

The King and his entourage descended *en masse* upon the great landowners of Hampshire, Wiltshire, Surrey and Essex. At every stop there were hunting parties and entertainments. While staying at Wilton, the Earl of Pembroke's country house in Wiltshire, the King visited Stonehenge and became very curious about the strange stone pillars in their mysterious circle. Since no locals could shed light on their origins, Inigo Jones, the Surveyor of the King's Works, was sent for. He opined that it was the remains of a Roman temple, an opinion at odds with the view of most antiquarians that the site went back to the Druids.

The controversy delighted James, who liked to think of himself as the learned king rather than the hunting king. The royal party then proceeded to Salisbury to visit the Gothic cathedral. By this time James was getting cranky. He was suffering from his legs, and news had just arrived that a Spanish army had invaded the homeland of his daughter's German husband.

James may have anticipated this disaster. Over his strenuous objections, his son-in-law Frederick, Elector of the Palatinate, a Protestant principality in Germany, had accepted the crown of Bohemia when it was offered to him by rebellious Protestant nobles. This had put him on a collision course with the Austrian Habsburg emperor who had suzerainty over Bohemia and was determined to keep it Catholic.

Now, not only were imperial forces getting ready to chase the foolish Frederick out of Bohemia, but the Spanish branch of the Habsburgs had moved in to deprive him of his hereditary German lands. James feared that he would be under pressure to go to his son-in-law's aid. How would this square with his hopes of marrying his son to a Spanish princess? In the eyes of the Venetian ambassador, who had followed the court to Salisbury, the King seemed "utterly weary of the affairs that are taking place all over the world at this time."

To amuse his unhappy master, Buckingham staged a comical play in the cathedral close. Buckingham himself played an Irish footman, his stepfather a tailor, and his uncle Northampton "a cobbler who taught birds to whistle." All played their parts well except Sir William Feilding, whose portrayal of a Puritan was thought to have "marred" the play.

Wherever they went, Buckingham's bride was presented with expensive wedding gifts, heavy silver salvers and bowls, and gold jewellery for which she was known to have a penchant. It took a while for Kate to realize that these were bribes for her husband's favour. When she asked George whether she should continue to accept them, he laughed and said "of course" - that was how people paid in advance for his influence with the King, although he did not always use it to their advantage. Should she accept these valuable things if he did not intend to help them? she asked. As his wife she had better get used to it, he told her, flashing that white smile of his.

By the end of the progress, King James was looking on Kate as a daughter. Her quiet manner was a relief after Buckingham's overbearing mother. And he took pleasure in Buckingham's obvious happiness with his bride, though he could foresee that she would not be able to keep him away from other women once the honeymoon was over. Every morning he sent his blessing to the couple.

His daily prayer, he said, was to hear that Kate was pregnant - he could hardly wait for "sweet bedchamber boys to play with me." To suit his newly married state and the high office of Lord Admiral, Buckingham had grown a small, pointed beard and a dashing, turned-up moustache that made him look even more handsome. It was a question who doted on him more, his wife or the King. The bonding between James and Buckingham remained as intense as ever, but as James aged prematurely and his health began to fail, it developed into more of a father-son relationship. James now lumped George together with Prince Charles and called them both his "sweet boys." There was ample room for Kate in this phase of their relationship.

Still, Kate had to adjust to the King's prior claim on Buckingham. After one day in London, James was on the move again between his palaces and his hunting lodges. Her time was taken up with her in-laws. Female relatives of the Villiers (some young and some not so young) poured into London from the country to be married off, thus there was the ongoing search for husbands. Buckingham's patent aim was to broaden his family's influence through a network of marriages to outnumber the Herbert and Howard clans.

Then there was the problem with the Purbecks. George's very reserved brother John, Viscount Purbeck, had suddenly turned loquacious and belligerent and, around the time of George's marriage, had been sent abroad. He was now at the Spa in the Spanish Netherlands, supposedly to drink the waters but, as everyone knew, to hide the signs of mental illness so as not to embarrass his illustrious brother. Meanwhile, the Countess of Buckingham suspected that his wife Frances was having an affair and she had conscripted the servants to spy on her. So far there was no break in the family connection but it engendered a great deal of unpleasantness at Denmark House, the Prince's palace that Charles had inherited from his mother, where the Villiers all had apartments. Kate was grateful she did not have to live among them.

One thing that made Kate very happy was the healing of the breach with her father. Over the summer the Earl of Rutland had paid 7,000£ in part payment of her dowry and had handed over the Helmsley estate with its stables to Buckingham. Moreover, he had made it clear to his son-in-law that he not only accepted him but relished the connection. Buckingham signaled that he too was ready to make up. In October he paid a visit to Belvoir Castle, bringing with him such distinguished guests as the great Scottish lord, the Marquis of Hamilton.

There, Buckingham convinced Hamilton to betrothe his thirteen-year-old son to his sister Susan's pre-pubescent daughter. (The betrothal had been sealed without the boy's knowledge and was to lead to his refusal to perform his marital duties two years later.) To spend time with George happened rarely enough for Kate these days, and to have him at Belvoir again was sheer joy for her. She could not find fault with her father's welcome to her husband, although her stepmother's welcome was far from warm. For the moment, even the stress and strain among the Villiers ladies was put aside when the Countess of Buckingham stepped out of her coach, followed by Lady Purbeck.

A few weeks earlier, Kate and George with his mother had been the guests of honour at a great feast at Syon House some miles west of London, tendered by the Viscount Doncaster and his famously beautiful wife, Lucy Percy.

The Viscount was the former Sir James Hay. He had been elevated to the peerage for his suave, albeit unavailing, diplomacy in the interests of the King's dispossessed son-in-law, the Elector Palatine. The Doncasters set the pace at court. Their extravagant entertaining was legendary, and predictably they were first off the mark to fete Buckingham and his bride. Syon House belonged to Lady Doncaster's father the Earl of Northumberland, but he being in the Tower of London and her mother deceased, she and her husband used this country house of white Portland stone with its acres of walled gardens as their own. With music and dancing and the rarest of food and wine, it was Kate's introduction to princely entertaining. While George was enjoying himself to the hilt, Kate, at seventeen, felt shy and somewhat intimidated by her hosts. Doncaster, slim as a stick, and (to Kate) foppish with his pointed toe and elegant gestures, was the model of perfect deportment and courteous to an extreme. A longtime favourite of King James, he had become a follower of her husband and Kate realized that she would be seeing a lot of the Doncasters. She noted that the men, including her own husband, could not take their eyes off the hostess with her large breasts, small waist, and full hips that were shown to advantage by the new style of swaying skirts that moved with the body. At dinner Kate intercepted a glance between Lucy and George that suggested an intimacy. She told herself she was mistaken.

In January 1621, King James summoned a Parliament, the first since the turbulent sessions in 1614 that had ended in dissolution. This brought George to London more often, and he and Kate began to have a home life. Kate found herself mistress of a houseful of servants, clients, and hangers-on. She got along well with Buckingham's men. She joked with them, made wagers with them, all the while earning their respect. Edward Hyde, a young lawyer destined to be the historian of the age, would later write that "beside her great extraction and fortune, she was of a very great wit and spirit." Having observed her in her home, he went on to say that she had a temper to match her husband's, and could be jealous, yet she could also be remarkably generous and understanding.

One of George's men whom Kate liked very well was Endymion Porter. Unfortunately, Porter had just been seconded by Prince Charles and was on the point of leaving. Kate had formed a friendship with his wife Olivia. Olive, as she was called, was the daughter of George's half brother by his father's first marriage. In the wholesale elevation of the Villiers clan, this gentleman had been made a baronet, but as he had four daughters and had not yet netted lucrative patronage, he gave but a small dowry of 2,000£. Urged by Kate, Buckingham provided an allowance for Olive.

Of all Buckingham's servants, the one Kate liked least was a Dutch immigrant painter of Huguenot descent named Balthazar Gerbier. At George's insistence, she sat to Gerbier for her portrait in miniature. Watching him dart around the room like a dancing master, she wondered how George could put up with this little man with his exaggerated her that he had been "an embryo in his mother's womb" when his Huguenot parents had fled Paris at the time of the St. Bartholomew Massacre and taken refuge in Holland. From her history books on the French wars of religion (had she not copied out excerpts in a notebook?) Kate knew that the massacre of thousands of Huguenots by rampaging Catholic mobs incited by the French king and his Italian mother had taken place in 1574. Gerbier was no older than George, who was born in 1592, so how could his mother have been pregnant with him? This lie discredited him in her eyes and further prejudiced her against him. When she told George, he said "yes, he is a knave but a useful one." She soon learned that Gerbier was more than the resident painter.

In fact, he was her husband's confidential agent. He kept the ciphers for corresponding with Buckingham's spies, and under cover of buying art Buckingham sent him abroad on secret missions. She was glad when George dispatched him to the Continent to buy paintings, though in her opinion these were mere baubles and not worth the price of a good horse.

It was obvious to observers that the Marquess and Marchioness of Buckingham were happily wed. A young painter named Anthony Van Dyck, on a brief visit from Antwerp, caught them on the wing like a pair of butterflies, dancing hand in hand in costume in a masque commissioned by Buckingham in 1621. Indeed, Kate was enjoying life as a young married woman in London. Squired by Prince Charles as well as George she "took the air in Hyde Park," attended cock fights at Whitehall, the horse races, and of course the Court masques. The three were often joined by Frances, Duchess of Lennox. a pretty woman with a piquant charm who had just married for the third time. Of august lineage, she had shocked her peers by first marrying a vintner.

Considered a love match as the only explanation, she was found on the vintner's death to have inherited a vast fortune. For her second husband, she reverted to her class with a marriage to the Earl of Hertford. When she put on airs in company, this droll gentleman was known to tease her, "Frank, Frank. How long is it since you married the vintner?" On his death in 1621 she announced she would marry no one but a king. Rumour had it that she aspired to fill the void created by Queen Anne's death and had her eye on the decrepit James. She came close to the throne with her third marriage to Lennox, the King's cousin, England's only duke. Now well into her forties, the Duchess of Lennox appeared still youthful. Although old enough to be Kate's mother, she completed the fun-loving quartet that was seen "going from one place of entertainment to another, turning up unexpectedly with a minimum of etiquette and in high spirits."

But Kate was keenly aware that she must soon get down to the serious business of life and produce a son and heir for Buckingham. To "breed" was every wife's purpose and duty. The fecund woman was praised by society while barren women were at best pitied, at worst scorned. One recourse for the childless was to go to a spa where it was believed the waters could induce fertility. Indeed, after the loss of her second son, a bereaved Lady Rutland had gone to drink the waters at Tunbridge Wells in the hope of getting pregnant. But the spa cure for her barrenness had not worked. The Rutlands blamed it on the curse of the Belvoir witches.

As the wife of the glorious Buckingham, Kate felt it was almost her sacred duty to procreate. She had to fend off intimate questions daily from the King and her mother-in-law. Rumours (false alas) abounded at court that the Marchioness was pregnant. George joked about it, but she knew that he was anxiously waiting to become a father.

The pitiable state of the childless woman apparently did not apply to Lucy, Lady Doncaster. Her only child, a boy, had died two weeks after birth and there had been no more babies, yet she was widely admired not only for her beauty but also as a hostess and a wit. Doncaster paid court to George assiduously and Kate found herself in Lucy's company more often than she wished.

A novelty that winter of 1621 was the "running masque", introduced to the court circle by the clever wife of the French ambassador Monsieur de Tillieres. Launched at the embassy, the masque was performed nightly at a series of different houses. Buckingham was most enthusiastic about the new craze and joined in the dancing every evening with other aristocratic masquers.

The hit of the show was a gigantic porter from the palace who made his entrance holding the Earl of Pembroke's diminutive page on his fist like a falcon. The Doncasters leased Essex House, one of the historic mansions on the Strand, where they entertained constantly. Indeed, the social event of the season was a lavish function at Essex House in honour of an ambassador extraordinary from the French king, Louis XIII. Living up to their reputation as style-setters, the Doncasters introduced the "ante-supper," another importation from France probably suggested by Madame de Tillieres. A Lucullan feast was set before the guests on their arrival, but before they could take a mouthful it was whisked away and a second feast was brought in. This one was to be consumed. Kate was shocked by the waste but George resolved to outdo their hosts as soon as he acquired a Thames-side palace he was angling for.

desperate for money, and only Parliament could give him the right to levy taxes by granting him subsidies. Not only had he emptied the Privy Purse that paid for the expenses of the royal Household, but he had also siphoned off funds from the Exchequer so that there was little money left to run the machinery of government. Although Buckingham had supporters in the Lords, he had no support in the Commons where the money bills originated.

In June, to his relief and Kate's, James prorogued Parliament for the summer. Kate had been upset by the sometimes ferocious criticism of George, but he reassured her that he would never be in any real danger because King James would dissolve any Parliament that tried to impeach him. Still, Kate had been surprised by the insecurity he displayed during his tribulations with Parliament. She realized that beneath her husband's apparent self-confidence and joking manner there lay uncertainty and even fear, and she attributed his frequent illnesses to this. In fact, after the parliamentary session he needed time to recover before he could join the King on the summer progress. Kate was happy that she could be a comfort to him. Only to her, not even to his mother, could he unburden himself.

Yet undeterred by Parliament's criticism of the patronage lavished upon him by King James, Buckingham had been looking for a suitable country estate. He had recently purchased Burley-on-the Hill in Rutlandshire for the considerable sum of 20,000£. In sheer grandeur it outdid nearby Belvoir, and that was why Buckingham had bought it. He wanted to show the Earl of Rutland that his daughter had not married beneath her, that although he did not have the Rutland heritage, thanks to the King's favour he was the greater man. Buckingham was planning a magnificent entertainment at his new mansion during the King's summer progress. The leading lords and ladies of the realm were invited, and he commissioned Ben Jonson to provide a masque in praise of King James, his benefactor.

The royal party arrived at Burley-on-the-Hill at the beginning of August. The rain that had followed the progress relentlessly suddenly ceased, and the mansion and its vast park were bathed in a welcoming sunlight. To her great joy, Kate was able to tell George she was pregnant. At the news, the King was as excited as the prospective father. He issued a barrage of instructions regarding Kate that were to be passed on to Buckingham's mother: "Let her never go in a coach upon the streets, nor never go fast in it. Let your mother keep all hasty news from coming to her ears; let her not eat too much fruit and hasten her out of London after we are gone."

Buckingham now had an estate suitable for a great lord. For Kate a large country house was no novelty, but she shared George's happiness in his acquisition. Ben Jonson's masque was an enormous success. Called "The Gypsies Metamorphosed," Buckingham played the captain of the gypsies with great panache, the role of a swashbuckler suiting his own personality only too well. James glowed with pleasure as Buckingham read Jonson's paean of praise for his kingly virtues and was visibly moved by the verses in which the favourite expressed his gratitude to him in flowery phrases. So much so that James (who was no mean poet himself) stayed up all night composing a sonnet in praise of George and Kate.

At the banquet the next day, James stood up with his hat in his hand (an unusual mark of respect from a monarch) and drank to the health of his hosts. He then proceeded to deliver his poem which he called "A Vow or Wish for the felicity and fertility of the owners of this house." The old aristocracy listened with distaste as the King declaimed his earnest wish that this "blessed couple dear" should parent a Buckingham dynasty. This seemed not unlikely as the news of Kate's pregnancy was out and James wound up by saying, "God send us a smiling boy in a while." The Venetian ambassador expressed the unspoken reaction of many guests that James's performance was less that of a king than a suitor. Writing to the Doge, he said "The King showed the favourite as much honour at Burley as he received from his Excellency." Blithely unaware of the negative reaction, George was delighted with James's public adulation of him. Kate was not so sure that it redounded to George's advantage, fearing it would only increase jealousy. In any event, the masque itself was so successful that it was repeated at Belvoir a few days later.

When Parliament reconvened in November, Buckingham made no attempt to face the opposition building against him. Instead, he accompanied James to Royston and Newmarket though this autumn they did not indulge in much hunting. At Royston, Buckingham took to his bed with one of his mysterious illnesses and when he recovered the King was indisposed at Newmarket. Buckingham kept the King isolated. When he was not standing guard in person, Kate, Sue, and his mother were on duty, hovering about the King like brooding hens. With no strong direction from the court, Parliament was left to its own devices and returned to the subject of Buckingham's misuse of patronage and his pro-Spanish policies; all this was rendering him frighteningly unpopular. Buckingham renewed his pressure on James to dissolve Parliament. It was dangerous enough that the Members of Parliament knew about the fortune he was making from his control over patronage in England, but Buckingham decidedly did not want his parliamentary enemies to learn of his similar dealings in Ireland.

He was making a fortune from Irish customs, of which he granted portions to sycophants such as Doncaster and Endymion Porter and to Kate in trust. On trumped-up title deficiencies, he expropriated the lands of the Old Irish proprietors and sold them to English planters. He was also selling titles, thus creating a clientage among the Irish peerage. In Dublin they were saying that Lord Buckingham planned to make himself Prince of Tipperary. It was with great relief that he welcomed the dissolution of Parliament at the end of the year, although the Commons had not voted the King a single subsidy.

Kate was deeply troubled by the growing animosity towards George in Parliament. Apparently more in tune with public opinion than her politician husband (perhaps by overhearing the servants' gossip) she feared that dislike of the favourite was spreading to the people. However, any advice she offered to George was disregarded. Through long habit Buckingham listened to his mother and to a lesser extent to his older sister Sue, but sharing the aristocratic male's contempt for women he had not awakened to the intelligence and common sense of his young wife.

Kate was also troubled by her husband's free-spending habits. Money had not been an object in her childhood home. Yet her father lived within his income and, as one example, had rented a London residence for the season rather than buying one. Her husband, however, was mad for property, boasting to her that he would become one of the greatest landowners in England. To further his aim, he made free use of Kate's present and future holdings, as he was permitted to do by law.

Buckingham had his country house, and now he set out in earnest to get hold of the London residence he wanted. York House, one of the venerable mansions on the Strand that bordered the River Thames, was the traditional home of the Lord Keepers of the Privy Seal. Francis Bacon's father had been Lord Keeper under Queen Elizabeth, and Francis had been born there. When he himself became Lord Keeper, later becoming Lord

Chancellor, he had moved back to his childhood home. He took great pride in his double right by birth and office to the historic premises. Meanwhile, Buckingham (a frequent guest) was looking at it as the perfect setting for staging lavish entertainments and displaying his growing collection of paintings. He decided he must have York House and, taking advantage of Bacon's fall from grace, managed to wrest it from him. The house needed a good deal of structural work and restoration before he and Kate could move in. He appointed his painter, Balthazar Gerbier, to be Keeper of York House, and in addition to his curatorial duties instructed him to fix up the old mansion and add a couple of wings, Gerbier being something of an architect as well as a painter.

In the meantime, a London townhouse was required for Kate's lying-in. Wallingford House, near Whitehall and overlooking the gardens of St. James's Palace, was a suitable residence and available for a mere 3000£. But at the moment Buckingham was running short of cash. He and his mother conducted a little charade to wring more money out of the gullible king. Making sure that James was within hearing distance, the Countess reminded her son in a loud voice that he must soon make preparations for his wife's lying-in. His murmured reply sounded despondent to the King's ears. James then burst upon the actors, and "conjured" (his own word) Buckingham to tell him the truth about his finances. With downcast eyes, Buckingham told him, "I must pay twenty thousand pounds for my land at Burley, and Kate's lying in is like to cost ten thousand." Besides this, there was the cost of Wallingford House. "All this must be borrowed," he sighed.

Not for the first time, James acted as Buckingham's advocate with the Lord Treasurer, the Earl of Middlesex. A City businessman brought into the royal administration by Buckingham, Lionel Cranfield was doing his best to clean up government finances but the extravagance of James and his favourite defeated him. James told Cranfield that "chancing to overhear" a conversation between Lord Buckingham and his mother, he had learned of his financial straits, and he feared that if this poor young man ran into debt there would be no turning back. Despite James's wheedling tone, the Lord Treasurer recognized it as the order it was. The King would pay for Kate's lying-in. Thus Buckingham's finances were freed up to purchase a great house in Essex dating back to Henry VIII's time. Above and beyond the initial cost of 22,000£, Beaulieu (renamed New Hall) required total modernization.

While Kate was patiently waiting to go into labour, she had two fathers fussing over her. King James was at Wallingford House "early and late" to enquire how she was and making a general nuisance of himself. A parade of Whitehall servants arrived with boxes of dried plums and grapes, violet cakes, chickens and game. "Your presents are so great we cannot eat them so fast as they come," Buckingham told him. As for the women hovering around the expectant mother, the Countess of Buckingham was the undisputed authority on birthing. She it was who chose everything from the midwife to the bed linen, proximity being to her advantage as she had moved into Wallingford House. The Countess of Rutland found herself of so little use to her stepdaughter that she made plans to go abroad to the Spa in Flanders.

In March Kate gave birth to a girl. Joy at her safe delivery was tempered by disappointment over the baby's gender. A boy would have ensured that Buckingham's title and the estate entailed would be passed down in his line. As Kate knew only too well, under the English law of entail a female could not inherit, thus if poor deranged John Villiers and his wayward wife had a son, he would be the ultimate heir. But Kate was confident that she would give George his son next time – and she was already looking forward to another pregnancy.

Rumours were circulating at court that the baby was to be named Jacobina after the King, but that was never considered for a moment at Wallingford House. George wanted the baby to be called Mary after his mother and Kate unhesitatingly agreed. She and her mother-in-law were growing increasingly close through their shared religion. Kate remained a fervent Roman Catholic in her mind and heart; she had accepted the Anglican Church only to marry George, but her conversion had been a sham. And at this stage, the Countess of Buckingham was a secret Catholic. Strangely enough, it had been her eldest son, the unstable John, who had induced her to change her faith. Following his return from the Continent, a Jesuit priest named Fisher had converted him. This priest was now in prison under the harsh anti-Catholic laws.

King James was well aware of the brewing Catholicism among the Buckingham clan. Several months earlier, he had arranged for the Bishop of London to hold a ceremony confirming them in the Church of England. Obediently, on the set day Buckingham, his wife and mother, and various members of their retinue went to the bishop's residence and were duly confirmed in his chapel. ("Just as children used to be" said one court watcher scornfully.) An elegant meal followed, with choice music and delectable food. A good time was had by all but the laying on of hands by Bishop Montaigne had no lasting effect on those who were crypto-Catholics.

On March 30 the baby was christened Mary, with King James her godfather. Buckingham, who usually showed little respect at christenings, laughing and winking at the ladies at the formulaic mention of combating weaknesses of the flesh, was on this occasion sober and dignified. Not only was the little mite in swaddling clothes his own firstborn, but Kate was lying very ill with smallpox at Wallingford House.

Smallpox, like childbed fever, lurked in every birthing bedchamber. The new mother, worn out from the ordeal of labour, was a natural victim. Kate was not strong and easily succumbed to the disease. There was deep distress in her circle. The fun-loving Duchess of Lennox herself fed Kate healthful broth each day, defying the danger of contagion. Prince Charles was so grateful to her for her care of their mutual friend that he presented her with a beautiful diamond chain.

This occasioned a display of jealousy on the part of the Countess of Buckingham, not untypical of her, that became the talk of the court. On hearing of the Prince's gift, Buckingham's avaricious mother was green with envy. She devised a plan to obtain the jewellery for herself. She dispatched a sycophant to demand the chain, asserting that he acted on behalf of the Prince of Wales. The Duchess of Lennox replied that she would only render up the Prince's gift if he himself came and asked for it. The Prince was so irate at his friend's mother that he threatened to leave the court if she was not expelled. The incident blew over owing to George's protection of his mother.

If he did not know it before, George realized how much his wife meant to him. Though well aware of his philandering, Kate's unshakeable love was the bulwark that sustained him in his tempestuous career. When she turned the corner and the physicians pronounced it safe to visit her, King James hurried down from the country to see her and his godchild. He had to know every last detail about the baby, especially about her nursing. As was the practice, she had been put out to a wet nurse. The Countess of Buckingham had found a decent woman, free of disease, among the family's poor relations, who was breast-feeding a son of her own. "Little to arrive at a settlement. Buckingham signed an agreement with his sister-in-law granting her a modest allowance with the stipulation that she never live with her husband again. Underlying Buckingham's insistence that the Purbecks not co-habit was his constant fear that he and Kate might not have a son, and a boy born to his eldest brother would inherit his title and estate. He did not keep his part of the agreement. Six months later, Frances still had not received a penny from him and had to turn to the King.

In the midst of this family feud, the Countess of Buckingham publicly announced that she had converted to Catholicism. James temporarily banished her from court for her apostasy, but some said it was because of the quarrel with her daughter-in-law.

CHAPTER SIX

King James's court was a nest of parading peacocks who passed the time exchanging ribaldry and seeking sexual conquest. Innocent as she was, Kate accepted George's philandering among the young maids-in-waiting as common practice of the courtiers. What was carefully concealed from her was the Duke's practice of debasing decent wives and mothers at court through a despicable subterfuge. He would set his eye on someone. His followers would approach the lady deferentially, informing her that the Duke of Buckingham was seeking her help or advice on an important matter and awaited her in one of the private receiving chambers. Flattered and taken in by the respectful tone of these courtiers, she would accompany them only to find herself attacked sexually by the Duke. The courtiers meanwhile stood guard on the door, just biding their time until they could ruin the lady's reputation. Modest maids-in-waiting were known to hide rather than encounter the Duke alone in the palace. All this was kept from Kate, but one aspect of her husband's extramarital behaviour she was well aware of.

Kate had suspected it. By Christmas 1622 she was certain. George was having an affair with Lucy Hay. She had come upon them kissing, not just a warm kiss such as George bestowed on every pretty lady but a ravenous embrace of the woman in his arms. He had never kissed *her* like this. Now other incidents took on significance, incidents that she had willfully dismissed from her mind: the frequent disappearance of the two from the rest of the party, careless remarks by Lucy that Kate had refused to interpret in order to avoid the anguish of discovery.

The court beauty could now preen herself as the Countess of Carlisle because her husband had received an earldom. True, James Hay was one of the King's favourite diplomats, but all honours were at George's discretion and Kate wondered if Hay's elevation in the peerage was not also payment for his acquiescence in his wife's affair. It was taken for granted that the courtiers would have mistresses; most wives accepted it. Kate thought she had come to terms with George's infidelity. She had even discussed it with her father who explained to her that her husband was one of those men who could not curb their lust. It did not affect his true love for her, her father assured her. But an affair with the haughty Lady Carlisle under her very nose at court was a different matter. To have to socialize with Lucy Carlisle was a trial for Kate.

After a particularly unpleasant evening Kate gave way to jealousy and temper, followed by tears. "Love only me," she entreated him. Buckingham was to hear this refrain throughout their married life. He would promise but both knew his word was not worth a penny.

The fact was that Kate had to accept the affair and, in any event, she still considered herself blessed to share her life with the finest man on the face of the earth.

Kate was the ultimate in the devoted wife. As she wrote him on one occasion, "Dear Heart, I cannot express the infinite affection I bear you. There never was a woman loved man as I do you." For her own peace of mind she tried to minimize his hurtful philandering. His only fault was loving women too much, she told herself. The marriage continued, outwardly as perfect as before, but with occasional bursts of jealousy from Kate and many tears in the privacy of her bedchamber.

Now that they had the proper mansion for entertaining, the Buckinghams assumed the lead in the social life of the court. The French ambassador's wife and her popular niece were returning to France, and this provided an excuse for a hectic round of feasting and entertainments over the Christmas holidays and into the new year. The King led off with a ladies' supper in honour of the departing guests. The following night Kate and George entertained at the refurbished York House. The French reciprocated at the embassy. Then it was the Carlisles' turn to offer one of their extravagant suppers at Essex House, at which Buckingham took so ill that he and Kate had to spend the night there. With the vomiting and runny bowels, Kate did not have to worry that George would sneak off to visit his mistress.

The Buckinghams and Carlisles jointly presented the French ladies with a parting gift of costly jewellery. All this hospitality and generosity did not fool the French ambassador. Monsieur de Tillieres was well aware that Buckingham and his master were hot on the trail of an alliance with Spain, France's rival. Writing home to France, the ambassador gave his opinion of Buckingham: "He exhibits debauchery, effrontery, irreligion and rapacity in the highest degree."

The cornerstone of the pro-Spanish policy was to marry Prince Charles to the one remaining unwed Infanta. But Madrid was dragging its feet. The impatient Buckingham was not content to let Ambassador Bristol in Spain negotiate the match through regular diplomatic channels. He convinced King James and the impressionable young Prince of Wales that the latter should go to Spain to woo the Infanta in person: he would accompany him. This scheme was not of Buckingham's devising. It had been put in his head by the Spanish ambassador, the Conde Gondomar, who had since returned to Spain. After initially agreeing to this knight errantry, James panicked. Once the Spaniards had his "baby" in their clutches, their demands would surely increase to the point that nothing short of his conversion would satisfy them. But James could not stand up to his favourite and his heir, and reluctantly agreed to their hare-brained plan.

On February 17, Kate saw them off at New Hall, the recently purchased country house in Essex. Sensible as always, she viewed the journey to Spain as both foolish and dangerous but she had been unable to convince George to reconsider. They would cross at Dover, he told her, where they would be joined by Endymion Porter and Sir Francis Cottington, then they would ride through France in disguise as simple "Jack and Tom Smith." They put on the false beards they intended to wear to show her. Kate erupted with laughter in spite of herself. They looked like performers in a comic ante-masque. But tears rolled down her cheeks at the thought of the dangers they could encounter – and of the loneliness in store for her. Off they dashed, with Kate waving until they were out of sight.

King James at Theobalds Palace was the first to hear of their safe arrival at Madrid on March 7. He immediately sent word to Kate. He decreed that church bells be rung and bonfires lit in celebration. At St.

Paul's churchyard, where the newswriters congregated, there was much condemnation of the Marquess of Buckingham for placing the Prince in peril in order to bring home an unwanted Spanish future queen.

At York House, Kate went about her duties as chatelaine with a heavy heart, making no attempt to hide her loneliness. In a letter to Buckingham, the painter Balthazar Gerbier reported "Madame so greatly deplores your absence that she cannot exist without having your image and shadow before her eyes." He had hastened to finish the life-size oil painting begun before his master's departure and it now hung in her bedchamber: "Madame keeps it as her sweet saint, always within sight of her bed." Unfortunately, he had been unable to finish the miniatures of Madame and baby Mary in time to catch the ship that was leaving Portsmouth with courtiers bound for Spain. Instead, he had sent the old miniature of Madame painted at the time of her marriage and the unfinished picture of little Mary, "the hands which crave a blessing on Your Excellency are merely outlined." Seeing the mistress drooping around the house, Gerbier offered his unsolicited advice that she should welcome his lordship's trip to Spain, it would give him the opportunity to cement his friendship with the heir to the Throne so that he would continue to be the favourite under the new regime that (considering the present king's health) could not be far away. This was little consolation for the grass widow but it proved to be true.

The King was lonely too. He sent over to York House for the miniature portrait Gerbier had painted in 1619, and he wrote his favourite that he wore it on "a blew ribbon under my wastcoate, nexte to my hairte."

One day, when Kate was feeling particularly sorry for herself, she had a visit from a woman she knew slightly from seeing her around Whitehall who had worse troubles. The woman introduced herself as the widow of one Murray, a Scot who had come to England with King James and had served in the royal administration ever since. The visitor told her they had seven children and the King had promised her husband that he would provide for his family if anything happened to him. Murray had died recently and his widow had gone to court many times to ask various officials if the King had made any provision for her and the children. She had been turned aside discourteously even by those courtiers who had been friends of her husband. Desperate, she had pleaded in vain for an audience with King James. She was now, she told Lady Buckingham, almost destitute, living on the charity of her few remaining friends. Kate told her not to despair and sent her away comforted with some money and the promise of help. Kate had been brought up to be charitable. She had the example of her father's sense of responsibility towards his tenants and her stepmother's attention to the servants' welfare. Kate immediately wrote to George in Spain, informing him of the King's broken promise and insisting he do something about it. When he received her letter, George wrote to James in no uncertain terms: "I am commanded by my wife to trouble you with a deed of honour and charity, to have a care of the widow, Mistress Murray, who you promised in her husband's time to provide for, and her seven children." This one charitable act signaled to the court that Lady Buckingham was a friend to those in need, and henceforth Kate would be prevailed upon to help numerous powerless people.

At the end of May, King James sent Buckingham the patent for a dukedom – the apex of the peerage. There was only one other duke in the realm (the husband of Kate's friend Frances who had just received a second dukedom, the very important one of Richmond). Kate was now a duchess. While it did nothing to brighten her days, it gave her some satisfaction that the Countess of Carlisle had to walk well behind her at all ceremonies. For his part, Buckingham (who had come to accept the King's largesse as his due) was truly overwhelmed with gratitude: "You have filled a consuming purse; given me fair houses, more land than I am worthy of, to maintain both me and them; filled my coffers to the full with patents of honour that my shoulders cannot bear more." Still, the King burdened those shoulders with more gifts. He ordered Secretary of State Conway to force the East India Company on some technicality to give the favourite 2,000£ and to deliver it to the new Duchess of Buckingham.

To start a dynasty with a dukedom! All the more reason for a son. Kate was hoped she was pregnant. She wrote George though warning him not to get his hopes up: "I can send you no certain word yet of my being with child but I am not out of hope, but we must refer all to God: as soon as I am quick, I will send you word if I be with child." King James too was hopeful. He wrote Buckingham that Kate was "a little sick these four or five days of a headache, and the next morning after a little casting, was well again. I hope it is a good sign that I shall shortly be a gossip over again." The prospect of a male heir had all Buckingham's entourage in a state of excitement. In his next letter to Olive, Endymion asked her to send him word "whether my lady be with child." But by July Kate knew she was not gift. It had cost him 500 guineas, he told Olive, and he had no money to buy another. The best he could do was to send her earrings and, as a token of his affection, an unusual feather. Not the best natured wife, and very suspicious of just how her husband was spending his money in Spain, Olive threw the feather away in pique.

When Kate heard that Buckingham was asking the King for more jewels to distribute as bribes and for gifts to the Infanta, she offered to send him a pearl necklace the King had given her. When James heard of it, he commanded her not to do so. "She would have sent thee the least pin she had," the King wrote Buckingham, "if I had not stayed her." But he could not stop her for long. She nagged him until he gave his permission. "The poor fool Kate hath by importunity, gotten leave of me to send thee both her rich chains," he told Buckingham in his next letter. He cautioned him not to give away any of her jewels because "thou knowest what necessary use she will have of them at your return." Kate's enhanced social position as a duchess would require her to bedeck herself in beautiful jewels. Besides, she had always loved jewellery. Not only that, "it was not lucky to give away anything I gave her," the King chided his favourite.

Kate prided herself on not appearing a jealous wife like Olive Porter. She allowed herself to be easily convinced that George was faithful to her (and to Lucy Carlyle) all the months he was in Spain. "Everybody tells me how chaste you are; and that you will not look at a woman, and yet how they woo you," Kate wrote George. Sir Francis Cottington, back from Spain in June, gladdened her heart by telling her that her husband had made a vow that he would not touch any woman until he saw her. Olive once showed Kate a letter from Endymion in which he said, "My lord and I live very honest, and think of nothing but our wives." The one wife believed it; the other simply laughed.

The truth was that Buckingham's philandering in Spain was notorious, but out of kindness the English courtiers conspired to keep Kate in the dark. Knowing his son-in-law, Rutland had sent him a salutary warning on his first arrival at Madrid: "If you court ladies of honour you will be in danger of poisoning or killing, and if you desire whores you will be in danger of burning. Therefore, my good lord, take heed." Like much good advice it was completely ignored. While Kate thought George irresistible ("yourself a jewel that will win the hearts of all the women in the world"), the Spanish women were not impressed with the English lord. Truth to tell, he had many rejections from the ladies of the court. By and large, he had to satisfy himself with servant women or even prostitutes. Indeed, he feared he had picked up a venereal disease. From one of his mistresses he received "a bitter affront" that turned into a scandal, leaving him humiliated before the entire Spanish court. Realizing that Kate would hear of it, he confessed the affair to her. She was completely forgiving: "Truly you are so good a man that, but for one sin, you are not so great an offender, only your loving women so well. But I hope God has forgiven you and I am sure you will not commit the like again."

Well aware that George was disliked and dishonoured at the Spanish court, Kate put little stock in a letter she received at this time from Tobie Matthews, a long-time friend of Buckingham's. From Madrid he sought to reassure her. "Some vulgar tongues may have told your Grace that the Duke is not much beloved here," but she should not believe it. "My lord hath been so fortunate this way that even his opposites in the treaty carry a great affection to his person, and set a fair stamp of value upon his parts; and this King proceeds nobly towards him, and the Infanta takes particular gust in him." According to Tobie, even the favourite Olivarez "desires nothing more than to oblige him." This well-meaning letter had an opposite effect on Kate. It ran so counter to what she was hearing from George himself that she discounted it entirely. For one thing, she knew Olivarez to be George's sworn enemy. Moreover, she had heard from others that Buckingham's easy ways with Prince Charles, speaking to him as an equal and slouching in undress in his presence, had rubbed the punctilious Spanish courtiers the wrong way and they had not troubled to conceal their lack of respect for him.

Being separated from George for so many months was a veritable purgatory for Kate: "I protest to God I have had a grievous time of this your grievous absence … my heart has felt enough, more than I hope it shall ever do again; and I pray God release me quickly out of it by your speedy coming hither again to her who does as dearly love you as ever woman did man." She grew very thin, her face became bony. Her personal physician feared she was in a consumption. As all the household knew, this Doctor Moore was more than her Ladyship's doctor. He was thought to be an Irish priest, some said a Jesuit, others a Dominican. He may not have heard her confession but he undoubtedly ministered to Kate's spiritual needs as a covert Catholic.

Perhaps uncertainty about Doctor Moore's medical qualifications made King James send the royal physician, Theodore Mayerne, to examine Kate. Trained at Montpelier in France and a successful practitioner in Paris, the enormously fat Mayerne had come to England in 1611 and immediately became the fashionable court physician. After examining Kate, he dismissed Moore's diagnosis, assuring the King that "it was but a vapour that came from her spleen" and was not serious. During her convalescence, James had Kate brought to the palace where she dined with him nightly in his bedchamber. Kate implored King James not to tell George she was ill: from his letters, she said, George was depressed enough without bad news from home. James promised on condition that she herself be merry. Kate replied that she had "a great deal of cause to be so, to see how firm your Majesty's affection is to my lord now in his absence."

When Buckingham learned of Kate's illness, he was furious both with her and with the King for not telling him. But his long scolding letter to Kate was so full of his love for her that she wept for joy:

"Never woman was so happy as I am, for never was there so kind a husband as you are; and God make me thankful to him for you, and I beseech him make me some way worthy of you. I protest I could not forbear weeping for joy when I read your letter, to see how much kindness was in it, and grieving to see how grieved you were at my sickness. It has been a great grief to me to think you should be so troubled; and but that I hope Sir Francis Cottington will satisfy you, I could never be merry till I heard from you again, for, I protest to God, anything I know troubles you, it is ten times a more grief to me; and I swear to you, when Sir John Epsley told me how much you were troubled, it went to my heart, and if I thought you were still so, I protest I could never be merry."

His assurance that he would soon be home was the "cordial" that cured her, she told him. Kate believed that melancholy was the cause of her illness and now she promised she would "grow fat" for her beloved husband's return.

In a relatively happy frame of mind, she joined the royal party at Hampton Court in August, taking little Mall with her. Having been weaned, Mall was now in the care of a dry nurse. Still an enthusiastic horsewoman, Kate rode with the daily hunt - "the shooting of deer is all our recreation," she told George. But a sigh escaped her when she recalled all the happy times they had enjoyed together at Hampton Court. She was very pleased to hear from the King that George, in his capacity as Lord High Admiral, had put her father in command of the fleet to bring the wedding couple to England. The Earl of Rutland had become one of Buckingham's most earnest followers. "I swear he loves you better, I think, than he does me," Kate told George. Knowing George's extreme devotion to his mother, Kate never failed to speak of her own love for the Countess: "I do as much love and honour her, I think, as you do almost; though I know, if my own mother were alive, I could not be so good a daughter as you are a son, yet I should love her very dearly too; and if my own mother were alive, I think I could not love her better than I do my lady, for I am sure I have been very much bound to her." The Countess of Buckingham was not at Hampton Court on this occasion. She had been forced to quit the court for a short while to go to Leicestershire to attend to her neglected husband who was suffering from early dementia.

Writing to George from Hampton Court early in August, Kate reported that his stepfather was growing worse but that his brother Purbeck was said to be very well. However, when she returned to London she learned that Viscount Purbeck was once again in "a distemper" and making scenes in public. She and his sister, Susan Denbigh, rushed to take charge of the poor fellow. Meanwhile, King James had ordered Sir John Hippisley and Sir Edward Conway, both Buckingham's men, to get Purbeck out of town at once so as not to cause embarrassment to the Duke. Kate had a great deal of sympathy for her afflicted brother-in-law.

She sent a letter to Conway (whom Buckingham had just made one of the two secretaries of state) saying that she and her sister Denbigh had spent a week with Viscount Purbeck and they believed that the best treatment would be to keep him privately in London. He was "so affected to the city" that they felt "any violent course" to move him would drive him quite mad. Moreover, he was "inclining towards his melancholy fit" in which phase he was easily handled. They recommended that Sir John Hippisley and some other of his friends stay with him in London for a few days until his "dull fit be upon him," then he would be amenable to do anything they wished. "This in our judgment is the fittest course at this present to be taken with him which we desire you will be pleased to let his Majesty know."

Kate and Sue had observed often enough that a manic phase was followed by a depressed state. Thus they understood his bipolar illness without being able to put a name to it. King James, caring only for his favourite's reputation, gave no weight to their advice. With a garden of flowery compliments, Conway conveyed the King's strict order to Kate that not only was the Viscount to be taken from London, "but that you will advise it and assist it with the most gentle (yet sure) ways possible:"

> "His Majesty therefore once more prays you that his former directions to Sir John Hippisley may be put in execution and the safest and surest for the good of the unfortunate noble person, and honour of your dear Lord, his Majesty's dearest servant."

Reluctantly, Kate and Sue allowed the Viscount to be moved to Hampton Court, at that time deserted of all but servants. Although he was under restraint, King James was still not satisfied and had the sick man removed further away to a spa in Warwickshire. A correspondent wrote the Earl of Rutland that the "best remedy for his disease must be in himself and not in waters of the fountain or herbs of the garden."

At the beginning of September, King James received word from his son and his favourite that they were coming home, but without the Infanta: "When we saw there was no more to be gained here, we thought it then high time with all diligence to gain your presence." Having little bargaining power in the adversary's camp, they had capitulated on every point. The marriage treaty specified that England's anti-Catholic laws were to be suspended and ultimately repealed; that the Infanta would control the education of any children until they were twelve; and, furthermore, that the bride must remain in Spain for at least a year after the wedding by proxy.

When James heard the terms, he blubbered for days but out of fear that Charles would be held prisoner, he authorized him to sign it. Although technically betrothed, Charles still had to make use of the perspective glasses to see his fiancée. Moreover, he heard that the Infanta was saying she would enter a convent rather than marry a heretic. No longer in love with a dream, Charles now listened to Buckingham's urgings that they go home. He left the marriage proxy with Ambassador Bristol, but as soon as he and Buckingham boarded the *Prince*, the Earl of Rutland's flagship, they sent word to the ambassador to withhold it until further instructions.

Kate was delirious with joy. On October 5, 1623, her father's flagship dropped anchor at Portsmouth. The Prince and the Duke stepped ashore to a chorus of cheers that would accompany them every foot of the way on their journey to the King. Buckingham had failed miserably but his very failure had made him a hero – the English people rejoiced that he had brought the Prince home safe and sound and, above all, single. The English gave thanks with one voice that they were not to have a Spanish Catholic queen. Though Buckingham and the Prince stopped on the way at York House to meet with the Council, Kate was not there. The King had arranged for the reunion to take place at Royston and had had Buckingham's wife, mother, and sister brought to him. Like the Biblical prodigal son, the "sweet boys" threw themselves at the King's feet. Buckingham kissed his womenfolk over and over again. Everyone cried tears of joy. Prince Charles looked very well. He had grown a short, neat beard and had matured in appearance and manner. Buckingham, on the other hand, looked ill. Kate gasped when she first saw him. His facial pallor was almost yellow and he had lost a good deal of weight. Now that he was home, she would bring him back to perfect health, Kate vowed.

Despite the rejoicing at his return, as he lay beside Kate in the darkened bedchamber he confessed that his failure to bring back the Infanta "hath almost broken my heart."

CHAPTER SEVEN

Kate thanked God that her prayers had finally been answered and George was home from that "wicked Madrid." He must never leave her for six months again, she told him: "I'm sure it would kill me: then might you have a finer and a handsomer, but never a lovinger wife than your poor Kate is." He assured her that being apart had been just as hard for him. Despite his philandering in Spain she knew he meant it. He had needed comforting, poor man. Worst of all, the Spaniards had sent him back to her a sick man, yellow with jaundice.

Charles and Buckingham had returned from Spain spoiling for revenge. Humiliated by their lack of success as lover and diplomat, they were dead set on going to war against Spain. They began applying unbearable pressure on James to reverse his foreign policy that had been based on friendship with Spain from the time he signed the Anglo-Spanish peace treaty at the beginning of his reign. War was unthinkable to him. But diplomats informed their home governments that the King of England was helpless to resist what was, in effect, a siege and an assault by his son and his favourite. Buckingham made sure that no Spanish diplomats or pro-Spanish courtiers gained access to James.

The Duke and the Prince were as close as brothers. Kate admitted to herself that the annoying Gerbier had been right when he predicted that the Spanish adventure would secure George's place as favourite in the next reign. On November 19, she and George held a feast at York House to celebrate Prince Charles's twenty-fourth birthday. Kate was pleased to see how the Prince looked up to George and she could tell it was apparent to everyone present. (Was it her imagination, or did Gerbier, who was acting as master of ceremonies, actually have the presumption to wink at her?) Buckingham had invited the Spanish ambassadors to the feast for the purpose of insulting them. Gerbier had been instructed to write a masque with some not very subtle disparagement of the Dons.

His "sweet boys" badgered James to summon Parliament until he agreed. This time Buckingham could anticipate hearty support from the House of Commons. The Members of Parliament, anti-Spanish and anti-Catholic, were as eager as he to end the marriage treaty. In an address to a joint session of both Houses on February 19, 1624, Buckingham "looking lean and yellow after his sickness" defended the way he and Charles had conducted themselves in Spain and predictably blamed the Spaniards for the breakdown in the marriage negotiations. To complete his self-justification, he accused the resident English ambassador, the Earl of Bristol, of treason. The speech was a triumph for him. Parliament sent King James a petition asking that the Spanish treaties be dissolved. On March 23, much against his better judgment, the King agreed to end the treaties. War with Spain was now imminent. The purported cause of the war was the Spanish king's failure to undertake the restitution of the Palatinate to King James's son-in-law – a proviso not insisted upon by Buckingham and Prince Charles during the treaty negotiations in Madrid.

Just when his popularity was at its height and his former critics were dubbing him the redeemer of the nation, Buckingham's ascendancy was threatened by the Spanish ambassador. Going secretly to King James, the Marquis de la Iniosa accused the Duke of a fantastic plot. He claimed that he planned to force the King into retirement or abdication, and to make Charles the veritable ruler. At the same time, Iniosa painted a lurid picture of Buckingham's licentious conduct in Spain. The Spanish ambassador's accusations against the Duke leaked out and soon it was the talk of Westminster and Whitehall. However Iniosa could not back up his charges and James, whose love for his favourite was now tempered by fear, had the Spanish diplomat recalled.

But all this had taken its toll on Buckingham and he collapsed. Kate had been worried about him ever since he came back from Spain. He had jaundice with accompanying weakness and fever, but it was more than that.

In a letter to King James he remarked that if it proved to be jaundice that could be cured. Obviously, he feared something worse. What was the illness he was dreading? Given his licentiousness in Spain, the obvious answer was venereal disease. But that was not what was causing him to cry in Kate's arms during the sleepless nights. He was suffering from a deep depression. Visitors would find him lying on a couch, unmoving, and he would "neither rise up nor speak." One perspicacious observer commented that he was "sick more in mind than in body." In fact, what Buckingham feared was madness. This was a deep secret known only to Kate and Bishop Laud; the latter had insinuated himself into the Buckingham household as virtually one of the family.

"I watched over my Lord Buckingham who was taking fits," Laud noted in his diary in May 1624. There are no further entries on the subject for several months because the Duke was away from London over the summer, but in September Laud wrote: "My Lord of Buckingham consulted with me about a man that offered him a strange way of cure for himself and his brother." Thus Buckingham believed he was suffering from the same malady as his older brother and, as the world knew, Purbeck was mentally ill.

King James was left in the dark about the true nature of his favourite's illness. Admonitions and advice came daily from Theobalds Palace in Herefordshire. "For God's sake be as wary as thou can with drugs and physicians ... take the air discreetly, and for God's sake and mine keep thyself very warm ... bid the drugs adieu this day, etc." James's own health was very poor. He could not stand on his legs for gout and his stomach was all but gone. He tried to lure his favourite to Theobalds, insisting that he would benefit from riding in the park. "I can take no pleasure in Theobalds Park till thou come." Buckingham put him off with faint excuses on blotted slips of paper that showed the disrespectful haste with which they were written or he left it to Kate to answer. In one letter written from Burley-on-the-Hill, Kate told the King that "my lord is all day long as stirring in his parks here as your Majesty is at any time in your park of Theobalds." Indeed, Buckingham no longer needed to hunt in Theobalds Park; he had his own extensive parks at Burley-on-the-Hill, and at New Hall where (as he told James) he had "found another fine wood that must in with the rest, and two hundred acres of meadows and plentiful springs running through them, so that I hope New Hall shall be nothing inferior to Burley." He was spending a fortune on New Hall. There were the new tennis courts and a bowling green, and he was planning to lay out a park that would be second to none in the kingdom with waterworks, a labyrinth, statuary, and rare plants. He first employed a gardener named "Genings" [Jennings] as "the fittest man for this business." But he soon replaced him with the renowned gardener John Tradescant who, from his travels in Russia and elsewhere, had introduced many new species of plants into England.

George's refusal to be at the King's beck and call certainly suited Kate. She nursed a long-standing grievance that her husband was always at court. How often had she begged him to stay a few days longer with Mall and herself? George adored his little daughter and Kate took advantage of his fondness. No doubt coached by her mother the precocious two-year old would say, "Lord, Father, I love thee well." In a letter to King James, in which he apologized for delaying a command appearance, he wrote: "Kate begins to make use of Mall's tongue, for she had made Mall so importunate with me to stay, that if necessity had not commanded me, hardly could I have refused her." Another time his excuse for arriving late was because of "a hearty taking my leave of my wife – the Prince will understand." Buckingham was a fond father and a lusty husband even in his weakened state.

Meanwhile, Prince Charles appeared lost without his constant companion. He urged Buckingham to come to London as soon as possible, but solicitously added "do not venture to come sooner than ye may with the safety of your health, and with that condition, the sooner the better." In June, Buckingham returned to court, "the dearness between him and the Prince continuing" a courtier informed a friend. His appearance shocked observers. Someone seeing him at Whitehall reported that he was "much discoloured and lean with sickness"; another, that he "looks ill and has quite lost his complexion." He remained in London for some weeks, meeting with the French ambassador and making plans for an expedition to intercept the Spanish treasure fleet. He was certainly not up to the tiltyard. His sporting activities were limited to matches of maw, a popular card game, with one of his cronies. As soon as possible, Buckingham retired to New Hall with Kate and Mall. Someone seeing him there did not think the Essex air was helping him: "He hath a spent body and is not likely to hold out long if he do not tend his health very diligently." After an exhausting visit from the King on his summer progress, Kate and his mother insisted on taking George to Wellingborough spa in Northamptonshire. This was a new spa and life there was very simple; all the aristocratic health-seekers, including the Queen, lived in tents. It was while they were at Wellingborough that Kate saw the first signs of improvement in her beloved husband's health. The devils of mental illness seemed to be retreating and George was recovering his passion for life.

During his months of ill health, Buckingham was occupied in finding a wife for the young prince. The Spanish Match was dead and when the Buckinghams hosted a grand feast at New Hall for the French ambassador, Monsieur d'Effiat, it was a sign that a French Match was in the offing. The prospective bride was the youngest sister of the French king, Louis XIII. Actually, the Prince and Buckingham had seen her on their way to Spain the year before. Taking a detour into Paris, they had put on their false beards and joined the citizenry who wandered freely around the palace. The Queen, Anne of Austria, was rehearsing a masque and among her ladies was her fourteen-year-old sister-in-law, Henrietta Maria. Charles had scarcely given this under-developed adolescent a second glance. At the time, he had eyes only for Queen Anne, whose blond beauty hopefully was a harbinger of that of her sister the Infanta whom he was on his way to wed.

To negotiate the French marriage treaty, the Duke dispatched his mistress's husband the Earl of Carlisle to Paris. Earlier, Henry Rich, Baron Kensington, had been sent to sound out the situation. Kensington was cut from the same cloth as Buckingham. Tall, handsome, and a notorious philanderer, he was having an affair with his hostess, the Duchesse de Chevreuse. The courtly Carlisle and Kensington, the ladies' man, were ideal for the duty of proposing marriage to the French princess on behalf of the Prince of Wales. This time Charles stayed home. After the Spanish debacle, the Prince and the Duke could not afford to fail again. The English diplomats were ordered to make no hard and fast conditions. Getting Charles a wife was the sole objective.

By the autumn of 1624, agreement was reached on the marriage treaty. Under the unequal terms, King James had to swear in a secret document that the penal laws against Catholics would be lifted - this, in the face of James's promise to Parliament that there would be no immunity for English Catholics in any marriage treaty. Henrietta Maria and her suite could practice their religion freely (Inigo Jones was completing the half-finished chapel at St. James's Palace originally intended for the Infanta) and any children would be in her care and raised as Catholics until they were twelve. For his part, King Louis merely gave a verbal promise that he would do what he could in the cause of James's daughter and son-in-law. In making the French treaty, the Duke of Buckingham was outplayed by the devious Cardinal Richelieu, who masterminded the negotiations for King Louis.

Buckingham's health had not proven equal to the strain of making the French match. He broke down again. People were saying it was a recurrence of the sickness he had brought from Spain. Any good effects of bathing and drinking the spa waters had dissipated by October and Kate was again nursing her husband at Wallingford House. At Prince Charles's urging, George joined him at Royston for a spell but spent the whole time shut up in his room. Yet of the two, George was the stronger man. Despite his impressive gravity and his measured speech (to control his stutter), Charles leaned on George for direction on everything.

By this time King James had become virtually irrelevant. Sinking into a premature dotage, he was clinging to George like a drowning man. Come to me, was his constant refrain. And he also craved the cosseting he was accustomed to from George's womenfolk. He gently chided Buckingham for ignoring his repeated requests to bring them to him. At last Buckingham announced they would all be coming: "Mall, Great Mall, Kate, Sue, and Steenie, shall all wait of you on Saturday, and kiss both James's and Charles's feet." Strange to say the King and the Duke referred to these women whom they loved and respected as "cunts" - the scatological term used by the most libellous lampooners. "I must quarrel with thee," King James wrote, "that though in both my former letters I prayed thee to bring the cunts with thee, thou has not so much as sent word whether they can come or not." And replying from New Hall, Buckingham said, "Tomorrow the cunts threaten to be early up, being of my mind, impatient to be with you." This casual use of such a word indicates the bawdiness of James's court.

From their private conversations, Kate knew that George's "grudgings" as they called his black moods, were aggravated by the disastrous news that Frances Purbeck had had a son. Early in 1624, the Countess of Buckingham had learned from her spies in the Viscountess's household that her daughter-in-law was pregnant. There was no doubt that her lover, Sir Robert Howard, was the father.

The Countess had sent a posse of retainers with her stepson, Sir

Edward Villiers, to break into Frances's bedchamber and threaten her with an examination by a midwife if she did not admit her pregnancy and name the father. Frances had disappeared after this invasion of her privacy, and nothing more was heard of her until the Countess learned of the birth of a boy. Understandably afraid of her in-laws, Frances had been living in a different parish as Mistress Wright, and had the baby registered at birth as "Robert Wright". As the law stood, he was the son of Viscount Purbeck, placing him second in line to the Buckingham dukedom after the Viscount. Even if a couple had separated, any child born to the wife was legally the husband's if he was "within the four corners" of the country and nominally had access to her. Viscount Purbeck had not stirred out of the kingdom over the past year.

This development was driving Buckingham to the brink, both physically and mentally. Kate was in misery seeing her adored husband in this state. But she knew the only thing she could really do for him was to produce a son.

Accustomed to get what he wanted from James, Buckingham went to the King and asked him to issue warrants for the arrest of Frances as an adulteress and for Robert Howard her paramour. The Prince sided with him but James refused to commit them to prison, pointing out that it would reveal the arbitrary power the favourite enjoyed from him. As solace, James and Charles gave Buckingham a Christmas gift of 30,000£ to help him pay down his debts, which, at the moment, amounted to 50,000£. Since James would not "bail him out" over the business of Lady Purbeck, in February 1625 Buckingham turned to the law courts. He wrote to the Lord Chief Justice, the Attorney-General, and the Solicitor-General, demanding that "the lady, by my humble and your like kind favour, may yet be kept in prison."

To oblige the powerful Duke, a preliminary hearing was held at Sergeants' Inn Hall on Fleet Street to examine Lady Purbeck and Sir Robert Howard on her alleged adultery. (Frances delighted the Town with her well-publicized remark that she "marvelled what these poor old cuckolds had to say to her.") The prosecutor was Buckingham's brother Christopher, the Earl of Anglesey. The defendants refused to plead (their right by a recent law) and having no witnesses to prove them guilty, the three law officials declined to send such high-ranking persons to prison, confining them instead to the comfortable homes of aldermen. They then handed this contentious issue over to the High Commission, the ecclesiastical court that dealt with matters of adultery. But not before Frances had her say. As recorded by someone present at the hearing, Lady Purbeck "complained that she had been treated in a very cruel manner, deprived of the comfort of her husband's company, loaded with the imputation of infidelity, her subsistence taken from her, and tho' endowed with a very great fortune, was reduced to such necessity as hardly to have wherewith to buy herself clothes." The account continues: "Standersby were so much the more moved at her distress, in that she had been married quite against her consent, to a man disordered in his senses, and the crime of infidelity urged against her." Sympathy in and out of the courtroom was all with the wronged Lady Purbeck. The overriding fact for Buckingham was that the so-called Robert Wright was still his heir.

But although Kate did not yet know it, she had conceived.

CHAPTER EIGHT

King James died on March 27, 1625. Shortly before his death he sent word to George to meet him at Windsor Park for some hunting and to bring Kate and Sue "with their bows." Kate regretted that they had not gone at once for it was at Windsor that the King came down with the fatal ague and was taken to Theobalds Palace. A sense of all he owed to his old master welled up in Buckingham, and he and his mother rushed to Theobalds. Finding that the royal physicians had given up all hope, Buckingham remembered a white powder that a local physician had prescribed for him at New Hall to cure an ague. He sent to this Dr. Remington in Essex for a dosage and, over the objections of the royal physicians, he placed a poultice made from the powder on the chest of the dying king and gave him a few sips of a posset (milk flavoured with spices, a traditional remedy for a cold). James's condition seemingly grew worse, and the royal physicians were murmuring among themselves in a corner. Prince Charles was sent for, and after receiving the last rites from Bishop Williams, the King expired.

George accompanied the new King in the coach to London, then passed the night with him in his bedchamber at Denmark House. When Kate received word from George, she realized that his life as the favourite of the young King Charles would keep him away from her even more than it had latterly under James.

It was around the time of King James's death that Kate became certain that she was pregnant. George was overjoyed. She and her mother-in-law were on their knees praying that this time it would be a boy.

The period of mourning for his father meant that Charles would not go to Paris for his wedding on the first of May. He was to be married by proxy with the Duc de Chevreuse, a distant cousin, standing in for him. Nor would Buckingham attend the wedding ceremony. The elaborate wardrobe that had engaged the attention of a host of tailors and clothiers was put away for the time being. Gerbier, advisor on all matters artistic and decorative in Buckingham's household, had taken pains to have his master outfitted in the most expensive and fashionable style to impress the French. For one suit he had designed a cloth to be woven with a pattern of roses and lilies to symbolize the union of England and France.

Kate was far from begrudging her handsome husband an expensive suit, but she resented the way Gerbier influenced him to spend money on building, furnishings, and especially art. At York House the multi-faceted Gerbier had designed and overseen construction of two symmetrical pedimented wings in the new classical style that Inigo Jones had introduced in England and was making major renovations to the interior of the old mansion. While George took great delight in his building, Kate was less than enthusiastic. With all the new parks and mansions and the burgeoning art collection at York House, they were heavily in debt and she tried to curb George's extravagance. Her efforts to economize were systematically undermined by the Keeper of York House. Gerbier was determined to make York House the finest residence in Europe. In his tug-of-war with the Duchess, he went directly to his master: "Monseigneur, beg of Madame that she will be pleased to furnish York House … and to dress the walls of the gallery; poor blank walls they will die of cold this winter." Buckingham duly gave his approval for the purchase of the tapestry hangings, and in spite of Kate's passive resistance the beautification of the venerable mansion continued. The chatelaine of York House and its Keeper were usually at loggerheads. "Madame has not given orders for the upholstery material of Persian cloth of gold, nor to mat the other bedrooms," Gerbier complained to the Duke in February 1625. "That should be done soon for new mats have an ill smell for a month or two."

Gerbier's purchases of paintings and sculpture arrived in profusion and just the sight of him stretching a newly arrived canvas on a wooden form aggravated Kate in her delicate condition. George took great pride of ownership in the dozen or more paintings Gerbier had brought back from a recent buying trip to France. He told Gerbier to try to open Kate's eyes to the beauty of these works by Titian, Tintoretto, Andrea del Sarto, and other great Italian masters, but she was blind to their charms. To her they were just a needless expense, and she took strong objection to hanging any erotic paintings on the walls of her home. George simply laughed at her prejudice and Tintoretto's *Danae,* with its luscious nudes, was given a prominent place. Most of the acquisitions, however, were religious subjects to which Kate could take no exception. A beautiful Raphael *Madonna* received her wholehearted approval, not for its artistic merits but as an object of veneration. When it came to practical matters such as the plumbing, Kate followed Gerbier's advice. Even though it would cost 400£ she agreed that lead pipes should replace the earthenware pipes.

There was no stopping George from purchasing more houses. He had recently acquired another mansion, this one in the village of Chelsea just outside London. He had gained possession of Chelsea House by bringing about the downfall of its owner, the Earl of Middlesex, the City businessman whom he himself had sponsored at court. Convicted of corruption by the House of Lords on weak, if not fabricated, charges, the disgraced Earl was fined 50,000£ and imprisoned in the Tower. But his real crime was that he had dared to disagree with the favourite over breaking off the marriage treaty with the Spanish Infanta. As Lord Treasurer, Middlesex knew only too well that England could not afford a war with Spain. In his fury at being crossed, Buckingham had brought down several other lords who stood by the treaty.

Following the royal wedding in May, Buckingham travelled to Paris after all to bring over the new Queen of England, the fifteen-year-old Henrietta Maria. Kate was pleased by reports that her husband's stunning good looks and gorgeous wardrobe was making a great impression on the French court. She felt it would help to balance his unhappy memories of Madrid. His open pursuit of the beautiful French queen, Anne of Austria, that astonished the French court, was kept from Kate. The manner in which they danced together left no doubt that the Queen was attracted to the handsome Englishman, still she was too prudent to encourage him when he accosted her as she strolled alone in a walled garden. Her screams summoned her attendants and the unfortunate incident spread all over Paris and to England with the returning courtiers. Kate may not have heard the scandal but his mistress certainly did, and rumour had it that Lady Carlisle was so angry with Buckingham that she was conniving with his worst enemy, Cardinal Richelieu, to see that he never got back to France.

Meanwhile, Buckingham's extraordinary performance in France had come to an end. He was on his back to England as escort for the young queen of England. She and her large entourage were expected to reach the French coast by the beginning of June, and the Countess of Buckingham, her daughter the Countess of Denbigh, and her granddaughter the little Marchioness of Hamilton, along with three other ladies of rank, had crossed the Channel to Boulogne to be on hand to welcome her. As it turned out, the welcoming party was kept waiting for some twelve days. Anne of Austria had taken ill on the way at Amiens, and this had delayed the royal progress. Undeterred by the failure of his first attempt to woo the French queen, Buckingham decided to take advantage of this unexpected opportunity. He stole into her bedchamber and kneeling at her bedside began to fondle her. No doubt in answer to her cries for help, a matronly figure appeared and sent him packing. His attempted seduction of the Queen of France remained a secret within the four walls of that bedchamber in the French provinces.

Kate's pregnancy had kept her at home, and she was looking forward eagerly to hearing about the new queen. The report she received from her lady relatives was that Henrietta Maria was tiny even for her age and of a sallow complexion, but that King Charles (himself a short man) seemed pleased with his bride on sight. Kate also received a typically saccharine description from Sir Tobie Mathew: "Madam, upon my faith," he wrote, "she is a most sweet, lovely creature, and hath a countenance that opens a window into the heart, where man may see all nobleness and goodness; and I dare venture my head on the little skill I have in physiognomy, that she will be extraordinarily beloved in this kingdom." Good Sir Tobie! He could not have been more wrong.

When George arrived at Burley before joining King Charles at Hampton Court, Kate quizzed him about their new royal mistress. He said that she was too devoted to her priests and to her governess Madame St. George, and he predicted Charles would have a hard time with his childish wife. It came out that he himself had already had a run–in with this Madame St. George at Dover. The French lady had taken her place as if by right in the royal coach to ride to Canterbury. Aggravated by her presumption, Buckingham had ordered her out to make room for his sister and Kate's uncle-by-marriage, Lord Willoughby, to serve as assistants to the admiral, Lord Wimbledon. None had any experience at sea.

Kate's delivery date was growing close. She was feeling fine in the good country air of Leicestershire, and Burley's proximity to Belvoir allowed her father to ride over often. Father and daughter were as close as they had been in her childhood. On November 17, Kate was delivered of a son. He was, of course, to be named after King Charles. A messenger was dispatched to Holland to carry the good news to the Duke, who was not expected back for some weeks. Meanwhile, the Earl of Rutland was so engrossed in looking after Kate that he failed to keep an appointment with the King. He excused himself in a note to Secretary of State Conway, explaining that he "forgot the day, being occupied with my daughter by reason of her Lord's absence."

As it happened, George returned earlier than expected. The Italian banker who was acting for the English Crown in Holland found the jewels difficult to pawn, and it would be a long time, if ever, before the money would be on the table. (Kate was just a little annoyed to hear that George had squandered 500£ of their own money on Arabic manuscripts.) Moreover, although the Dutch readily agreed to sign a treaty with England to fight Spain, the French ambassador at The Hague informed the Duke of Buckingham that King Louis wished to "divert" him from his intention of coming to France. As he had attempted to cuckold the French monarch, this should have come as no surprise to the Duke. There was nothing for it but to return to England. So it was that in mid-December, after paying his respects to Charles in London, George arrived at Burley to see his Duchess and his new son. He was full of gratitude to Kate. With this boy the entail was secured and he could put "Robert Wright" out of his mind.

As a bonus for making the French match, George received 80,000£ of the dowry. This windfall was an answer to Kate's prayers. In spite of their great wealth in country estates and London property, they were short of ready money. And George was an incorrigible spendthrift. Like all his class, he took advantage of the fact that, practically speaking, the peerage could not be taken to court and sued. This resulted in tradesmen dunning the lords to the point that they would run after their coaches or station themselves in the street opposite their gates. Their lady wives often bore the brunt of this form of persecution as an easier prey because an irate nobleman might well bring his scabbarded (or possibly unsheathed) sword down on the head of a persistent creditor. Buckingham's extravagance included lavish gifts of jewellery and other luxury items for ladies of their set. "For God's sake," Kate wrote George on one occasion when she was being dunned, "send me 400£ to pay for the ring and cross you gave Lady Exeter. They haunt me so for the money that I cannot stir out of the house." She could only imagine the jewels he was squandering on Lucy Carlisle.

The plague was over and Kate planned to go to London after Christmas. The baby was to remain with his nurse at Burley until spring to keep him safe from the foul London air. Kate hated to leave the precious infant, but for several reasons she felt it necessary to take up residence in London. George would certainly need her in the coming months. Parliament was to be recalled early in the new year and his unpopularity since the failure of the expedition against Spain was alarming. A landing on the Spanish coast at Cadiz had turned into a farce. Instead of sacking the town for its gold, the thirsty English soldiers discovered a fort stocked to the rafters with wine and had made themselves hopelessly drunk. The expedition had no better luck at sea. The Spanish treasure fleet made it safely to port, Admiral Wimbledon having misjudged both its route and the time of arrival from New Spain. Poor command and fierce autumn storms resulted in only a few of the English battleships and merchantmen making it back to Portsmouth. Unpaid, disease-ravaged soldiers and mariners roamed London streets menacingly. Naturally, the Lord High Admiral would be held responsible for the many men and ships lost in the Cadiz expedition when it came up in Parliament. In the taverns people were calling Buckingham a coward for not taking out the fleet himself. George had found it necessary to make public an unconvincing medical report stating that he was in no condition to lead the expedition.

Kate had another reason for moving to London. During her absence in the country, Buckingham's renewed affair with the Countess of Carlisle had made that lady virtually his consort. Suitors were turning to her for her influence with the favourite and her chambers at court were frequented by all the most powerful courtiers. Kate heard such tales constantly. She felt it imperative to challenge the mistress and to reassert her rightful position as Buckingham's wife. She could not put a stop to the relationship. She had pleaded with him many times to love her only, but George would reply that limiting himself to one woman was not in his nature.

CHAPTER NINE

As the second year of Charles's reign began, the main subject at court was not the brewing conflict with the House of Commons but the King and Queen's unhappy marriage. Charles was at his wits end with his young wife. Most of the time she barricaded herself in her own quarters and he could only speak to her through a mediator. Henrietta Maria's childish behaviour suited Buckingham very well. Originally he had confidently expected to bring the young Queen under his influence as he had Charles, however it was clear to him by now that the sorry incidents that had taken place between them meant he could never win her over. She showed this even in small ways. For one thing, she did not invite Kate to her intimate little suppers. This snub bothered Buckingham more than it did Kate. As Henrietta Maria was openly his adversary, his objective was to feed Charles's discontent with his wife. When Charles complained to his friend in confidence that his wife was refusing to sleep with him, Buckingham taunted the young king (who may have been a virgin at the time of his marriage and was very unsure of himself sexually) that if he could not control his wife he could not control Parliament.

The palace rang with high-pitched French voices that to English ears sounded like the squeaking of the mice under the rushes. Charles blamed the "monsieurs," as he called the several hundred French priests and servants that had come over with Henrietta Maria, for turning his wife against him. It had reached such a pass that she refused to take part in his

Coronation. On February 2, 1626, Charles was crowned at Westminster Abbey with all the pomp and ceremony of age-old tradition, but without his consort.

Katherine, Duchess of Buckingham, was seated in the front row as befitted her pre-eminence to view the historic event. The procession entered the Abbey in pairs: first the London aldermen, then in sequence eighty Knights of the Bath, the Sergeants at Law, the judges, bishops, the peerage in their ermine robes, the officers of state holding the swords, globe, and sceptre associated with their respective offices, two bishops carrying the golden cup and the communion plate. With beating heart, Kate watched her adored George step through the portal looking like one of the magnificent knights of old in the storybooks. Charles had appointed him Lord High Constable of England for the day, an ancient post revived only for Coronations. Kate was as dazzled by this man, who had been her husband and bedmate for almost ten years, as when she had first met him. Conscious of Lady Carlisle sitting some rows behind her, she wondered if his mistress was feeling the same proprietary pride as she was. For Kate, the entrance of the King was almost anti-climactic, though she heard a collective intake of breath when the slight but dignified figure in white satin with a train of purple velvet walked into the Abbey under a canopy supported by the four Barons of the Cinque Ports.

Another slight stir riffled through the Abbey when Bishop Laud handed Charles the staff of King Edward the Confessor. This ceremony was the function of the Dean of Westminster and Bishop Williams held that deanery. But Williams had fallen into disfavour with the Duke for speaking his mind at the last Parliament, and had been stripped of his office as Keeper of the Great Seal. As one of Williams' disappointed clients remarked, "Anyone on whom the Duke's hatred lights is to be pitied." No one was exempt from the Duke's hatred, no matter how illustrious. Walking beside him in the Coronation procession was the Earl of Arundel, Earl Marshal of England. In a few days Arundel would find himself in the Tower of London simply because Buckingham regarded him as among those lords who were no friends to him. The Archbishop of Canterbury, an elderly man bent over with arthritis, performed the traditional ceremony: at the High Altar he read out the Coronation Oath to each part of which the King assented, he then officiated at the robing and anointing of the King; his final duty was to escort His Majesty to the Throne, where he placed the crown upon his head. All this Archbishop Abbott performed with fitting dignity, but he too had attracted Buckingham's hatred and was soon to be sequestered from his official duties. Of all the prelates, it was the officious High Churchman, William Laud, who basked in Buckingham's favour.

The rise of Laud and the fall of Abbott was precipitated over a doctrinal matter. The Archbishop had refused to license a sermon by one Sibthorpe, vicar of a Northamptonshire parish. Uneducated in theology, this vicar nonetheless enjoyed the patronage of Buckingham's favourite prelate, William Laud. The sermon exalted the doctrine of the divine right of kings. Preaching before a gathering of judges, Sibthorpe opined that "Kings had power to put poll money upon their subjects' heads." This, of course, was intended to sanctify the King's power to raise money without Parliament's authority, at this time through forced loans. Thinking it could earn him favour at court, Sibthorpe had the sermon printed and presented it to Buckingham. Knowing that the Puritan archbishop would never endorse it, Buckingham saw the sermon as an opportunity to get rid of Abbott who was a thorn in his side. The old archbishop was in poor health and unequal to a contest with the powerful favourite, yet knowing the consequences he refused to license the objectionable sermon. And so he was dispossessed of his duties and banished to a country residence to remain out of sight until death. This was a colossal act of ingratitude on Buckingham's part because it was Abbott who had launched him on his career as royal favourite.

It was not only mutual detestation and conflicting views of kingship that separated the two prelates, Abbott and Laud. There was also an underlying religious difference. Laud adhered to the Arminian doctrine of free will while the elderly Archbishop was a strong proponent of the Calvinist dogma of predestination, the universal position of the English church at the time of his appointment by King James. Schooled by Laud, Buckingham had become an Arminian doctrinally. As far as Kate was concerned this was the lesser of Protestant evils and in 1626 the Duke and Duchess of Buckingham were entertaining the leading Arminium bishops, Richard Montague and John Cosen, at intimate dinners at York House. Kate always invited her sister-in-law Sue Denbigh and their joint protégé Lady Falkland, wife of the Lord Deputy of Ireland, an intellectual lady who was trying to decide between Arminian Protestantism and Catholicism.

On February 5, the newly anointed King Charles was on his way to open Parliament at Westminster Hall. Once again he rode in lonely splendour. As the royal coach passed through the arch of Holbein's Gate on to King's Road, Charles looked up at the gatehouse to see his wife standing in the bay window with her French ladies dancing and cavorting in the room.

Kate dreaded this session. She feared that the Commons would resume its concentrated attack on George. Though George reassured her that Charles would keep him safe, had he not dissolved the last Parliament because of the Commons' hostility to him? Still Kate was very uneasy.

In fact, Charles's unshakeable support of Buckingham in this his second Parliament was to destroy any hope of obtaining the subsidies necessary to finance another expedition against the Spaniards. The Cadiz disaster had given fresh cause for the Members of Parliament to oppose the Duke in 1626. The opening thrust came from a little known MP named Doctor Turner. Disingenuously, he posed leading questions about the Duke that he acknowledged were no more than common gossip. Had the Duke impoverished the Crown by the gifts and offices bestowed upon his relatives? Had the number of recusants increased because the Duke's mother and father-in-law were Papists? Was the Duke's staying home the cause of the bad success of the Cadiz expedition? There was no dispute that these questions were grounded upon unproven "common fame" but learned lawyers on the front benches gravely distinguished between this and rumour, declaring that "common fame" was the voice of the people and should be heard. It was resolved that "common fame is a good ground of proceeding for this House."

Sir John Eliot, House Leader and a gifted orator, turned Turner's questions into formal charges. He began the parliamentary attack with the fiasco at Cadiz. The King had suffered much dishonour in the eyes of the world, Sir John told the House, and many men and ships had been lost. Speaking in a scathing tone, he said that the Duke who commanded all by sea and land had sent a deputy to take out the fleet while he stayed safely at home. He charged that honours and judicial places were sold, land alienated from the Crown, and all this to enrich the Duke's family and friends. Eliot concluded with a reference to Buckingham's attempt to pawn the Crown jewels in Holland: "I hear nothing said of our jewels. I could wish they were within these walls."

Kate saw that George was extremely hurt. Eliot had been his travelling companion on the Continent when they were young men. They had maintained their friendship, or so he had thought, and he had made Eliot vice-admiral of Devon. Now this treachery! Perhaps he did not know that Eliot had beheld the starving, dying sailors returning from the Cadiz disaster, the sight of which had brought him to tears.

Charles tried to stop the attack on his favourite before it went further. Summoning the Commons to Whitehall, he warned them off: "I must let you know that I will not allow any of my servants to be questioned amongst you, much less such as are of eminent place and near unto me. I see you specially aim at the Duke of Buckingham." The Commons responded with a Remonstrance in which they flatly declared that "it hath been the ancient, constant, and undoubted right and usage of parliaments, to question and complain of all persons of what degree soever, found grievous to the Commonwealth in abusing the power and trust committed to them by their sovereign."

On March 13, 1626, Kate's aunt, Lady Scrope, wrote to her brother Sir George Manners that "where the last parliament did end, this hath begun." But this session, not only the Duke but her husband and her brother Rutland were targets for the Commons' wrath. "These are the three they are desirous to remove," she told Sir George with foreboding. The Puritan majority in the Commons denounced Lord Scrope and the Earl of Rutland as "Popish recusants" and demanded they be dismissed from their offices. It was asserted that the Earl of Rutland, who was Lord Lieutenant of Lincoln, Rutland, Northampton, and Nottingham, with other offices in York and north of the Trent, favoured his Catholic tenants over the Protestants on his vast estates. The incidents cited were that he had given a license to a known Papist at Helmsley to keep an alehouse, and that he had hired a "Popish" schoolmaster to teach his tenants' children. This was not the first time the Commons had taken aim at Rutland. In 1624 he and his wife had been named as Popish recusants.

This year he had taken the Oath of Allegiance recognizing the King as head of the Church of England in the vain hope of avoiding penalties as a Catholic. As for Lord Scrope, Lord President of the North, the Commons charged that in spite of his official position that should have made him the upholder of the Church of England, he never went to York cathedral on important occasions, never received the Sacrament (and in fact was seen to walk out with his servants), and on fast days was "publicly riding abroad with his hawks." Moreover, his two daughters were brought up Roman Catholic. There was some good news, however, for the family. The King had told the Duke that if he fell, he would fall with him. "If this be true," Lady Scrope wrote, Buckingham was safe "which I wish for my Lady's sake." Royal protection would cover her brother Rutland and her husband as well, she said hopefully.

Bowing to the strong anti-Catholic sentiment in the House of Commons, Charles issued new recusancy laws. Accordingly, when English Catholics emerged from the French Ambassador's chapel one Sunday, peace officers were waiting to arrest them. And Jesuit priests, living in Anglo-Catholic houses, suddenly found themselves apprehended. This enforcement of the penal legislation affected the Duke's own household. The Catholic Doctor Moore, Kate's physician and spiritual advisor, received notice from the Commissioners for Recusants that he was to be indicted for recusancy. This could mean at the least a heavy fine and sequestration of his personal property. Despite Kate's pleas, Buckingham refused to get him excused. "But you take care of all your people," she insisted. "To please me, I pray you have this indictment stopped."

"No, my dear Kate," was the response. "I have discussed it with the King and we decided that a show of favouritism for my servants would give the Commons another stick to whip me with."

Doctor Moore was summoned and Kate stood by, a reluctant witness, while the Duke issued instructions to him. "You are to suffer yourself to be indicted for recusancy and permit yourself to be convicted on His Majesty's promise to me that you should not be prejudiced by the conviction." He continued. "Thanks to my patronage you are not a poor man. You have the King's word and my word that if your land holdings are sequestered you will be able to lease them back at a nominal rent." Moore put his trust completely in his master but Kate was worried for her good servant. She had knowledge of too many royal promises unkept. Perhaps it was in a rebellious state of mind that, at this very moment, she stood bail for the court appearance of a Jesuit priest who had been discovered on a search warrant in the house of "one Payne."

Although the zealous Puritans in the Commons denounced her father and her Aunt Elizabeth's husband, nothing entered the record about the Duchess of Buckingham's pro-Catholic activities. Kate made no attempt to conceal her true feelings. She was known at court as one of the

"Romanizing ladies," grouped together with the Catholic Countesses of Arundel and Derby, yet lip service to the Established Church seems to have been all that was required of her. Unlike her mother-in-law, Kate was admired and well liked. Known for her good sense and high morality (both attributes not widespread among the ladies of the Court), she enjoyed an unimpeachable reputation. Mention of her name was usually followed by "Heaven bless her for her worth." Even the lampoons that eluded official censorship, did not sully her as they did other great ladies. Scurrilous verses were circulating that Buckingham's fifty-six year-old mother was having an affair with the much-younger Bishop of Lincoln, John Williams.

Early one morning in March, York House received a visit from one of Buckingham's men, Sir John Hippesley. The unfortunate man had been despatched to tell the Duke that the Commons was passing articles of impeachment against him and that his response was required before ten o'clock. For Kate this was not unexpected. George had prepared her for an impeachment, at the same time reassuring her that Charles would protect him. Buckingham smoothly put off his adversaries for the time being. His one fear was that the Earl of Bristol would be given a hearing in the House of Lords. If the former ambassador to Spain were permitted to speak he could give damning testimony of Buckingham's conduct in Madrid in 1623, then even the King might not be able to save him. Buckingham had so far managed to muzzle Bristol. Since his return from Spain two years earlier, the Earl had first been imprisoned in the Tower and then confined to his country house. But the angry, influential peer was stirring up the opposition, and Buckingham convinced Charles that Bristol should be charged with high treason.

On the first of May, the Earl of Bristol was brought to the bar of the House of Lords. The essence of the charge was that when the then Prince Charles was in Madrid, the Earl had "cunningly, falsely, and traitorously" tried to persuade him to convert to Catholicism and further that he had agreed to a term of the marriage treaty promising full liberty to Jesuit priests in England. However, Bristol turned the case on its head by charging the Duke with high treason on the same grounds. He testified that he had informed King James of the Duke's "unfaithful service" and that the King had promised to hear him on his return from Spain. "I pray God," he said in a meaningful aside, "that that promise did him no hurt for he died shortly after." (This struck home with their lordships who were all aware of the rumours about a white powder administered to the dying King James by the Duke and his mother.) Bristol continued. On April 19 of this year, he had petitioned Parliament to hear his accusations against the Duke. Instead, he found himself accused of treason. On being told by the Attorney General that the charge came "out of the King's own mouth," the Earl said he would have humbly submitted to his Majesty and would not have upheld his own honour and religion were it not for the sake of his posterity. He asked only that he and the Duke be heard on an equal basis. Overriding the King's objection, the Lords ordered that both treason charges be heard before they made a decision.

Bristol presented the Lords with a wealth of documents to prove his unimpeachable behaviour in Spain and in his other diplomatic posts. When the King and Buckingham saw they were on weak ground to obtain Bristol's impeachment, they attempted to move the case into the courts where tame judges would do their bidding but the Lords firmly retained jurisdiction.

The Duke's white face showed the strain he was under as Bristol levelled twelve charges against him. He grimaced and clenched his fists but did not interrupt until the Earl turned to his scandalous behaviour in Madrid. Rising to his feet, he asked permission to speak. He did not deny his licentious behaviour in Spain, he said, but he requested silence on this distasteful matter "so as not to hurt my wife, as these things touch her and not others." Out of respect for the Duchess, Bristol quickly moved on.

When Bristol wound up his case, the impeachment proceedings against the Duke commenced before both Houses. Whereas in the Parliament of 1625 the Lords by and large had supported the Duke, in 1626 there was barely a handful in the Upper House that were not against him, and these few were men within his patronage network. The Commons were after his blood. A great debate had taken place in their own chamber as to whether a new charge could be added concerning "a plaster and a posset applied to King James in his sickness when the King's physicians had agreed on other directions." When put to the vote, the yeas had it by an overwhelming majority.

On May 8, the eight members of the Commons charged with arguing for the Duke's impeachment lined up at the bar of the House of Lords. They were all of the gentry class, university-educated or lawyers with considerable parliamentary experience. Following a prologue delivered by

Sir Dudley Digges setting out Parliament's privileges, each in turn spoke to one of the counts against the Duke, beginning with his purchase of the Admiral's place with the King's money. They then proceeded to his mismanagement of the navy, accusing him of extortion and graft. Particularly odious to the Puritan majority was the fact that he had loaned ships to the French king that had ended up being used against La Rochelle, the Huguenot stronghold. Another of his accusers dwelt upon the unmerited and lucrative honours for Buckingham's family. Yet another dealt with the enormous amount of money he had personally received "from the public treasure in a time of want", allegedly 162,995l. over ten years that could have been used to supply the fleet. Moreover, half the Irish customs went to him personally. (Here was the realization of Buckingham's worst fears that a parliamentary investigation would uncover his Irish depredations.)

Nevertheless (said his accuser) by his own admission "his costly furniture, sumptuous feasting, and magnificent building" had left him 100,000£ in debt. Finally, he was accused of "a misdemeanour of so high a nature, as may justly be called, and is, by the said Commons, deemed to be an act of transcendent presumption, and of dangerous consequence" – the plaster and posset he gave to King James of blessed memory against the advice of the royal physicians.

After two days of charges, Sir John Eliot delivered the epilogue, comparing the Duke of Buckingham to the Roman Sejanus who had betrayed the emperor. Immediately after the session, Charles had Digges and Eliot committed to the Tower, however as Members enjoyed immunity while Parliament was sitting he had to release them. The Lords had earlier achieved the release of the Earl of Arundel on the same grounds.

Ignoring the Lower House, Buckingham responded to the impeachment charge before the House of Lords only. He had an innocent explanation for each count. Where these fell short, he claimed he was just carrying out instructions from the late King James. On receiving a copy of his answers from the Lords, the Commons, not bothering to hide their contempt for the favourite's responses, declared that "they did not doubt they would bring judgment against him according to the laws of Parliament unless his power and practice again undermine our proceedings." As they feared, Charles promptly dissolved Parliament. Unhampered now by parliamentary immunity, Charles ordered the Earl of Bristol to the Tower.

Although the King had saved the Duke from earthly punishment, to the credible mind of the day it seemed as if the Heavens had marked him out for retribution. In June 1626, London was experiencing one of the heaviest rainstorms in living memory. Graves were uncovered by the rivers of water and corpses were washed along the streets as if they were swimming. The rain was so heavy that the coach in which the Duke and Duchess were riding with some company from Whitehall to YorkouseH House overturned and they were thrown out on the road. No one was seriously hurt. The worst that happened was that the Earl of Rutland lost his beaver hat. Yet it could be seen as a portent. A few days later, a heavy wind that was churning up the Thames turned at York House and whirled above the mansion in rising circles until it dissipated. Witnesses of this phenomenon described it in wonder and all who heard about it believed it was God's judgment on the Duke.

Meanwhile, Charles was less concerned with the Commons' disobedience (for so he regarded the late session) than he was with the wayward behaviour of his young wife. Among other stories of her priests' bad influence on her, Charles was told that Henrietta Maria had made a barefoot pilgrimage to Tyburn and prayed on her knees for the souls of the Roman Catholic priests executed on the gallows there. Whether true or not (he never asked her) the story was widely circulated. Thus not only was she making his home life an agony, she was undermining his kingship. After threatening to do so for months, he made up his mind to replace her French retinue with English ladies-in-waiting, as George had been pressing him to do for some time.

Shortly after the dissolution of Parliament, Charles went to the Queen's Side (her apartments at the palace), something he rarely did, and entered the room where Henrietta Maria was laughing and playing games with her French servants. Taking her firmly by the arm, he marched her over to his apartments. He half pulled her into a room, locking the door behind him, and informed her that he was sending her servants back to France because they would not let her be a wife to him. At the same time Secretary of State Conway accompanied by the Yeomen of the Guard entered the room where the French were vociferously demanding to go to their mistress. He told them that they were to be moved to Denmark House to await His Majesty's pleasure, and "howling and lamenting as if they were going to execution" they were dragged out bodily by the Guard.

When the Queen understood that her people were being evicted at this very moment, she ran to the window and shattered it with her fists. A few days later, Charles, accompanied by Buckingham, Carlisle, and Holland, went in person to Denmark House to inform the French retinue that they were to be sent back to France.

Well now, George said to Kate afterwards, you are to be a Lady of the Bedchamber to Her Majesty. Along with Kate, Buckingham secured the appointment of his sister, the Countess of Denbigh, his thirteen-year-old niece, the Marchioness of Hamilton, and his mistress, the Countess of Carlisle. Henrietta Maria was to be surrounded by Buckingham women. The Countess, George's mother, was also admitted to the Queen's bedchamber although as a Catholic her son felt it better not to make it official. The Earl of Rutland was chosen to be the Queen's Lord Chamberlain – an honourable post he at first refused, but at the urging of Kate and George he finally agreed to take it. (To accommodate his new, unwelcome appointment, Rutland at last purchased a London mansion from Lord Dorset.) The Queen was permitted two other Catholics and Lord and Lady Savage, very close friends of the Rutland family, were appointed. Kate's reaction was mixed. On the one hand, the post of Lady of the Bedchamber was the highest honour a woman could achieve at court. On the other hand, it meant that she would have to be in the company of Lady Carlisle on a daily basis.

CHAPTER TEN

In her on-going struggle to economize, the chatelaine of York House was clearly losing ground to the Keeper of York House. Though he had narrowly escaped impeachment, Buckingham continued his magnificent lifestyle. After all, he was still the chief minister and the most powerful subject in England. Balthazar Gerbier gleefully wrote his good friend, the Flemish artist Peter Paul Rubens, that "all the machinations of his enemies have never been able to turn the Duke from his old penchant for painting and the other arts." Gerbier was less pleased that the Duke had brought over the Italian painter Horatio Gentileschi to paint a ceiling mural at York House and had installed him in a fine lodging adjoining Gerbier's own residence by the gatehouse. The two artists were continually arguing *fortissimo* much to Kate's displeasure. Moreover, the Duke had commissioned Inigo Jones to construct a vaulted ceiling in the principal saloon where the cream of the collection was exhibited. Kate was unhappy about this because of the noise and the dust that could be harmful for Baby Charles who was not strong like his sister. But a great French noble, the Marquis de Bassompierre, was expected early in October, and George was planning a lavish banquet for him. Accordingly, York House had to measure up to the sumptuous *hotels* of the *Faubourg Saint-Germain* and the *Marais* quarter where he had been entertained in Paris.

Buckingham's main objective these days was to betrothe four-year-old Mall to the elder son of the Earl of Montgomery, a boy not much older than she. Not only were the Herberts extremely rich but their connections included some of the foremost families in England. The animosity of the lords during his recent ordeal in Parliament had shown the Duke how desperately he needed a family connection with men of high birth. Marrying off his relatives had so far done nothing to enhance his position. Despite her efforts, his mother had failed to find a rich wife among the nobility for his younger brother Kit. (One young noblewoman eloped rather than marry him.) In the end the Countess had to settle for the daughter of a wealthy commoner in her own county. A marriage with the Herberts of Wilton would be a good foundation for Buckingham's ambition to build a dynasty. At a time when the aristocracy's average dowry was 5,000£ to 10,000£, Mall's dowry was 25,000£. But the Herberts could not be "bought" just with money. Part of the dowry consisted of giving the Earl of Montgomery the choice appointment of Lord Chamberlain, the top official in the royal Household. It was a position the Earl of Carlisle had coveted and expected to get. Instead, he was named a Gentleman of the King's Bedchamber, the male equivalent to his wife's position in the Queen's household. This disappointment alienated Carlisle from Buckingham in a way that the latter's sleeping with his wife had never done.

Observing her little daughter playing happily, Kate had to ask herself whether she and George were doing the right thing for her. Arranged marriages were usual among the nobility but seldom with a child so young as four. Of course, Mall would not live with her husband until both were past puberty. But what if she disliked the Herbert boy and fell in love with someone else? Goodness knows there was an example in their own family of the tragedy that could result. But if Frances Coke and John Villiers were a disastrous mismatch, what of Lucy Percy's love match with James Hay that had soured to the point that she was now the mistress of Kate's own husband? Kate sighed. She herself had married for love. Indeed, it was that enduring love that made her support a marriage contract between these children, notwithstanding her reservations. George felt he needed the alliance with the Herberts therefore he must have it.

Upstairs in his own quarters lay the little lord who was to establish the Buckingham dynasty. George had transferred one of his own titles to the baby and henceforth the eldest son of the Dukes of Buckingham was to be styled Earl of Coventry. At eight months Charles was showing himself to be a very different child from his lively sister. He was placid and did not at all mind the swaddling clothes in which he was wrapped from his toes to his armpits. Whereas with Mall, when the nurse would start to wrap the long band of cloth around her, she would scream and kick so hard that at four months they stopped swaddling her and before long she was on the floor crawling like a little animal. Kate was considering taking Charles out of swaddling clothes not because he was too active but because he was not active enough. However, her mother-in-law and her stepmother were vehement that this would be harmful before he was a year old. Usually at odds, on this the two strong-willed countesses agreed.

Wrapping the legs tightly was essential to keep them growing straight, they told Kate. If he was allowed to put his weight on the floor, his legs would become as bowed as those of an old seaman. To counter their traditional thinking, Kate pointed to Moll's perfectly-formed limbs. She smiled to herself at the thought that if King James were alive, she would have had to answer to him too. Nursery matters had seemed to interest him more than matters of state!

There was another little person in the house who provided Kate with a good deal of pleasure. She had gone one day with George to see the kennels at Oakham in Leicestershire where his bull-baiting dogs were kept. This sport was a great favourite with the nobility. Even women attended these gory events. Kate met the keeper of the animals and three of his sons, heavy-set, burly fellows like their father. Then she caught sight of a dwarf, perfectly formed but no more than two feet tall. The embarrassed keeper introduced him as his youngest boy, a seven-year old named Jeffrey. The little fellow had a handsome face, a surprisingly refined manner, and Kate fell in love with the exquisite creature. To his father's great joy, she said she would take him into her service. Little Jeffrey Hudson became a favourite in the Buckingham household. Kate dressed him in silks and satins and gave him two men to wait upon him. So petted and spoiled was he that when his countrified father came calling Jeffrey refused to see him. When the Duke heard of this, he almost turned out the boy who was saved only by the Duchess's pleas.

In July of 1626 Kate took up her duties of the Bedchamber. Until now she had seen little of the Queen. Her Majesty's pert manner in the French way was not to Kate's down-to-earth English taste. Henrietta Maria was interested in gossip, personal beautification, clothes, and entertainment (she was mad for masques), all of which was of limited interest to Kate. The

Queen was spending more time with the witty, sophisticated Countess of Carlisle who taught her to dress and, shamefully, to paint her face, than with the Buckingham women. Nevertheless, the Florentine agent visiting the Queen at Denmark House at the beginning of October found her "cheerful and happy" in the company of the Duchess of Buckingham, the Marchioness of Hamilton, and the Countesses of Rutland, Buckingham, and Denbigh.

With their new appointments, Kate, her mother-in-law, and sister-in-law Susan Denbigh became extremely influential at court. Courtiers and hangers-on sought out "the Buckingham ladies" for favours. Kate found this very bothersome; she had no desire to help greedy aristocrats (other then her in-laws) attain royal patronage. For her, satisfaction lay in using her influence to help worthy people who did not have the rank or money to help themselves. Kate maintained friendly relations with Buckingham's men in office so that when she solicited their assistance they were happy to oblige her. In the last month of pregnancy, she had made a wager with Sir John Hippesley, Lieutenant of Dover Castle. He was delighted to win from her "two skins, two pockets, and two pair of gloves," and since the Duchess was soon to give birth he approached Edward Nicholas, a known favourite of the Duchess. If Nicholas could get these things "before she be brought a' bed" Hippesley offered to share his winnings with him.

Meanwhile, Kate's male relatives were worrying about her safety. The King was raising forces to fight on the Continent in the war against the Spanish and Austrian Habsburgs. London streets were already full of unpaid soldiers and sailors, a terror to the costermongers who tried to protect their barrows from their depredations. Rape and robbery were common. Now more men would be pressed into service and there would be more unrest. On October 31, 1626, Kate's cousin, Sir Henry Manners, wrote to another cousin, Sir Charles Manners: "Let the Duke have a care of his house in this time of mustering soldiers in London."

One day in October while Buckingham was attending a meeting of the Privy Council, angry sailors, survivors of Cadiz, destroyed his empty coach. Mutiny was in the air. In December a large body of sailors marched on the Court with cudgels, demanding their arrears. Then, as Kate's cousins had feared, that winter six captains forced their way into Wallingford House when she and George were at dinner. Taking no heed of the dozens of cowering servants, they ordered the Admiral, "Pay us, so we can pay our mariners." Fearing for his wife and children, Buckingham went to his strong box and paid up.

At the end of March 1627, little Charles took seriously ill, just how ill even the doctors could not say. All they would tell the distressed parents was that he was not yet out of danger. King Charles sent over the royal physician, now enobled as Sir Theodore de Mayerne, however Kate placed more confidence in her own Doctor Moore. Standing by the bedside of her sixteen-month-old son, Kate thought back over their short-lived relationship. Of all the ladies around him, relatives and nurses, he had seemed to recognize that she was his mother. It tore at her heart to remember how he had locked eyes with her. Her thoughts inevitably went back to her little brothers. They had been about the same age as Charles when she had seen them lying in their sickbeds. She had been only a child then, but she vividly recalled watching Henry gasping for breath in his last days and, two years later, a seemingly lifeless Francis who, nevertheless, had dragged on for six more years. As worried as she was, she had to keep up a semblance of hopefulness for George's sake. He had gone to pieces.

On April 2, the news spread at Court that the Duke's only son had died and that the family was utterly grief stricken. The extent of their grief was somewhat unusual. Infant mortality was so high that most families accepted the death of one or more of their children as inevitable. But the Duke had no other son and his dynastic ambitions were notorious. The establishment of a great family and the wherewithal to accomplish this was his legacy from King James. Had not the old king expressed his wish at Burley-on-the-Hill in 1622 that this "blessed couple" should parent a Buckingham dynasty? To the sorrow of his family, the infant Earl of Coventry was buried in Westminster Abbey in a little chapel on the north side of Henry VII's monument. In due course, Buckingham would arrange for a patent giving Mall the title of Duchess of Buckingham in default of male issue.

With the death of the son and heir, Buckingham and his mother resumed their persecution of Frances Purbeck. Two years had gone by since the judges had referred Lady Purbeck and Sir Robert Howard for trial before the High Commission. When Charles was born, the Duke had let the case lapse. Now, he was proceeding with a vengeance. He relished the thought of Frances being paraded through the streets in the white sheet of the adulteress. He was full of animus against her lover as well. Sir Robert had been elected to Parliament and throughout the impeachment trial he had lounged in his seat with a sneering expression as the Duke's reputation was torn to shreds. Buckingham reflected with grim satisfaction that he would wipe that sneer off his face. To prepare for the trial, the Countess of Buckingham would be busy for the next few months assembling witnesses.

While mourning her son, a heartsick Kate returned to her duties as a Lady of the Queen's Bedchamber. Although King Charles was still complaining about his wife to his best friend, Kate told George that from what she could see the Queen was softening towards the King. George had better ingratiate himself with the willful Frenchwoman. Kate decided to buy the Queen's favour. She made Henrietta Maria a gift of a handsome coach and six fine horses costing 20,000 crowns. She had to sell some of the land she had inherited from her mother to pay for it.

While a wife retained possession of her property, the use of it belonged to her husband and she could not dispose of it without his permission. George was only too happy to give his permission for this purpose. Although he did not tell Kate, he was also using his mistress to improve the Queen's opinion of him. Lady Carlisle's influence with Henrietta Maria was growing every day and he felt a good word from her in the royal ear could sway the Queen in his favour.

Deprived by Parliament, King Charles was raising money for the Spanish war by exacting forced loans. Officials in the counties estimated the worth of the landed gentry and each was assessed accordingly. The peerage was exempt although Charles made personal appeals to the lords. Many squires who refused to pay up were threatened with service in the army or the navy. Jail was another weapon used by the King against objectors. Five knights determined to bring on a test case and, refusing to pay the forced loans, were brought before the courts. The judges, loyal to the Crown, found against them on the grounds that the King's writ was the law.

Like every autocratic action of the government, the extra-parliamentary forced loans were blamed on the Duke. His unpopularity, fed by the charges against him at his impeachment trial, was taking on frightening proportions. Kate was doing everything she could to help him – sometimes without his knowledge. A Commission of Inquiry into naval affairs had been set up by the Privy Council. It was only a sop to pacify the Commons and Charles and George intended to let the Commission lapse. Kate (who had more sense than both of them) felt strongly that this was a mistake. She sent a trustworthy young man named Sir Guildford Slingsby secretly to Secretary of State Conway. He told the Secretary that the Duchess feared that letting the Commission fall posed a danger to the Duke. If the abuses in the administration of the navy that the Commons were complaining about went unremedied, she believed they would be laid on the Duke. The Duchess would acknowledge herself beholden to the Secretary if he would further this view with the King and the Duke. Conway was a creature of the Duke's. As he once said to him, "It is impossible for me to forget who made me." He was unlikely to take a divergent position to his patron.

Conway was used to receiving appeals from the Duchess. Kate was well known by this time for her charity and compassion. People in trouble came to her and she used her influence for them with state officials, most of whom owed their appointments to her husband. In the winter of 1627 she undertook to help "poor, distressed" Lady Falkland, wife of the Lord Lieutenant of Ireland. A personal friend of Kate's, she was a regular guest at the York House dinners for Arminian bishops. As it happened, Lady Falkland owed money to the banker Burlamachi and was in danger of going to jail for debt. Indeed, she was a most unfortunate lady. Her husband, finding that her Catholic leanings increased his difficulties in his Irish post, had shipped her back to England.

This was a poor return for her having mortgaged her jointure to establish her husband in vice-regal style; for this wifely "kindness" her father Lord Tansfield, Chief Baron of the Exchequer, had disinherited her. In 1626 she had converted to Catholicism and was subsequently banished from the English court for going to mass at the Queen's chapel. Since then she had drifted around London, shabbily dressed and with "an abstracted demeanour." She complained to all who would listen that she had "no meat, nor drink, nor clothes, nor money."

As a member of the nobility she was an embarrassment to King Charles. He thought to send her to her mother who lived far enough away in Essex, but the arrangement was unpalatable to both mother and daughter. In March 1627 Lady Falkland wrote a desperate letter to Secretary Conway. If she was to be "confined" in Essex, she desired that it be near her sister. She entreated him to speak to the Duchess and the Countess of Buckingham on her behalf, and to believe them rather than "those pestilent servants of her Lord, whose misinformation have begotten her miseries." Although Lady Falkland claimed that Susan Denbigh had promised to convert with her and had let her down, apparently she did not hold this against her for she continued to enlist her help.

Kate was fond of Lady Falkland, not least because she was a Catholic. Also Lady Falkland's children "were near to her in blood" as Viscount Falkland's sister was married to Uncle George Manners. Moreover, Kate who was known as a friend to women authors admired Lady Falkland, a writer of some renown, a translator of Latin classics and the author of a play, *The Tragedy of Miriam,* said to be the first play authored by an Englishwomen ever to be published. Responding to the pleas of this lady, Kate wrote to Secretary Conway asking him to kindly speak to the King and, if necessary, to get the Duke to do the same. Ultimately, the "business between Lady Falkland and Burlamachi" went to the Privy Council which, in turn, referred it to Sir Edward Nicholas, Secretary to the Admiralty. The sympathetic Kate requested Nicholas "to show all the lawful favour he can" to the unfortunate Eliza Falkland who was "a lady whom she so much respects."

Her intervention was successful. King Charles ordered Secretary Conway and the Chancellor of the Exchequer, Sir Richard Weston, to arrange with Viscount Falkland's agent in London to supply his wife's needs. Her husband agreed to allow her 500£ a year but he never paid it. As it happened, Viscount Falkland was recalled from Ireland shortly afterwards for corruption. He soon became mortally ill, putrefying with gangrene, and his forgiving, rejected wife hurried to his side and nursed him through his final days.

Not all those Kate endeavoured to help were worthy of her intervention. In February 1627, Sir John Hippesley, the Lieutenant of Dover Castle, dismissed an employee, one Peter Cannon, because of his dissolute life, claiming that Cannon was bringing the Admiralty into disrepute. Cannon's wife appealed to the Duchess with her own version of events that absolved her husband completely. Hippesley heard that she had made the Duchess believe her. Indignant at the prospect of having this blackguard back, he sent a letter to the Duke giving his reasons for the dismissal and expressing the hope that "my Lady Duchess has not spoken for him to have him restored." In this instance, Kate's charity was misplaced.

At times Kate ventured into the field of criminal justice, as in the case of two Berkshire men convicted of murder by the local coroner. She and her mother-in-law were convinced that the men had killed in self-defence and the two ladies were attempting to get a pardon for them. That this extraordinary intervention was based on more than women's intuition is indicated by the fact that the Earl of Dorset (not known for humanitarian impulses) was endorsing their efforts. After signing the pardon, King Charles had second thoughts and stayed it.

All the Buckingham clan turned to Kate to approach the Duke on their behalf, even his mother. Kate reminded him that he had promised "two Baronets for my Lady." This would be ready money for the Countess as baronetcies sold for a goodly sum. Kate also nudged him "to remember her sister Washington's business." (Buckingham's half-sister Anne was married to Sir William Washington.) Then there was some "business" for a distant cousin, Dick Turpin.

To every favour she asked of George he gave his consent in an offhand way. He was clearly distracted. In fact, his mind was occupied with a daring action that he was confident would redeem his reputation and make him the most popular man in England. Brimming over with optimism, he was readying a large fleet to go to the relief of the Huguenots whose stronghold, the city of La Rochelle on France's west coast, was under siege by Louis XIII's troops.

The Duke was under strong censure for having lent several English ships to the King of France during James's reign, which it now appeared were to be used against the French Protestants. In fact this was one of the charges against him in the impeachment, so by going to their aid he expected to earn enthusiastic praise from the Puritan Members of Parliament. This would not be another Cadiz. He himself would go as Admiral of the Fleet and Commander-in-Chief of the land forces. To show that such was his intention, a coal-ship was being converted into a luxurious home afloat for him. Carpenters were building stalls for oxen, milk cows, goats, and coops for fowl and poultry to provision the troops.

Kate, his mother, and his sister, were frantic at the danger this adventure posed for George. They begged him on their knees not to go, saying it would be his ruin. He told them he was doing it to bring peace to Catholics and Protestants in France. When this was greeted by a skeptical retort from his mother, he told her she would have thought differently if he were going to the aid of the Catholics. He strode out leaving the women weeping. Their pleas proving of no avail, they decided to intercede with

King Charles to stop him. The opportunity would arise at a banquet at York House.

Unable to shake off her grief over the loss of her baby son, Kate was in no mood for the frivolity of a York House banquet, but George insisted on entertaining the King and Queen before his departure for La Rochelle. On a beautiful evening in early May gilded and painted barges bearing the coat-of-arms of their owners arrived at York-stairs. From these stepped out several hundred gorgeously attired members of the nobility and aristocracy. Last to arrive was the royal barge. Passing through a new watergate like a small triumphal arch, the guests walked up the garden path escorted by footmen carrying flambeaux to the mansion blazing with lights. Once inside, the guests outdid each other in praising the recent changes and acquisitions – the coffered vaulted ceiling, the rich hangings, the equestrian portrait of the Duke by Rubens hanging in the Great Chamber. York House had become so magnificent that the Marquis de Bassompierre, arbiter of taste at the French court, had said on his recent visit to London that it was "the most richly fitted up" of any palace he had ever seen. At the banquet, every culinary luxury was set before the guests – swans, salmon, oysters, turkeys, sturgeon, crabs, musk melons, sugar loafs, washed down with claret, sack, muscadine, Rhenish wines and Spanish sherry. The *piece de resistance* was a huge pie borne by four footmen. When set down on the table, to the delight of the guests Kate's dwarf, tiny Jeffrey, sprang out. The Queen was in raptures. She hinted so broadly that she wanted the boy that the Duchess gave him to her on a silver platter. Jeffrey kneeled before his new mistress and the company rose to toast Her Majesty and her miniscule servant. A masque followed in which the Duke performed the principal role. As he capered to the lilting music of mandolin and lute, he was pursued by jumping figures wearing masks of dogs' heads with open mouths: the audience understood that these represented the barking of the ignorant mob.

Before the evening was over, King Charles was taken aside by Kate, who together with her mother-in-law and sister-in-law pleaded with him to forbid the Duke to go to France. They argued the dangers of the sea crossing, the fighting, and the fact that if he was killed he left no male heir. In spite of the King's courteous attention, it became apparent that he was as keen on the expedition to relieve the Huguenots as George was.

CHAPTER ELEVEN

On May 31, 1627, the Duke of Buckingham set sail from Dover with twenty-seven ships. It was an abortive start. On board, he was informed that there were no shoes, shirts, or stockings for the sailors and no surgeons' chests. He ordered the captains to put ashore at Portsmouth to equip the fleet.

Around this time, family retainers were noticing that the Duchess "pukes a little which makes us hope she is with child." In fact, she was. When George returned briefly from Portsmouth she implored him not to leave her in her condition. He was kindness itself, and before the tearful interview was over he promised her on his oath that he would not go to France. He left her on her knees thanking God for His mercy, despite her apostasy.

Happy but just a little uneasy, she dashed off a short note to George, begging him not to deceive her and to love her only. For her part, "it was impossible for a woman to love man more than I do you." An unexpected visit from Sir Sackville Crow, Buckingham's treasurer, dashed her hopes. He told her that the Duke was going to France but that he would come to see her before he left. Then on June 26 she learned that he was setting sail the next day. The Countess of Buckingham found her "so troubled because the Duke had failed in his promise to see her again" that she sent an urgent message to her son at Portsmouth that "a word or two from you in excuse would revive her much." But George slipped off without a word. Kate wrote her husband an uncharacteristically angry letter:

"I confess I did ever fear you would be catched, for there was no other likelihood after all that show but you must needs go. For my part, I have been a very miserable woman hitherto, that never could have you keep at home. But now I will ever look to be so, until some blessed occasion comes to draw you quite from the Court. For there is none more miserable than I am now; and till you leave this life of a courtier, which you have been ever since I knew you, I shall ever think myself unhappy. Even when I am with child I must have so much cause of sorrow as to have you go from me, but I never had so great a cause of grief as I have now."

Then she revealed the true depths of her despair. "If I were sure my soul would be well, I could wish myself out of this miserable world," she wrote her husband. However being a realistic woman, she soon faced the facts:

Since there is no remedy but that you must go, I pray God send you quickly that you may be quickly at home again; and whoever wished you this journey beside yourself, that they may be punished, for it will be a source of a great deal of grief to me. But that is no matter. Now there is no remedy but patience, which God send me! I pray God send me wisdom not to hurt myself with grieving. Now I am very well, I thank God, and so is Mall."

But there was still more to get off her chest: "I would to Jesus there were any way in the world to put you off this journey with your murderers ... but you have sent yourself and made me miserable. God forgive you for it."

She told him she would never put him on his oath again nor ever believe him. Her mother-in-law took her part completely. In a letter to her son the Countess wrote: "God hath blessed you with a virtuous wife and sweet daughter, with another son, I hope, if you do not destroy it by this way you take: she cannot believe a word you speak, you have so much deceived herself."

Even in the midst of her misery in the certain knowledge that George would go to France, Kate had the heart to promote the careers of two of George's young cousins. The boys were asking to go with the expedition "for they would rather venture their lives than stay behind," she wrote George. "I hope you will put them in someway for their advancement for they deserve very well."

On June 27, the Lord High Admiral set out from Portsmouth with a fleet of ninety ships. He landed his forces of some 9,500 infantry and cavalry on the Isle of Rhe, two miles off the mainland facing La Rochelle. The first objective was to capture the island that controlled the approach to the town. Under Buckingham's direct command, the English forces began a siege of St. Martin's, the French government's principal fortress on the Isle of Rhe.

Undeterred by Charles's refusal to stop George from going, Kate appealed to him in the name of their long friendship to order George to come home. Charles may have humoured her with some vague promises because she believed he had agreed. But when weeks went by and she heard nothing, she wrote to Hippesley to remind the King to issue the recall order. The Duchess's intervention was a well-kept palace secret. Perhaps because it was never acted upon.

In the midst of her worry about George's safety, he sent her a macabre souvenir of the campaign. It seemed that the governor of St. Martin's fortress had despatched a man to kill Buckingham. The assassination attempt failed and George sent Kate the knife meant to murder him. Kate believed in her husband's narrow escape but many English were skeptical. Indeed, the Duke was criticized at home for being too friendly with Toras the French governor. Stories came back to England of Buckingham and Toras entertaining each other and of "presents and compliments" passing between them. This example of *noblesse oblige* while English soldiers were being killed and wounded did not go down well with the ordinary Englishman. It was generally held that "civilities to an enemy seldom produced good effects." Kate understood popular opinion and likely shared it. When George sent over a bottle of orange water that he said was a gift to her from Toras, Kate thanked him but said she dared not use it, coming from the French governor.

A gift she could accept with a clear conscience came at the same time from the Queen's sister, the Duchess of Savoy. It was a cabinet chiefly of rock crystal objects, pieces of cloth of gold and silver, vases with jessamine water, and such-like to a value of 20,000£. Its hodgepodge of pretty, useless things appealed to Kate who had never developed a taste for painting and sculpture as her husband had.

While George was fighting on the Isle of Rhe Kate sought to arrange a patronage appointment for the Denbigh family. The fines imposed upon

Catholics under the recusancy laws yielded considerable revenue and to collect the moneys two receivers were appointed, one for the North of England and one for "South of the Trent." These were lucrative sinecures and before he left, Buckingham had granted the latter post to his nephew George Feilding, Sue's second son. However in Buckingham's absence the Treasurer, Lord Marlborough, had stayed the grant, insisting that the moneys collected go directly into the Exchequer; in the hands of a receiver there could be precious little left for the royal treasury. Seemingly untroubled that the receipts would come from penalizing Anglo-Catholics, Kate wrote to Secretary of State Conway asking him to move the King to order the Lord Treasurer to allow the grant to "her servant, George Feilding." But with the Exchequer virtually empty and anticipated taxes and loans three years hence already spent, Charles was anxiously looking for money to finance the Rhe campaign. He rescinded the grants and ordered that the recusants' revenue should be kept apart for the navy.

Kate was doing everything she could to aid her husband's campaign. By mid-September George was complaining bitterly of a lack of supplies from England. Kate hurriedly sent him two hundred pounds' worth of supplies for the winter. At the same time, George's appeal to his mother to lend him some money to purchase supplies had gained him nothing but a good scolding. For him to wage this war in the name of religion, "to make God a party to these woeful affairs," she told him, was deplorable and "would turn all Christian princes to bend their forces against us, that otherwise, in policy, would have taken our parts." Shortly after these very different family responses some supplies arrived belatedly from England. The Countess made it very clear to Buckingham that he could thank his wife for them. Kate, she wrote, "works carefully in sending moneys with the supply that is now coming, though slowly: it would have been worse but for her."

By November, things were looking better for Buckingham's campaign. He had it on reliable intelligence that the besieged garrison was almost starving in the fortress. Victory seemed at hand when at the last minute the French navy broke through the blockade of English ships and the defenders of St. Martin's fortress were re-supplied. After this setback, it reached Kate's ears that the Duke was considering the precipitous action of invading the mainland to launch an offensive against the French army besieging La Rochelle.

It was to keep an eye on George and to prevent this kind of rash action that Kate had sent her personal physician and spiritual advisor, Doctor Moore, to accompany the expedition. "I should think myself the most miserablest woman in the world if my lord should go into the mainland …to venture himself beyond all discretion," she wrote the doctor. "I pray keep him from being too venturous, for it does not belong to a general to walk the trenches; therefore keep a care of him." She added, "He is not any whit the more popular man than when he went; therefore you may see whether these people be worthy for him to venture his life for."

It was quite evident to his mother as well that George's purpose in going to France to make himself a popular hero had misfired. "I hope your eyes will be opened to see what a great gulf of businesses you have put yourself into," the Countess of Buckingham scolded, "and so little regarded at home, where all is merry and well pleased, though the ships be not victualled as yet, nor mariners to go with them. As for moneys, the kingdom will not supply your expenses, and every man groans under the burden of the times." Both women agreed that not only had he not gained anything but he was in danger of losing his hold over the King. Without Buckingham to complain to and goad him on to quarrelling with her, Charles was getting along famously with his wife. Buckingham was well aware of this. In a postscript to a letter in August, Charles wrote that "my wife and I were never better together; she was showing herself so loving of me, by her discretion on all occasions, that it makes all wonder and esteem of her." All the courtiers were talking about the royal couple's newfound marital bliss.

On the Queen's side at the palace the Countess of Carlisle ruled as the undisputed favourite. The young queen took great delight in her malicious wit. Lady Carlisle excelled in what the courtiers called "Characters" – word portraits that were nothing less than character assassinations. Kate did not believe for an instant that this ambitious woman was using her favoured position to help reconcile George and Henrietta Maria. Indeed, she had no doubt that if George fell out of favour with the King, Lady Carlisle would end their affair. She sent a warning letter to George urging him to hasten home, "both for public and [our] private good in Court." Lady Carlisle was diminishing the Buckingham family's interest by her almost insulting treatment of his sister Susan and even herself. "Your great lady that you believe is so much your friend uses your friends something worse than when you were here, and your favour has made her so great as now she cares for nobody."

Only one person in the Queen's retinue stood up to the Countess of Carlisle, and that was the smallest one of all – Jeffrey Hudson. He felt so secure in the Queen's affections that he was quite outspoken to all the courtiers, serving in a way as her court jester. One June day little Jeffrey fell out of the window at Denmark House. He was bruised and battered but with no broken bones. Henrietta Maria was so upset that she would not even get dressed that day.

Kate need not have feared that George would launch an offensive against the French army at La Rochelle. Such an action was preempted in November when the superior forces of Louis XIII crossed to the Isle of Rhe and routed Buckingham's dispirited troops, causing tremendous casualties during their retreat. He himself had fought bravely throughout the entire campaign but his generalship had lacked strategy and even day-to-day tactics. As just one example, the English forces had attempted an assault on the fortress with ladders several feet too short. Of the more than 9,000 cavalry and infantry the Duke set off with, he returned on November 12 with no more than three thousand men, most of whom were diseased or wounded.

When Kate heard the news that he had landed, she went on an all-night vigil. In a touching expression of her deep love for him, she sent off a note to Plymouth where he remained a few days after the failed expedition. "I have been still every hour looking for you that I cannot now till I see you sleep in the nights, for every minute, if I do hear any noise, I think it is one [a messenger] from you to tell me the happy news what day I shall see you." She was lightheaded with relief (and sleep deprivation), her only thought to have her beloved husband returned to her.

Charles, too, was overjoyed to have Steenie back. He sent his own coach to Plymouth to bring him to London where the entire court, some on horseback others in coaches, was lined up to welcome him home. In reality, he was a defeated general returning to what should have been disgrace, but because the King willed it he was received as a conquering hero. Charles would hear no criticism of the Duke's conduct of the war and assumed the blame himself for the delay in relief supplies and troop reinforcements. The result of the failed expedition to relieve the Huguenots of La Rochelle was that Buckingham had now involved England in two wars - with France as well as Spain. Although he was unpopular before, the Rhe disaster had brought down upon Buckingham's head the people's wrath. He even acknowledged as much to his wife and his mother. In this mood, he was determined to see the ruin of his sister-in-law, Frances Purbeck, and her lover, Sir Thomas Howard.

On November 19, 1627, their case was heard by the court of High Commission. A parade of witnesses, including the midwife who had delivered Frances's baby, had been assembled by the Duke of Buckingham and his mother, yet all that this evidence proved was that Lady Purbeck had had a baby. There was no conclusive proof that her husband was not the father. The court did, however, find the Viscountess Purbeck guilty of adultery with Sir Robert Howard. She was fined 500£ and sentenced to do penance. Failing a son from his pregnant Kate, Buckingham had to acknowledge to himself that Robert Wright was still second in line to his dukedom. Still, it would be almost enough satisfaction just to see the woman he so passionately hated walking barefoot from Paul's Cross to the Savoy hospital in the white sheet of the adulteress. But first he would have to find her.

After the trial Lady Purbeck simply vanished. The Christmas festivities came and went and all of January with no sign of her and her child. Finally, just before Lent Buckingham's spies ran her down at a house in the Strand beside the Savoyard embassy. It was Shrove Tuesday and the street was filled with roisterers in carnival costumes and curiosity-seekers attempting to scale the garden wall for a glimpse of the notorious lady. Constables were summoned and took up stations on the street in front of the house, but the beleaguered lady could still escape through a rear exit.

To enter the garden at the back of the house they would have to go through the embassy's garden. The ambassador who was enjoying Shrove Tuesday pancakes with Balthazar Gerbier, Buckingham's factotum, at first refused permission but at repeated requests from a gentleman representing the Countess of Buckingham "craving permission for the officers of the law to pass through his house and garden," he agreed to allow in one constable around the dinner hour. Meanwhile amid all this hubbub, a coach pulled up before the house, a slim, fair-haired figure dashed out carrying something wrapped in a blanket, jumped into the coach and was off in a minute down the street. A hue and cry that this was Lady Purbeck sent the constables and the mob chasing after the coach. When they caught up with it, the "lady" turned out to be the Ambassador of Savoy's young page in women's garments. Meanwhile, another coach arrived at the door and the real Lady Purbeck, clutching her little son, made her escape from under the nose of the constabulary.

Buckingham and his mother gave up the chase after this although Frances was known to be in Shropshire with Sir Thomas Howard. For once again "Robert Wright" was no longer a threat. Kate had produced a son for George on January 30, 1628.

On February 8, the bells of Westminster Abbey and the church of St. Martin's-in-the-Fields were ringing "full merrily" as baby George Villiers was christened at Wallingford House by Bishop Laud. His godfathers were King Charles in a celebratory mood wearing "a long soldier's coat, covered with gold lace, and his hair all gaufred and frizzled," and the Earl of Suffolk. (The choice of the latter indicated that the Duke's vendetta against Sir Thomas Howard had taken a benign turn for the present Earl was his brother.) Queen Henrietta Maria had accepted the invitation to be the baby's godmother but preferred to remain in the palace hardly two steps away, sending as her deputy the widowed Duchess of Richmond and Lennox.

Kate had continued her advocacy for the unfortunate even during her lying in. Hearing of an English soldier who was a prisoner in France after the Duke's return from the Isle of Rhe, the good-hearted Kate sent off a letter to Sir John Hippesley. "The Duchess desires that one of the prisoners left behind in France be ransomed," Hippesley informed Secretary Conway. Kate's good works kept Buckingham's appointees busy.

CHAPTER TWELVE

It was well-known at court that the Buckingham women detested the Countess of Carlisle. A courtier explained the reason to a friend: "The Duke's wife, mother, and sister hate her not only for the Duke's intimacy with her but also that she has the Queen's heart above them." Although the Duchess took precedence over the Countess, Henrietta Maria made it very obvious that Lucy came first with her. Kate would arrive at the Queen's side of the palace to find the two laughing at some joke no one else shared. The Countess of Carlisle had been granted a pension of 2,000£ and her own chambers at Whitehall. Because of her influence with the Queen, and the Queen's growing influence with the King, all the great men frequented her salon. As the Duke's wife, Kate too was an important figure at court, but she admitted to herself that her rival was more amusing and much more beautiful. Actually, she was not vying with Lucy Carlisle over power at court; she was in a contest with her for Buckingham's love. "Love me only," she pleaded with George.

The truth was that George's extra-marital passion was not for his mistress but for the Queen of France. In spite of the costly failure of the Rhe campaign, Buckingham was planning to go to France again the following summer to relieve the Huguenots, still under siege by Louis XIII's army at La Rochelle. Balthazar Gerbier, who understood his master very well, was of the opinion that Buckingham had a personal motive as well as reasons of state. Love was drawing him across the Channel - "the poet's Cupid was the boatswain of his ship." It was Gerbier himself who had brought the message back to his master in January 1627 that the French would not accept him as English ambassador. Louis XIII and Richelieu would not let the English duke into France so he would force his way in. Kate would not have disagreed with Gerbier entirely. That her philandering husband would aim to seduce the consort of the French king did not surprise her. And irresistible as he was in her eyes, she would have expected him to succeed.

To outfit another fleet, Parliament had to be called to vote taxes. Almost immediately after its opening in March 1628, Parliament voted the King five subsidies for the navy. However before the legislative proceedings were completed and the taxes levied, a new bone of contention arose. This was the billeting of soldiers on the country. Members of the Commons came to Westminster with an unprecedented number of complaints from householders of robberies and rapes by strangers living under their roof.

Charles's response was that he would look into the situation. What with billeting, forced loans, imprisonment without trial, one Member of the House declared, "I more fear the violation of public rights at home than a foreign enemy." On the promise of the subsidies, Buckingham sent out his brother-in-law, the Earl of Denbigh, to begin the summer offensive for the relief of La Rochelle. As an admiral, Denbigh failed ignominiously, bringing the fleet back to England at the first reverse. This, the fourth failed naval expedition, destroyed any confidence in Buckingham's ability to command the navy, let alone to run the country. Sir Edward Coke, the venerable leader of the parliamentary opposition, denounced him as "the grievance of grievances."

Unable to touch the Duke because of the King's protection, his servants bore the brunt of it. Balthazar Gerbier chose this inauspicious moment to apply for naturalization. His application was rejected peremptorily. In fact, Gerbier felt so threatened by the popular hatred of his master that he began carrying a revolver when he went into town and seldom sallied forth without a man to protect him. He was not exaggerating the danger. One Doctor Lambe, a charlatan said to be in Buckingham's employ, was beaten to death on the street by a mob shouting that they would do the same to the Duke if they had the chance.

In Parliament, Charles was demanding immediate passage of the subsidies bill while the Commons was insisting on redress of its grievances first. Unmoved by Charles's assurance that they could trust him to take care of their complaints after he received the subsidies, the Members drafted a Petition of Right for the King to sign. The rights for which they sought royal approval included an end to billeting soldiers in private houses, to violations of habeas corpus, to forced loans, and to taxation without Parliament's approval. Charles saw this as a gross trespass on his prerogative, but to save his friend Buckingham from another impeachment charge he signed the Petition with no intention of observing it. Fearing with good reason that the Petition would be ignored, the Commons prepared a Remonstrance detailing Buckingham's sins of commission and omission and attributed "the miserable condition of the Kingdom to the Duke's power and abuse of power."

The highly respected jurist John Selden intoned that "it would be a breach of duty to the King if the Commons did not deal clearly without sparing any how near and dear soever they were unto him, if they were hurtful or dangerous to the Commonwealth." The Remonstrance alleged an increase in popery which it attributed to Buckingham, his mother, and his friend Bishop Laud whose Arminianism, with its emphasis on ritual, was simply "a cunning way to bring in popery." The military disasters, decay of trade, and the failure to guard the Narrow Seas, the scarcity of gunpowder in the Tower were all laid at the feet of the Lord High Admiral. The Remonstrance concluded with this message to the King that it was impossible for one man to manage so many and weighty affairs, that it was not safe to continue the Duke in his great offices or in "his place of nearness and counsel about your sacred person" and that he should be dismissed.

In response, Charles staunchly defended Buckingham's innocence, demanded that the Remonstrance and all debate pertaining to it be struck from the parliamentary record, and at the end of June he prorogued Parliament to October. Nevertheless, the Remonstrance acted as tinder to set alight the public anger.

The Duke's arrogance was such that he appeared scornful of the Commons' attack on him. He was reported to have said to guests at his table, "Tush, it makes no matter what the Commons or Parliament doth, for without my leave and authority they shall not be able to touch the Hair of a Dog." He denied this vehemently, even asking for time in the House of Lords to repudiate the statement attributed to him, yet Kate and his inner circle had heard him make such remarks many times. Certainly there was reason enough for his self-confidence as King Charles had shown that he would dissolve or prorogue Parliament when the barking dogs were nipping too closely at the Duke's heels. Yet Kate knew (and the knowledge did not go beyond their bedchamber) that George was a frightened man. All his old insecurity had returned and was making him ill. His life hung on a thread, that of the King's favour. Though Charles had never been more staunch to him, the King's new uxoriousness made Buckingham fear that Henrietta Maria would triumph over him in the privacy of the royal bed. One other saw behind the confident front that Buckingham presented to the world. The Archbishop of Canterbury, George Abbott, who had been disgraced and sequestered from all his offices by Buckingham, said of him that "the keys of England hang at his girdle; yet [he] standeth in his own heart, in such tickle terms, as that he feareth every shadow, and thinketh that the lending of the King's ear unto any grave and well-seasoned report, may blow him out of all! Which in his estimation, he thinketh is settled on no good foundation but the affection of the Prince; which may be mutable …"

A big problem that worried Kate more than it did George was their shortage of ready cash. Indeed, the Buckingham finances were in such a state by the summer of 1628 that they closed down York House temporarily and took up residence at Burley-on-the-Hill to save the expense of living in London. "Pray for me," Kate wrote Olive Porter, "I do not doubt but we shall be merry again in York House. We shall by living here a while redeem ourselves out of debt, I hope in Jesus." Kate had discovered that she was pregnant again. She assured "Sweet Cousin" Olive that she was feeling fine. She told her that the local doctor had sent a favourable opinion on her state of health to Doctor Moore.

Henrietta Maria had gone to the spa at Wellingborough with her ladies. Before leaving, Sue Denbigh had written Kate to ask a favour. She had received the King's promise to give her chaplain the living of Halifax. But if the Lord Chamberlain would get him sworn one of the King's chaplains and Secretary Conway would secure him a prebend in Windsor or Canterbury, she would resign her claim for Halifax. In her absence, would Kate look after this little patronage matter? Of course she would. Sue was doing very well at court. She had a good head for business and now as Mistress of the Robes handled the Queen's private finances. Indeed, the warrant for 2,000£ for the Queen's extraordinary expenses in her present progress to the spa was made out to the Countess of Denbigh. This *de facto* position as Her Majesty's personal treasurer had given Sue a good deal of prestige, making her second only to the Countess of Carlisle on the Queen's Side.

At the moment, Kate was seeking a patronage plum for one of her own dependants. Once again she found herself involved in the criminal justice system. A man in Essex was accused of murder and if convicted he would lose not only his life but his lands and goods would be appropriated by the Crown. These would then be granted away or sold to the highest bidder. A longtime servant, John Baker, had come to Kate and begged her to use her influence to get the appropriated estate for him. She decided she would not approach the King herself on such a matter but would work through an intermediary. Accordingly, she wrote to Endymion Porter to present her suit on behalf of Baker for which Endymion would get a commission. Using his entrée at court, Porter made a good living out of representing suitors or to squeeze payment out of the Exchequer. Some found his commissions too high.

During the parliamentary recess, Buckingham was busy organizing the next expedition to relieve La Rochelle. He would take the helm again soon after Denbigh's botched attempt. The court was abuzz with the Lord High Admiral's upcoming campaign. Nothing was more thrilling than a new military campaign for courtiers who would experience none of it personally. Buckingham strode around issuing orders, the personification of the gallant wartime commander, seemingly brimming over with confidence. But on the eve of leaving for Portsmouth, he called Bishop Laud aside at court and took him by the back stairs up to the gallery behind his lodgings where he was assured of complete privacy. "If I should die," he said, "I want you to see that the King looks after my wife and children." The utter seriousness with which he spoke caused Laud to feel that he expected to die in battle. While expressing his hope and belief that such a stewardship would not be necessary, he assured the Duke that in the unlikely event he would devote himself to the Duchess and the children.

Kate was resigned to his going this time. Her only demand was that George allow her to accompany him to Portsmouth before he sailed. The old Countess was not so easily put off. In spite of his high position, she still took a mother's liberty to scold him when she felt it necessary. Now, fearful that her golden boy was going to his death, in their private talks she warned him that he would be forgotten and forsaken by the court that now grovelled before him. There were stories of a loud quarrel between mother and son shortly before he started out for Portsmouth. He was said to have walked off with a grim expression on his face, leaving his mother "overwhelmed in tears and in the highest agony imaginable." Neither had mentioned it to Kate.

On the 22nd of August the Duke and Duchess set out for Portsmouth attended by a great company of the nobility in coaches or on horseback. Kate brought her sister-in-law, Kit's wife Elizabeth the Viscountess Anglesey, along for company. It made a nice change for Elizabeth who had to put up with Kit's drinking. (At one point, King Charles had suspended Anglesey from his post of Chief Steward of the Honour of Hampton Court, saying he would have no drunkards in his chamber.) At Portsmouth Buckingham took his womenfolk to Captain Norton's house on High Street where the ducal party was to stay. The hall was full to the rafters with people waiting for the Duke. Wherever he was, whether at York House or Whitehall or Hampton Court or the racetrack at Newmarket, he was always surrounded by courtiers, suitors, creditors. On this day the crowd was swollen by the nobility that had come to see the Lord High Admiral off on his second expedition to La Rochelle.

Kate was in the nauseous stage of early pregnancy and tired from the trip, she spent the rest of the evening quietly in her bedchamber. The following morning she woke to find George already up. Her maid came in to tell her that His Grace had gone downstairs to take his breakfast. Suddenly, there was a tremendous hubbub. Running to the gallery that overlooked the hall in her nightgown, Kate saw her adored husband splayed out on the floor in a pool of blood. The glint of a knife lay near his body. She started screaming. She tried to throw herself over the railing but was forcibly restrained by Viscountess Anglesey and the maids.

One horrified bystander, the courtier-diplomat Sir Dudley Carleton, sent off a hurried note to the Queen: "Ah poor ladies, such were their screechings, tears, and distractions, that I never in my life heard the like before, and hope never to here the like again."

Below, the scene had turned into a melee with everyone shouting "Where is the foul murderer? Who is he?" A short man in the buff tunic of a soldier spoke up, "I am the man. My name is Felton." He made no attempt to escape, even when some men drew their swords against him. He was taken away to the governor's house where he was soon discovered to be a lieutenant who had served in the Cadiz and Rhe campaigns. He took a high line, declaring that "it was the hand of Heaven that gave the stroke, and though the Duke's body had been covered over with armour he could not have avoided it." That the assassination was a premeditated act was confirmed by a paper sewn into his hat declaring that the reason that moved him to this act was no grudge of his own, though his pay was in arrears and he had been bypassed twice for a captaincy, rather it was for the public good since Parliament had branded the Duke an enemy of the state.

King Charles was staying some four miles away and the army officer who was despatched to inform him of the Duke's death found him at prayer. The dreadful message was whispered in the royal ear but to the messenger's surprise, the King remained in the chapel until the end of the divine service. Afterwards, it was as if he awoke to the tragedy. He issued a barrage of orders including an order to take the Duchess to a safe place immediately under heavy guard, obviously fearing a conspiracy against the Buckingham family.

At Belvoir Castle, the Earl of Rutland was handed a letter brought at a gallop describing the dreadful event at Portsmouth. Without further ado, he mounted his horse and rode post haste towards London. Encountering Lord Scrope's secretary, he told him that he was on his way to comfort his daughter. He showed him the letter and asked him to convey its contents to his sister Lady Scrope.

Bishop Laud was not far behind the Earl of Rutland in rushing to Kate's side. He felt a special responsibility, having pledged himself to the Duke to look after Kate and the children in the event of his death. As well, the news of the assassination touched him as a personal tragedy. Writing to Secretary Conway, he called it "the saddest accident that ever befell me." Kate was not as fond of the little bishop as George had been. She resented his efforts to stamp out what he called popery, but his genuine sorrow and grief over "the abominable murder of his dear lord, the Duke" offered her some much needed comfort at this time.

Kate's grief was such that she was virtually inconsolable. Religion provided no consolation. Had she not forsworn the true Catholic God? At times she tortured herself with the thought that her horrendous loss was punishment for that abandonment. She cried without let up and the household was awakened by her moans. George had been the light of her life. Her world without him was inconceivable. His absences in Spain and France had nearly killed her but then she could look forward to his eventual return. Now there was no hope of ever seeing him again. How could she bear it, she asked herself. Friends and family told her that the baby growing inside her was a tiny image of himself, a keepsake as it were left to her by her adored husband. Nothing aggravated her more than this well-meant sympathy. She recalled the player at the Globe theatre declaiming about an infant "mewling and puking in his nurse's arms." How could this little manikin replace the joy of lying in the arms of her glorious lord and lover? As the weeks went by, however, Kate's common sense and forbearance gave her command over herself, allowing her to bear her loss with dignity, in public at any rate.

Charles wished to give his friend a funeral even more magnificent than King James's, but he was talked out of it. Sir Richard Weston told him flatly there was no money in the Exchequer for this. It was also explained to Charles that the late Duke was so hated by the people that such a display would invite a violent attack on the cortege as it made its way from Wallingford House to Westminster Abbey. In the event, the funeral took place under cover of night, followed by no more than a hundred mourners and accompanied by a guard of trained bands shouldering their pikes and muskets in readiness for an attack, not trailing them at their heels as was usual in funeral processions. In fact, the coffin was empty. For fear the mob would break open the coffin, the actual burial in the Abbey had taken place secretly the day before.

The popular hatred of Buckingham was such that the assassin Felton became a hero. On his way to the Tower he was cheered as the saviour of his country. At his trial the judges refused to allow him to be put on the rack, ruling that torture was illegal (notwithstanding that it was used daily). His execution was relatively humane without the "drawing and quartering" - the butchering of the still living body - that was usual in cases of convicted murderers. But Felton himself believed harsh punishment was justified and offered to have his hand cut off – an offer grimly accepted by King Charles but rejected by the judges. Felton had recanted even before his trial. He sent a message to the Duchess of Buckingham expressing his contrition and begging her forgiveness. In an act that put her charitableness to the test, Kate replied that she forgave him. At Tyburn, just before his hanging, he praised the Duchess "for being so noble as to forgive him that heinous crime." He could have been content, he said, for his body to have suffered exquisite torture to have given her satisfaction. His corpse was hung up in chains two miles out of Portsmouth. It was in the same garments he was wearing when he killed the Duke. This was at the wish of the Lady Duchess.

Her father was Kate's mainstay in the days and weeks following the assassination. He it was who took six-year-old Mall on his lap and staunched her tears with stories of her father happy in Heaven. He took over the burden of financial matters that in her distressed state of mind was beyond Kate. Rutland worked closely with the executors who included his good friend Lord Savage and several of Buckingham's retainers. A financial accounting would have to be given presently to King Charles. A week after the Duke's murder, letters such as this one to Captain Pennington were sent out: "The Duchess's affections being such as she is unable to look into the Duke's estate, she has desired the executors to do so." The captain, an old sea dog employed by the Admiralty even before Buckingham became Lord Admiral, was asked to send a brief account "of what monies he has received from the Duke and for what service it was intended and has been issued." Buckingham's financial transactions were so intermingled with government business that it would prove virtually impossible to separate them.

Shortly before setting off for La Rochelle in 1627 Buckingham had made a will bequeathing all his property to his wife during her lifetime: the three London mansions, with Chelsea House, New Hall in Essex, Burley-on-the-Hill in Rutlandshire, as well as nineteen houses on the Strand and some dozen other country properties from which Kate would draw the rents until the second Duke, the baby George, reached his majority. Buckingham gave her the power to dispose of his personal estate outside the entail and left her well fixed with 4,550£ a year from Irish customs and a pension of 6,000£. The will was a testament of his love for her. But wealth tied up in property did not cover the Duke's expenses and he left a debt of 70,000£. Although strapped for funds, over the next few years King Charles would pay off the outstanding debts of his late favourite. (In fact, Rutland and the executors had urged Charles to forego a lavish funeral for the Duke and to use the money to help pay off his debts.) In disposing of Buckingham's multiple offices, the King reserved one sinecure called Roper's Office for Kate. A jealous courtier said that she would find it "an excellent cordial because the gold will be most predominant."

The greatest boon for Kate was that the King granted her the wardship of the young Duke. Mothers were seldom given the wardship of their eldest son. Technically the heir became the ward of the King, and the Court of Wards either granted the wardship to a male relative or sold it to a non-family member. Wardships were worth paying for. They allowed the purchaser to use the property (such as collecting rents from the tenants) although on achieving his majority the ward received the principal of his inheritance or what was left of it. In Kate's case, Charles made the wardship a free gift.

In the early days of her widowhood, Charles visited her constantly. He promised to be "a husband to her and a father to her children." Seeing the King's great concern for the Duchess of Buckingham, Queen Henrietta Maria made it her business to console the widow as well. A month after the assassination, Kate received word from the palace that the Queen was coming to pay her respects. For this formal occasion, Kate marshalled the members of the Villiers family and they were all present with the exception of Viscount Purbeck who was kept out of sight in the country in the custody of a caregiver. As they awaited the Queen in the Great Chamber at York House, Kate looked around at these people who had been her family for eight years. There was her mother-in-law, a commanding figure in an enormous, old-fashioned ruff. Standing by her side was her youngest son Christopher, Earl of Anglesey, sober for once Kate was pleased to see. Kit resembled George but, Kate thought, only as a pale imitation. Susan Denbigh, George's older sister, was sitting beside her; they had been through thick and thin together during her married life and Kate sincerely hoped that their close relationship would continue.

The sweet little Marchioness, Sue Denbigh's daughter Margaret, or Mary as they called her, was dandling Baby George. Poor Mary, now fifteen, would love to have a baby of her own but her husband, the Marquis of Hamilton, would not co-habit with her. The over-proud young Scottish lord was so incensed at having been matched with a daughter of the Denbighs, mere gentry until raised to the peerage by Buckingham, that he betook himself to Scotland and would not come down. King Charles hoped to lure him by offering him Master of the King's Horse, a choice appointment that had opened up with George's death. Pretty Mall, standing at her mother's knee, was George over again. She had his looks, his grace, and his charm. The thought came into Kate's mind that, unconsciously, they had all arranged themselves in the Great Chamber much as they appeared in the family portrait that the Dutchman, Gerrit Honthorst, had painted a few months earlier. Remembering that George had instructed the painter to show him holding her hand, Kate could hardly restrain herself from weeping.

At the appointed hour, the Queen arrived with a large suite (inappropriate, Kate thought, on a condolence call). Kate was relieved to see that the Countess of Carlisle was not among them. The court beauty had been struck down with smallpox just around the time George was murdered. Henrietta Maria had been so distraught that she had had to be physically restrained from going to her favourite lady's bedside before the period of contagion was past. Her friends said that Lady Carlisle was left unmarked by the disease but Kate understood she wore a mask so how could anyone know. Henrietta Maria was fulsome in her expressions of sympathy to the Duchess of Buckingham, offering to do anything she could to help her. Yet Kate felt that the purpose of the visit was to gratify the King. The Queen was so anxious to please her loving husband these days that she even took his side in the war with her brother, King Louis XIII.

The royal couple continued to give Kate their personal attention. She had moved to the house in Chelsea with the children and the King and Queen would stop in on their way between Hampton Court and London.

The Countess of Buckingham's seeming lack of emotion after the death of her adored son had surprised Kate. Her mother-in-law had received the news of his assassination with a composure that had continued up to the day of the Queen's visit. The truth was that the Countess had foreseen on that cursed day of their quarrel that her son would die. She had already buried him in her mind.

Susan, on the other hand, had given way to undignified behavior that was quite out of character for her, crying and declaring her "everlasting grief" to everyone. She even prattled of a mysterious "vision" she had had foreseeing his death. Indeed, she seemed to mourn her brother more than she had her son Philip who had died nine months earlier. (At the time, George had arranged for the fifteen-year old boy to be buried in the Henry VII Chapel in Westminster Abbey beside his own infant son, Charles.) George, ten years younger than she, was her idol. Where would she and her not very bright husband have been without his patronage? The Feildings boasted that they were descended from the House of Habsburg through extinct German aristocratic families. Knowing the claim to be false, Sue nevertheless vouched for it. Really the only thing that counted in their rise had been the fact that she was the sister of the great Duke of Buckingham.

Kate felt that her own grief would never end. But with the world at large, it was as if the great Duke had never lived. At court they spoke no more of him other than to bid for his offices and honours. Like the whirlwind that had circled above York House until dispersing into the atmosphere, his meteoric rise had ended in nothing.

CHAPTER THIRTEEN

Gossip had it that the widowed Duchess of Buckingham had returned to the Roman Catholic Church. In fact she had not. In a tract dedicated to her in 1630, an Anglican cleric named Giles Widdowes described himself as her chaplain. Indeed, she and her father were both attending the Established Church of England. The Earl had not converted back to Protestantism but he told his friends he went to church to avoid paying recusancy fines. Despite her yearning to return to the bosom of what was to her the true church, she dared not do so because as a widow she was vulnerable. She had to retain the King's favour. With the exception of his wife who flaunted her Catholicism in the face of Protestant England, Charles was coming down hard on the Anglo-Catholics to conciliate a Puritan Parliament. With anti-Catholicism on the boil in his realm, Charles announced that he would turn all Papists out of his service. This included the lord lieutenants of the counties with two exceptions, the Earl of Rutland and the Earl of Worcester because, said the King, "he held them to be very good subjects."

From her father Kate learned that the new session of Parliament that convened on January 23, 1629, was as obstreperous as the previous ones when George was alive. The King's request for a money vote was put off day after day while the Commons ranted against the Arminian faction in the

Anglican church, calling them crypto-Catholics and Bishop Laud the worst of them. The delaying tactics enraged Charles, in particular when the House petitioned him for a day of fasting to show solidarity with the Protestant churches abroad. Charles had pledged large contributions to the Protestant forces in the religious war raging on the Continent and was in a desperate hurry to meet these commitments. Contemptuously, he told the House that while it was England's duty to help their Protestant brethren, "fighting would do them more good than fasting." Both sides were increasingly confrontational. Sir Dudley Digges and Sir John Eliot harped on the familiar theme of royal officials collecting taxes unauthorized by Parliament (this time it was the customs duties known as tonnage and poundage) and without the Duke to take the blame the King was unshielded from these attacks.

Yet open and direct criticism of the monarch was regarded as sedition, (and indeed unthinkable to the average Englishman) and Members of Parliament continued to address Charles as their "most gracious sovereign" and they, his "most dutiful subjects." Following a brief adjournment, the Commons returned with a Protestation declaring the collection of tonnage and poundage illegal and condemning any merchants who paid the duties as enemies of the kingdom. Charles did not mince words. He declared that he was dissolving Parliament because of the "disobedient and seditious behaviour of those ill-affected persons of the House of Commons, that we and our regal authority and commandment have been so highly contemned, that our kingly office cannot bear, nor any former age can parallel." The session ended in a disgraceful scene with the Speaker being held down in his chair so that he could not dissolve the House and the King's messengers pounding on the locked door of the chamber. Charles grimly determined never to call a Parliament again but to govern on his own.

On April 2, 1629, Kate was delivered of a healthy baby boy. Though it was expected that she would name him Charles (the first baby of that name having died), she chose to call him Francis after her father. The bittersweet event earned the baby a poet's commiseration. "Nourished with sighs and frights, and form'd with feares/ And then baptized in thy mother's teares," the poet enjoins little Francis to "teach these eyes againe (blest child) to smile/ and never let another cloud beguile/ Us of the Comfort of those glorious beames/ nor Lett such sunnes as those sett in sadd streames/ Instruct her teares to smile by thy sweete power/As when the sun vouchsafes to gild a shower."

Kate asked George's close friend Bishop Laud to officiate at the christening. She was growing ever closer to this bishop who had recently been promoted to the diocese of London. She found his High Church practices very like those in a Catholic church: the priest in his surplice and cope, the use of the cross in baptism, the kneeling at communion, the ring in the marriage ceremony and, above all, Laud's insistence on moving the communion table from the middle of the choir to the altar end of the church. All of which made him extremely unpopular with the Puritan-minded parliamentarians. For his part, Laud admired Kate sincerely, praising her in his diary as "that excellent lady who is goodness itself."

Her tragedy had changed Kate, her heart hardened. Whereas before George's murder she and her mother-in-law had tried to get a pardon for two convicted murderers in the belief that they had killed in self-defence, now even the most pathetic appeals from relatives of a convicted murderer could not move her. In July 1629, one Captain Stamford had been sentenced to death as an accessory to a murder. He and other disbanded officers had attempted to release a soldier in the Fleet Street prison by force and this had led to a fight with the constables guarding the prison. The tumult had spread along Fleet Street and Stamford and another captain had killed a constable. Kate knew Stamford. He was one of Buckingham's men and was a familiar figure in his entourage. After his sentencing, his mother and father came to Kate and pleaded with her to save him from the death penalty. She answered that she would never open her mouth for a murderer after the foul murder of her lord. In fact, this was not Stamford's first murder. Some years before, he had murdered a night watchman but, no doubt through Buckingham's intervention, had been granted clemency by King Charles. This time Stamford was executed at Tyburn.

Unlike the Dowager Duchess of Richmond and Lennox, Kate's old friend Frances who was profligate with gifts of money and jewels, Kate made no attempt to retain her prominence at court. She stepped down from her post as a Lady of the Bedchamber. Towards the end of 1629, however, she made the occasional appearance at the Queen's apartments in Whitehall Palace. The magnificent Lady Carlisle was nowhere to be seen. It seemed she had fallen out of favour with the Queen and had been banished from court. The French ambassador, the Marquis de Chateauneuf, an extremely proud and overbearing aristocrat, had neatly turned the wittiness that so delighted Henrietta Maria against her. Incensed to learn that Lady Carlisle had amused the Queen's circle with one of her "Characters" using himself as her subject, he vowed to take revenge. The ambassador was on very close terms with Henrietta Maria his countrywoman, he alone among ambassadors was allowed to sit on a stool in the Queen's presence, and he told her, vengefully and probably untruthfully, that Lady Carlisle was making sport of her behind her back. Henrietta Maria believed him and ordered Lady Carlisle out of her sight. The expulsion came to an end after the new year but Kate could see that the Queen was spreading her favour more widely. She had come to rely upon sensible Susan Denbigh, her Mistress of the Robes, to manage the finances of her household, and was finding platonic playmates among her young male attendants such as Henry Percy, Lucy Carlisle's brother who was undismayed by his sister's banishment.

To a certain extent, Buckingham's death empowered his widow. Kate had always done George's bidding, now she was free to do things her way. While keeping the art collection virtually intact (she exchanged a few erotic paintings with the King for religious subjects), she attempted to get rid of the curator Balthazar Gerbier whom she had always disliked. In a codicil appended to his will, Buckingham had left Gerbier a small annuity, the keepership of York House, and the house that he and his family occupied at the east side of the gatehouse for a further thirty-one years at the nominal rent of "one pair of gloves on the birthday of my son George, Earl of Coventry." On the pretext that Gerbier could not inherit because he was not a naturalized citizen, Kate refused to give him his inheritance. As it was, Gerbier was outraged at his scanty reward for twelve years of extraordinary service. When he learned of the Duchess's attempt to deprive him of even that much, he took his case to Lord Dorchester who had replaced the ailing Conway as Secretary of State. Informed of the situation by Dorchester, Charles promptly naturalized Balthazar Gerbier by letters patent so he could inherit.

Although Kate was unjust to Gerbier she went out of her way to find good positions for other faithful servants of the Duke's. There was William Burden who, she wrote the Secretary of the Navy, "served her late dear lord many years." She asked that he be given the cook's place on the *Mary Rose*. She was up against competition from another sponsor who wanted the cook's place for one William Sparkes but it is likely that Burden was chosen to oblige the Duchess.

She made her greatest efforts on behalf of the chief porter of the Tower of London, William Bold. This gentleman was claiming a part of the Tower precinct where some hundred tenants of the King's resided, and these families had signed a petition against him. The Lieutenant of the Tower, Sir Alan Apsley, could not understand why Bold was claiming anything more than the house he lived in and one house on the bulwarks of the Tower. For some reason Bold's weak claim had received royal approval but when the matter came up at the Privy Council the grant was stayed. At this point Kate entered the fray. She wrote to Secretary of State Dorchester begging him to help Bold "as an act of justice and friendship to the memory of her dear lord who esteemed Bold's service." Clearly Kate was not acting on the merits of the case but simply doing what she knew George would want her to do.

She was proving to be very businesslike. Two days before the birth of her baby she had sent a servant to Captain Pennington with a note asking him to hand over to the bearer ten pieces of tapestry hangings along with a tent that had been delivered to him for the Duke's intended voyage to La Rochelle in 1628. She included a receipt for the same. After the traditional month spent in her bedchamber receiving visitors, she took hold firmly of business matters. Coming upon a list signed by Sir Sackville Crow, Buckingham's one-time treasurer, she saw that George had pawned some of his own jewels in Holland in 1625 "for his Majesty's service." This, of course, was at the time he and Charles were attempting to raise money for the Spanish war by pawning some of the Crown jewels. She immediately brought the matter to Charles's attention and he ordered that the Duke's jewels should be redeemed and delivered to the Duchess.

There was money owing to George from his years as Lord High Admiral and Kate began reeling in these outstanding debts. As Admiral, George had been entitled to a share of the booty from all prize ships taken during wartime. She asked Edward Nicholas, the Secretary of the Navy, to procure her a note of all prize ships brought into the port of London, or any of the outports, since the war with Spain. Nicholas, who had got his start as Buckingham's secretary, was devoted to the memory of the late Duke and admired his widow immensely. No doubt to Nicholas's surprise (for corruption was endemic in the Admiralty), he received payments out of the blue for accounts overdue to the late Duke. He found that these had been solicited directly by the Duchess. As was to be expected, her father was her best advocate. While taking the waters at Bath, the Earl sent for one William Willett of Bristol and sternly charged him with the fact that his daughter had received no account of moneys owing since the Duke's death. In a letter to Nicholas the wayward Willett excused himself for not paying money due to the Duchess and promptly paid up.

At least on one occasion she found herself on the opposite side at the Admiralty Court. The goods salvaged from shipwrecks had been granted by patent to various favourites of the Duke who then took a share; as his beneficiary, this partnership continued with Kate. One such partner was Sir Thomas Walsingham, a knight of the shire for Kent. A Rotterdam ship bound for Venice had been wrecked off the shores of Kent and Walsingham's men had hurried down to take possession of its rich cargo. Notwithstanding his patent, the Admiralty Court seized the goods. An irate Sir Thomas wrote Nicholas that by this means the Duchess and he "would lose their shares and right of place." He asked the Secretary of the Navy for advice. As it happened, Walsingham died before the year was out and his patent died with him.

Charles was governing without Parliament. His shrewd Treasurer, Sir Richard Weston, had unearthed old forestry laws and other royal exactions unused for centuries to bring in revenue. Notwithstanding the Commons' express refusal to authorize him tonnage and poundage, Charles continued to collect the custom duties, claiming the right based on precedent from previous reigns. Those merchants who would not pay the duties were imprisoned. The Privy Council issued new regulations for particular types of trade so that only those affected were moved to complain. A decree forbidding the dressing of flesh on Wednesdays, Fridays, and Saturdays was of no consequence other than to butchers, inn-holders, and victuallers, who were hauled before the Privy Council and fined if they did not comply. But Charles and Weston could only go so far. The hated practice of forced loans had to be abandoned as too incendiary. In these ways and by scrimping, Weston was able to generate sufficient revenue for the royal government in peacetime. He had impressed on Charles that independence from Parliament depended on keeping out of the wars that were raging on the Continent. In 1630 England signed peace treaties with France and with Spain.

Without the shadow of Parliament hanging over him, Charles created a refined and elegant court that mirrored his own personality. Deeply in love with his consort, he catered to her love of entertainment and participated with her in the court masques that were becoming more gorgeous (and more costly) every year. In the autumn of 1629 Henrietta Maria discovered she was pregnant. Having had a miscarriage the year before, she would not take the risk of descending from "the Heavens" in one of Inigo Jones's contraptions operated by pulleys and levers, but contented herself with reigning over the festivities in the role of the fairy queen, safely seated on a throne.

Kate rarely went to court these days. Memories of Buckingham were too painfully vivid. How he had shone at all the festivities! The handsomest man, the best dancer, the royal favourite. Seeing the Queen's happy marriage only intensified her misery over her loss. "Unfortunate" was the way she described herself henceforth, signing her letters "Your unfortunate friend, cousin, aunt, etc." Indeed she was a sad figure in her widow's weeds – a simple black gown with a wide, plain white collar, and a miniature of her dear departed on a black velvet ribbon. She looked for traces of George in her children, seeing them in little George's mischievous smile, in baby Francis's brilliant blue eyes, and in Mall who grew more like her father in manner and appearance all the time.

Charles was generous with patronage for Buckingham's family. A good part of England was composed of watery low-lying lands known as the Fens, where the inhabitants walked about on stilts and fished rather than farmed. Gradually, these marshes were being drained to create arable land that dramatically improved the rents. Much of it was Crown land and Charles granted rents from a large section to Kate and her uncle, Sir George Manners, in trust for the second Duke. The King asked that the rents be used for the baby Duke, or for payment of the late Duke's debts, or for his other children who had been left unprovided for. To include a male trustee was prudent. Although technically a widow could administer her own property, women often found their grants or inheritances challenged by rival claimants unless placed in trust with a male relative or friend. Kate was to find that the male relative could prove to be the rival claimant.

CHAPTER FOURTEEN

Mall was in a state of excitement. The King and Queen's new baby was to be christened at St. James Palace and she was to take part in the procession to the Chapel Royal. She would carry the train of the Duchess of Richmond who was acting as proxy godmother for the Queen of Bohemia. A very self-confident child, she was not overly nervous but her mother worried that an eight-year-old might drop the Duchess's heavy ermine-trimmed velvet train.

On May 29, 1630, an august gathering was seated in the two galleries of the Chapel Royal awaiting the baby who, should he survive the hazards of childhood, would be the next king. Kate was very pleased that the great honour of presenting the infant had been given to George's niece, Susan's daughter Mary. (Susan herself had been appointed the little prince's governess for the great day.) With measured step, the young Marchioness of Hamilton entered the chapel under a canopy held aloft by the four barons of the Exchequer. A tiny girl, she looked even smaller walking between the Lord High Treasurer and the Earl Marshall, both tall men. But she was perfectly composed holding the ermine pillow on which the royal infant lay. Nodding his approval, a smiling Bishop Laud was waiting at the altar to perform the ceremony. Christened Charles after his father, the baby was dark complexioned with black hair, a throwback to his Italian ancestors through his grandmother, Marie de Medici.

The young Marchioness had carried off her demanding role without a misstep. She was now living with her reluctant husband and, hopefully, was pregnant. To Kate's relief, Mall had held the heavy velvet train with seeming ease and had never once stepped on it - the hazard for trainbearers. Kate knew that her little daughter would never forget the grandeur of the occasion that marked her introduction to court life. This was indeed the life cut out for her through the marriage George had arranged. As it happened, her future father-in-law, the Earl of Montgomery, had just inherited the earldom of Pembroke on the sudden death of his older brother. With his double earldom, the high office of Lord Chamberlain, and as master of Wilton, the Herberts' great estate in Wiltshire, he was one of the most powerful and richest nobles in England. As his elder son, Mall's betrothed was heir to all of this.

George had provided brilliantly for his daughter and his niece by marrying them into the highest ranks of the nobility. From the grave he provided Susan's second son George with an earldom. Richard Preston, the Earl of Desmond, had two daughters but no sons, and in 1622 Buckingham had obtained the reversion of the title for this nephew, his namesake. When the Earl of Desmond died in 1628, the title passed to George Feilding but Preston's wealth remained with his under-age daughter. Susan's plan was to get the wardship of the heiress and to marry her to George. However, the Court of Wards awarded the girl to her great uncle, Lord Sheffield, and he, in short order, married her to the heir of the Earl of Ormond. Thus Susan's plans were foiled (the result might have been different if Buckingham were living) and she had to seek another wealthy bride. She found one in an heir to the deceased Sir Miles Stanhope. Bridget Stanhope became a ward of the Court and this time Susan was successful in her bid for the wardship. In April 1630, the young woman was married to George Feilding, Earl of Desmond. This was only one example of the Court of Wards literally selling brides.

George was a prize example of a spoiled, feckless son of the aristocracy. His days were frittered away at court. One day in the Queen's apartments, and in Her Majesty's presence, he had an altercation with a page named Croft. George started it by saying to the other youth, "Your hose are too short." Young Croft replied, "So is your nose." This moved George to hurl an insult at Croft who retaliated by knocking him down. George ran crying to his father. The Earl of Denbigh took this childish episode as an affront to the family honour and encouraged his son to call out young Croft. George sent Croft his glove - "throwing down the gauntlet" being the traditional challenge - and the two frightened youths had a duel in Hyde Park. Both survived. Still, they had broken the law against duelling and there was a trial of some sort without consequences to either. England was getting too hot for the tempestuous Earl of Desmond. Now eighteen years of age, it was arranged that he would go abroad for several years. Kate invited his wife to stay with her at York House and Bridget accepted gratefully. The young woman was only too happy with the whole arrangement for she disliked the husband she had been forced to marry.

Another marriage that had got off to a bad start was turning out more satisfactorily. On March 6, 1631, Mary Hamilton gave birth to a daughter. Sue's gentle child now had her own baby. The christening was a happy affair so different from that of Kate's fatherless Francis the year before. The godmothers were the Queen and the Countess of Buckingham; Lord Treasurer Weston was godfather. Shortly afterwards the Marquis of Hamilton left for Scotland to raise a troop to take over to Germany to join the forces of the King of Sweden, the brilliant Protestant leader in the war against the Catholic Habsburgs. While King Charles would not bring England into the continental war even to recover the Palatinate for his sister and her family, he encouraged his subjects to go over and fight. To finance the expedition, he had given Hamilton 40,000£ and the Scottish wine customs for eleven years, which would yield about 20,000£ a year. The Swedish king had lately recovered all the towns in the Lower Palatinate but two, and hopes were running high in England for the Protestant cause.

If George Feilding was a problem, his older brother Basil was the pride of his parents and a great favourite with his Aunt Kate. In 1629, the King raised him to the peerage as Baron Feilding. This gave him the opportunity to sit in the House of Lords before the King swore off parliaments. Basil was now soldiering in the Netherlands with the Prince of Orange, who was engaged in the brutal, bloody war with the Spaniards that seemed endless. Basil's derring-do, however, was matched by his father's adventurous travels. In 1631 the Earl of Denbigh, no longer a young man, took ship on an East Indiaman bound for India. Other than merchants working for the East India Company, few Englishmen undertook the perilous voyage to visit the court of the Mogul emperor. It would be two years before he returned to the familiar soil of England, reportedly weighed down with jewels from the Great Mogul.

Denbigh, his son, and his son-in-law would eventually come home, but one who was gone forever was Christopher Villiers. George's youngest brother had died in 1630. The most that could be said for him was that he left behind a son to carry on the name. The old Countess had now lost her three sons, two to death and one to madness. Still, fate had left her unbroken and unbowed. She entertained lavishly. Writing to her father on April 16, 1631, Kate reported that the Countess of Buckingham threw "a great supper" for the King and Queen the night before. Although well into her sixties, rumours continued to swirl about her relationship with the much younger Bishop Williams. Kate did not know what to make of it. All she did know was that the Bishop's coach was almost daily to be seen outside the palace gatehouse where her mother-in-law resided.

As eager as her mother-in-law was to keep in the royal swim, her father was just as eager to get out of it. Although the King had ordered his nobles to stay in the country and attend to their estates, he made an exception for Rutland whom he liked to have at court. Once when the Earl, still Henrietta Maria's Grand Chamberlain, failed to answer the royal command to be at Greenwich Palace to greet the King and Queen, it had fallen to Kate to apologize for his absence. She was relieved to report that the royal couple had graciously accepted her apology. Clearly, her father put his private life ahead of royal commands. Had he not "forgotten" an appointment with King James in the excitement of his grandchild's birth? Kate's family was his primary concern. But he also took his responsibilities to his tenants very seriously. While some landowners were known for their hard dealings with their tenants, the Earl of Rutland was a benevolent father figure to his. His wife matched his good works, looking after the health and welfare of the servants and of the wives and children of the tenantry. Indeed, Lady Rutland's burden of care extended to her brother-in-law George's household at Fulbeck. Informed that one of his servants was feeling under the weather, she recommended garlic: "She thinks it would be good for you," the sick man was told, "and she says she would take it herself." Especially after Buckingham's death, Rutland spent his time at Belvoir rather than Whitehall. Horse breeding and the hunt were his daily activities, which he shared with other landowners of the surrounding counties. First among them was his brother George, another crony was William, Earl of

Newcastle, at Welbeck Abbey in neighbouring Nottinghamshire.

Kate's alliance with George's mother and sister had survived his death, but an action of Sue's threatened to disrupt it. In 1631 she erected a monument to her late brother in Portsmouth Cathedral. She did this knowing that Kate was planning a magnificent monument for him in Westminster Abbey. Kate had already commissioned a carver, Isaac Besniers, to do the marble work. The Portsmouth monument was a far simpler affair – a marble arch with a tall urn in the niche and two carved figures below of angels blowing their trumpets. It was nothing compared to Kate's extravagant plans. But it was the message on a tablet between the trumpet-blowing angels that disturbed Kate. Written in Latin, it celebrated the life of the Duke of Buckingham, decried "his monstrous murder in this very town," and ended with the words that the Duke's "bowels," together with his sister's, "are buried here." To Kate's certain knowledge no part of her husband's remains had been removed at Portsmouth before he was embalmed at London, and the effect of this outrageous assertion by his sister was to push his wife aside as the principal mourner of the late Duke. However, in the interest of family solidarity, Kate forgave Susan for the offending tablet and the Buckingham ladies continued to present a united front until death broke up the triumvirate.

"The three Buckingham ladies," as they were known around the court, were a force to be reckoned with. They worked together to further the family interest and because King Charles revered Buckingham's memory they had great influence. Kate had succeeded in getting a Denbigh relative, another George Feilding, appointed Registrar of the Admiralty. This would provide a steady source of income for life. Meanwhile a relative of the Chancellor of the Exchequer, Sir Francis Cotttington, was trying to oust him from the post. Kate jumped in to the rescue. On July 22, 1631, she sent a letter to Secretary of State Dorchester: "The late Duke had bestowed upon her servant, George Feilding, the office of Registrar of the Admiralty. Of late, one Mr. Cottington has used means to obtain a grant of the place, so as to put George Feilding from office or force him to a suit in law. To prevent which, he has become a petitioner to the King." She "entreated" the Secretary to second her "Sister Denbigh in procuring a dispatch of this business" by speaking to the King. Within a few days Kate was thanking Secretary Dorchester for "his favour to her servant Feilding." George Feilding would perform the office of Registrar of the Admiralty with distinction for many years.

Indeed, she continued to find places at the Admiralty for Buckingham's family or faithful dependents. In October 1631, she was seeking to get the purser's place on the *Adventure* for "poor William Kifferd, the Duke's servant, who would have had that place if the Duke had lived." Although the Lords of the Admiralty were informed that Kifferd had no experience for the post, they gave it to him to gratify the Duchess.

As for Kate's own interests, she still had not been fully recompensed for naval expenditures the Duke had paid out of his own pocket while Lord High Admiral. A case in point was the construction of the *Lion's Whelp*. This ship had cost 7,000£ and Captain Pennington confirmed that the Duke had advanced money for it. The Duchess had received 4,500£ from the Exchequer but there was some question whether the remaining 2,500£ came from the Duke and was owed to his heirs or whether it fell to His Majesty. The matter was settled, presumably to Kate's satisfaction, for she signed a release on April 2, 1632.

Kate had been living in the house at Chelsea, then in 1631 she decided to move back to York House. To have the place to herself, she first had to get rid of Horatio Gentileschi. The temperamental Italian painter continued to occupy the premises near the gatehouse that the Duke had made available to him in 1626. Kate needed the space for her servants. Otherwise, as she told Secretary Dorchester, she would have to keep a family at Chelsea just to look after the laundry.

She spoke to Gentileschi and found he was not averse to leaving. "If he could have the money due to him from his Majesty," she wrote Dorchester, "he would willingly leave England and begone into his own country." But Charles paid nobody unless it was absolutely necessary and Gentileschi stayed on. At least the house nearby formerly occupied by Gerbier was vacant. King Charles had appointed Balthazar Gerbier his Agent in Brussels, and to Kate's relief, the painter had departed with his wife (a sweet woman to whom Kate had no objection) and his many children, who had raced around the grounds of York House like a tribe of wild Indians.

Naturally, everything at York House reminded her of George and their life together there. The house was a very different place now. Instead of a setting for magnificent entertainments, it was a home for children and for women such as the young Countess of Desmond who needed mothering.

York House was a sanctuary for the former Bridget Stanhope, her only fear that her husband would come back from abroad and take her away. Other women too found a protector in the kind, generous Kate. The writer of religious tracts, Alice Sutcliffe, would later say that the Duchess of Buckingham had been "more than a mother" to her and a source of strength in a world unfriendly to women writers: "She valued a woman's writing more highly than others did." In 1634, Alice dedicated her "Meditations of Man's Mortalitie, or a Way to True Blessedness," to Kate and Sue Denbigh. In the dedication, she asks the Duchess to protect her "against mocking Ishmaels" who may criticize her work because it was "not usuall for a Woman to doe such things."

As well as the dedicatory epistle, the book included acrostics praising Kate and Susan and lamenting the Duke of Buckingham's death. The author also offered an encomium to the Earl of Pembroke and Montgomery for encouraging her to write and publish the "Meditations". Pembroke, a patron of Shakespeare who dedicated his First Folio to him and his brother, was ahead of his time in patronizing a woman writer. On the one hand, his recognition of women authors augured well for Mall since the Lord Chamberlain was her future father-in-law and Mall was given to scribbling little tags of verse. However Kate was doubtful that Mall would find in him a kindred spirit. Pembroke was a domestic tyrant with such a wild temper that Anne Clifford, who had taken him as her second husband, was planning to leave him because of his "lunatic behaviour." This intellectual lady made poor choices in husbands. Her first husband, the Earl of Dorset, had boasted that he could hardly read or write.

Kate's relationship with her only daughter was as close and loving as any such could be. They whiled away the time reading to each other. For Mall, Sir Philip Sidney and Edmund Spenser had opened a door to her own future. Kate's taste ran to history and religious tracts. Whatever the book, mother and daughter read aloud to each other with equal delight.

On April 19, 1632, the Countess of Buckingham passed away at the age of sixty-three. Kate would miss her. In many ways she had replaced the mother Kate had longed for and never known. To the world of the court, however, she was "a rapacious and predatory old termagant." All the stories of her misdeeds were freshly circulated, including the scandal of her second marriage. After the death of her first husband, the estimable Sir George Villiers, she had been forced to depart from Brooksby as the manor house had passed to his eldest son by his first marriage. A comely and still young widow, she found a new husband in a sickly man of eighty who had made his fortune as a wool merchant in Nottinghamshire. Shortly before he died, she had her servants break into the wool house and load a train of packhorses and wains with the wool, along with various household goods, to sell at market before the children of his first marriage could take possession of their rightful inheritance.

A local knight intercepted the caravan and the stolen goods were returned to her mortally ill husband. Her actions were known far beyond Nottinghamshire as the case had come before the Star Chamber in the early years of the century. Then there was her infamous attempt to purloin the gold chain that Charles had given to the Duchess of Richmond and Lennox for her care of Kate when she had smallpox. This had earned her a short banishment from court. But she was most notorious for kidnapping the richest girl in England to secure her as a bride for her son. When this gossip came back to Kate she smiled, for without such tactics on his mother's part she and George might never have wed.

The Countess was buried in Westminster Abbey with full honours beside her first husband, the father of the Duke of Buckingham. In due course a marble monument was erected over their graves in St. Nicholas Chapel, he in plated armour and she in an ermine mantle. Not content with her undeserved peerage, the epitaph carved on her side of the tomb read that she was "descended from five of the most powerful Kings of Europe." (These pretensions, which her daughter Susan Denbigh inherited, had amused the court for years.) Considering her avariciousness, her estate was far smaller than expected - not above 1,000£ a year. She had divided it between her grandson, Lord Basil Feilding, and the Angelsey children. Kate was to face a much greater loss before the year was out.

CHAPTER FIFTEEN

The Earl of Rutland had seemed well enough throughout the spring and summer of 1632. He was leading his usual life at Belvoir, attending to his duties as Lord Lieutenant of the county, looking after his tenants, and improving his stables. The Earl of Holland had recently given him a stallion for breeding purposes; Sir George Manners had immediately sent over a mare from Fulbeck for a "leap" of this fine animal. (With the mare he sent a crown to be divided between the stallion's groom and "those who help in the covering.") As well as his passion for hunting, Rutland had renewed his interest in falconry. A friend had sent him two hundred ducks' eggs, which had now hatched, to feed his hawks and the birds were affording him good sport.

Sadly, in the autumn he fell ill and Dr. Matthew Lister one of the royal physicians was called in. Another physician, Dr. Samuel Turner, was also consulted. Kate hated the sight of this man. When she visited her father and found him there she could hardly be civil. She held him to blame for unleashing the attack on Buckingham in the Parliament of 1626 that had led to the impeachment charge. But her father claimed the physic Turner prescribed was helping him, so for her father's sake she smiled and chatted with this villain. By the end of November the Earl was thought to have recovered and was on his way to court when he took desperately ill at an inn at Bishops Stortford in Hertfordshire. Knowing he was nearing his end, he sent for his daughter, his wife, his brother George, and his good friend Sir Thomas Savage.

With heavy heart Kate rushed to the inn to find her father at death's door. "Sweetheart give me your hand," he said to her. "Now I pray God bless you and your children. It grieves me I shall see none of them before I die, but I leave them my blessings." He issued a paternal injunction regarding Mall. "You know there was a match wished by your husband between my Lord Chamberlain's son and Mall, which I desire may go on."

Then running his gaze over the long faces around the bed, he proceeded to give them his directions. He wished to leave one of his finest horses to His Majesty. "The King's equerry should go to my stable and choose either my best hunting horse for the hare or my best buck hunter." His gaze fixed on Lord Savage. "Present my humble service to his Majesty," he said to his old friend, "letting him know that never King had a more faithful servant or a more loyal subject than myself nor never subject had a more gracious Sovereign. I am infinitely bound to his Majesty for his ever gracious favours unto me."

Aware of the conflicts that could arise between the dowager and the heir when an entailed estate passed out of the immediate family, his dearest wish was that there should be no dispute between his wife and his brother. Should there be any, he enjoined Lord Savage to decide it. "If you cannot," he told his friend, "I pray you to commend my love unto my Lord Keeper, and my desire is that your two Lordships should decide it."

He was very concerned over two thousand pounds he owed to one Sir John Ayres. An honourable man all his life, he could not die in peace unless he was assured that this debt would be repaid. He told Sir George and Lord Savage, both executors of his will, that they would find a thousand pounds in his iron chest at London, and his servant Robert Cook could give them five hundred pounds that were in his custody. The rest, he told his executors, was to be taken out of his estate. He also wanted Dr. Lister to be given fifty pounds for the care he had taken of him in his sickness.

"For my funeral I would have it such as my ancestors have had, which will be no great charge, for that my tomb is already made, and I would have my body, so soon as it is embalmed, to be removed forth of the inn."

Kate wept her heart out when two days later he died at the inn. Although he was fifty-four he had many good years ahead of him, she said through her tears. Once more she and the children were deprived of a beloved male protector. Soon the embalmer arrived to do his evisceration work then the body, encased in lead, was shipped to Belvoir. The funeral was a simple affair in accordance with the Earl's orders. He was buried in St. Mary the Virgin Church where he had worshipped. The stonemason had made the tomb according to the Earl's directions and when it was erected in the church it caused some surprise to the mourners. In the first place, the inscription on the tomb revealed that the Earl had gone to his grave convinced that his sons had been killed by witchcraft: "In 1608 he married ye Lady Cecilia Hungerford, daughter to ye honorable Knight Sir John Tufton, by whom he had two sons, both of which died in their infancy by wicked practices and sorcerye." The second surprise (experienced most poignantly by his widow) was that instead of the usual two recumbent figures on top of the tomb there were three: the Earl had had the carver show him lying between both his wives. Out of kindness to her stepmother, Kate concealed her satisfaction at this evidence of her father's enduring love for her mother.

The Earl of Rutland had worried that his will might cause a breach between his wife and his brother. As it turned out, it was his daughter and the new earl who were soon embroiled in as nasty a family quarrel over inheritance as the court had witnessed in many a year. Although her father had made Kate his heir general, her uncle was claiming that all land, castles and manors, including property that Sir Francis had bought personally, belonged to the entailed estate.

Kate had anticipated something like this. During her father's illness she had confided to the Earl of Holland that she feared her uncle would attempt to deprive her and her children of their rightful inheritance. Henry Rich had reason to help Kate because he owed his earldom and his prominence at court to her late husband. In 1624 Buckingham had sent him to France as joint ambassador with the Earl of Carlisle to negotiate Charles's marriage to Henrietta Maria and this had established him as a leading courtier during Charles's reign. Handsome and charming like his benefactor, he had become a favourite with the King and Queen and professed to have enormous influence with both. Holland had assured Kate that he would speak to the King and get him to side with her against her uncle. However, it appeared that Charles did not intend to become engaged in a money dispute between the Duchess and one of his earls. Holland had exaggerated his power and he was clearly embarrassed. Kate tried to save his feelings. In a letter to Kate he said he was "glad to hear from her that he had then done for her and her children as much as could be expected from him." He lashed out at Dr. Turner, going so far as to suggest that the physician had poisoned her father to enable her uncle to succeed to the earldom prematurely: "Sir George Manners is beholden to the knave," he wrote, "for if physic can hasten a man's end, Turner has taken pains to make him Earl of Rutland." Although Kate detested Turner, she did not take Holland's accusation seriously.

Having no doubt that her uncle intended to deny her her legacy, Kate retained the services of the eminent barrister Richard Lane. He, in turn, consulted with a former solicitor-general with Buckingham ties, as well as two other persons skilled in the law. The sum of their learned opinion, as conveyed to Kate, was (predictably with lawyers) that she go to court. "They desire peace," Lane wrote, "but do not think it can be effected without answers in Court and sight of writings." At the end of January 1633, Kate started legal proceedings against her Uncle George.

This course of action required courage, however having suffered so many slings and arrows of fate in recent years the once gentle, submissive Kate had plenty of that. She might have been discouraged had she dwelt upon the experience of other women who had dared to insist on their inheritances. This had embroiled them in interminable court proceedings and left them open to censor and ridicule.

A case in point was that of the Countess of Pembroke and Montgomery – Mall's future mother-in-law. Born Anne Clifford, she was the only surviving offspring of the Earl of Cumberland. However her father had left the title and the landed estate to his brother. Although she had received a not ungenerous cash settlement by his will, Anne and her mother had refused to accept the disposition on the grounds that the original deed dating from King Edward II stated that the estate would pass down to "an heir of the body", that is to a biological offspring regardless of sex. For years Anne had fought for her rights in the courts. She had been opposed by no less than King James and the Archbishop of Canterbury, and above all by her first husband, the Earl of Dorset, who had made her life a living hell. His domestic cruelty came to an end with his death in 1624 but her second marriage to the Earl of Pembroke and Montgomery had been no improvement. He it was whose violent temper led him to "lunatic behaviour" at home and in public. Both husbands believed that if she would renounce her inheritance the fortune would come to them as the closest male relative. But Anne Clifford never wavered in her battle to obtain her rights. The price she had to pay was high. In the male dominated world of her time she was a pariah.

Indeed, among the aristocracy Kate, too, had her critics. Like Anne Clifford, she was upsetting the natural order (epitomized by the rule of entail itself) whereby the woman must yield to the man, no matter the merits of the case. One knight wrote another that "the Duchess of Buckingham hath put in an information into the Court of Wards, against the now Earl of Rutland, whereby she endeavours to overthrow the late earl her father's will, and thereby to recover all his personal estate, with the Castle of Belvoir, and divers other lands, as heir general, from the new earl." Had Kate seen this letter she would have denounced it as a complete misinterpretation of her father's intention. How often had he announced in company that he was leaving her his personal estate, and that his greatest desire was that she should have Belvoir Castle!

The long legal wrangle began. Both sides knew that the estate would be plundered if the wardship officials got their hands on it, so Kate did not press on. However, she used the Court of Wards to threaten her uncle whenever negotiations seemed about to break down. The lawyers' letters were soon flying. In May 1633, Kate received a proposition from the other side that was totally unacceptable to her. She responded in no uncertain terms: "I ...perceive that my uncle has no desire of a good conclusion between us, for firstly he would make me give up my legacy for the land, which I conceive the law casts upon me, and secondly I am sorry they proceed from my uncle, that he should have so mean opinion of my right, to be such as I could accept of." Then came the threat: "Therefore I desire him to know that tomorrow I must begin with my course to move in the Court of Wards." Still Kate held off. With the failure of a negotiated settlement, Kate and her uncle agreed to ask the Lord Keeper, Sir Thomas Coventry, to establish a panel of judges to arbitrate their dispute.

Though King Charles had not taken sides in the dispute over her father's will, he showed his great care for the widow of his never-to-be forgotten bosom friend. Reluctant to appoint a Lord High Admiral to replace Buckingham, in March 1633 Charles set up a commission of three to administer the admiralty. It was noted at this time that he handed over "the entire yearly revenues of the Admiralty to the wife and son of the late Duke of Buckingham, who enjoyed them when alive."

Queen Henrietta Maria, too, made a point of publicly showing favour to Kate. In June 1633, King Charles went to Scotland for his Coronation (having little interest in his northern kingdom, he had put it off for eight years) and while he was away Henrietta Maria visited York House with a large entourage. The occasion was the boat races on the Thames for which York House gardens provided an excellent view. Although six months pregnant with her third child, to the delight of the courtiers the playful queen decided to take part herself in a race. She challenged Sir George Goring to race his barque against hers. The stakes were set at 500 crowns. The little Queen stepped into the royal barque and the rowers set to heartily. Boats filled with ladies and cavaliers followed the contestants up the Thames. To the cheers of the large gathering, Her Majesty's boat came in ahead.

Kate had been living quietly away from court, but after the famous boat race York House was besieged by courtiers and hangers-on who came to pay their respects to the wealthy widow. The only ones that gained admittance were those who had remained faithful to the memory of her departed lord. None was more welcome than Edward Nicholas, Secretary of the Admiralty. Nicholas never referred to the dead admiral as other than "my dear lord and master." Although Kate had not yet paid him Buckingham's legacy of 500£, he was her staunch friend at the Admiralty. They had a close platonic relationship that allowed him to tease her. Referring to those courting her favour, Nicholas wrote her a joshing letter: "If I had as much ability to serve you as I have unfeigned affection, I would press hard amongst the number that now since your Ladyship becoming a favourite throng at your doors to attend you."

The Lord Keeper's award was very slow in coming. A year went by since the matter had been handed over to him. In May 1634, an exasperated Kate wrote to Sir Thomas Coventry more or less demanding a final answer to end the dispute between herself and her uncle. This jogged the Lord Keeper and his judges into issuing the award. Despite the fact that he had agreed to have the panel decide the apportioning of the estate, her uncle would not accept the award as it stood. He particularly objected to Nottingham Castle being "devised" to the Duchess. In a letter to Kate, he insisted that no final arrangement was possible until a Mr. Beresford came to town "for many things have to be inserted in the award which lie only in his knowledge."

It was obvious to Kate that her uncle had "an aversion" to ending their dispute and she told him so bluntly. He denied the charge and tried to play upon her sympathy: "The burden will be so heavy by the debts, legacies, and charges of my brother and my own that I shall not be able to live as I should. I have but the remains of a short time …" He asked her "to reflect upon the contents of my last letter and to treat with my Lord Keeper concerning the same." As for the Lord Keeper and the judges, he was sure he could satisfy them "touching this respite."

His apparent belief that he could change the award to suit himself infuriated Kate. She sat down and immediately wrote him an angry letter. "I cannot forbear any longer, for I see you have no disposition to agree to anything unless I give away my father's legacy, which he intended for me absolutely." She asserted that Lord Savage had provided papers to the judges that confirmed her father's intentions. She gave her uncle an ultimatum. "If you have any inclination to agree to this award I will be at York House tomorrow, and if not, I must go on to the Court of Wards."

This time her uncle took the threat seriously. Within days it was known that a settlement had been reached between the new Earl of Rutland and the Duchess of Buckingham. The childless Earl was to have 7,000£ per annum and Belvoir Castle was to go to his successor, his brother John. "All the rest falls upon the Duchess and her children," a correspondent informed the Lord Deputy of Ireland, Sir Thomas Wentworth. There were a few small pockets of land that remained in contention. To tie up these loose ends, King Charles appointed a commission to report upon what part of these lands "has descended to Katherine, Duchess of Buckingham, in fee simple, and which of them belong to the old entail."

Kate was particularly pleased to have acquired Hemsley Castle and its stables. Now it would remain in the Villiers family and be passed down to young George. She was thinking dynastically for the stud as well. From her husband's favourite Spanish Barb, she bred a mare that she named Bald Peg in the hope of perpetuating that stock.

Her father had prepared her for the difficulties of rural estate management. The tenant farmers were constantly in arrears with their rents, but he would not dispossess them. And nowadays he had to pay them for farming the demesne land, a service they owed the landlord under age-old feudal law. At most, he said, his bailiffs got a turkey at Christmas. It seemed as if only those landowners who had set up industrial works enjoyed a ready cash flow. Nottingham Castle had a profitable ironworks, its furnaces fueled by cutting down trees on the heavily wooded estate. King James had granted the Nottingham estate to her father personally in 1622 so it was not part of the entail. Kate was distressed to learn from the steward that months before the settlement the new Earl and the Dowager Countess of Rutland had taken away all "timber, tiles, slate, bricks, iron, lead, and glass." The steward had made an inventory at their command but it had never been shown to the Duchess before.

Sad to say, Kate was alienated from the good lady who had brought her up. She was resentful that her stepmother was in league with her uncle. But the hard fact of life for the Dowager Countess of Rutland was that she was dependent on her brother-in-law, the new Earl, to pay her jointure and to give her the small manor near Belvoir that was her dower house. With some reluctance, Kate was suing her stepmother as well as her uncle for half of the funeral expenses and the honorariums for the Lord Keeper and the judges.

CHAPTER SIXTEEN

The monument Kate had commissioned for George's grave in Westminster Abbey was finished. An elaborate sculpture in marble and bronze, it had been two years in the making. Although Isaac Besniers had begun carving the marble figures in 1631, the bronze work had been delayed because Hubert Le Sueur had first to complete an equestrian statue of King Charles for the Lord Treasurer's park at Roehampton. Kate had ordered the sculptors to extol the Duke's military greatness as Lord High Admiral and General of the King's land forces (Kate knew that was how he would like to be remembered) and for herself she had them portray him as a family man. Effigies of the Duke, the Duchess, and their children were arranged on a sarcophagus adorned with weeping angels and with grieving figures kneeling at the four corners, two of which were Neptune and Mars. The Duke's gown was embroidered with anchors. At his feet was the figure of Fame. Reshaping his life to suit his wishes and hers, Kate had his epitaph read "charissimus omnibus" - beloved by all. Kate took great satisfaction in seeing the completion of this sumptuous tomb. She felt it made up for the shameful funeral accorded her husband.

Buckingham's monument in the Abbey was for posterity, but he would also live on through the children she had given him. Kate decided to have a family portrait painted. She commissioned the court painter, Anthony Van

Dyck, a Flemish immigrant who had been a pupil of the great Rubens. The King so admired Van Dyck that he had knighted him and given him a fine residence in Blackfriars. Van Dyck's portraits of the Queen flattered her outrageously. With each new portrait, Henrietta Maria became more exquisite. The courtiers outdid each other in praise of her beauty. Kate shook her head in disbelief when she looked at the tiny (and somewhat misshapen) young woman with buckteeth who was the subject of this adulation. Perhaps the artist could even turn *her* into a beauty! She had always been too thin (a continual source of despair since George liked his women plump like the Countess of Carlisle), and now when she looked in the glass Kate saw a small, pinched face staring back at her. And was not her nose getting longer? Mercifully, the children all resembled their handsome father. The painting was a memorial to the adored husband and father. On the wall behind the family group a portrait of Buckingham gazes down on them and Kate is holding a miniature of him close to her heart. She had insisted on wearing black for the sittings and her expression is sad beyond words. The children all look grave. Looking at the portrait Kate was sure there would be no more children and that her life as a desirable woman was over.

A letter to Basil Fielding, Buckingham's nephew, expresses this sense of finality, her feeling that her life had ended with George's death. " For the affection that my dear lord bore you, I must ever own it, for whilst I breathe I shall ever show my true love to him and ever continue to deserve the title of your constant, loving but most unfortunate servant and aunt."

Although York House resounded with the cheerful sounds of children's laughter, one pleasant voice was missing. Bridget, the young wife of Sue Denbigh's second son who had been living with Kate for two years, had been forcibly removed by her husband. One morning, shortly after his return from the Continent in 1634, the Earl of Desmond had gone to York House and demanded that his wife come away with him at once. The young woman, still in her nightclothes, refused to leave. The brutal fellow took her away weeping and half undressed, and forced her into a coach waiting at the door. The story soon got out that while at an inn en route to Leicestershire, she had attempted to escape by borrowing clothes from a milkmaid. Kate heard from Sue (without entirely believing her) that Bridget was settling down in her new life as the Countess of Desmond.

As the beneficiary of three fortunes, the Duchess of Buckingham was considered one of the richest landowners in England. Her land holdings were vast but rents were slow to come in. Keeping up York House, Burley-on-the-Hill, New Hall and the other mansions in the accustomed style was running Kate deeper into debt. Living with the extravagant Buckingham she had evidently acquired a taste for luxury. Accordingly she was running up large bills with tradesmen for wine, rare foodstuffs, gold jewellery; but there were no new paintings and no new mansions. Like most of the landed aristocracy, Kate was short of ready cash and to meet her high expenses she was borrowing money.

To obtain the necessary loans, she turned to George's old retainers especially those who owed her a favour. George Feilding, William Bold, and William Kifferd were expected to pay for her past patronage retroactively. By 1634 Feilding, Bold, her accountant Thomas Fotherley, and William Alcock, the administrator of the Duke's goods, had co-signed bonds and bills with Her Grace, totalling 7,000£. Should she default, the creditors would fall back on them, and they on her. There were mortgage payments and surveying costs for her land holdings. A relatively small item to be paid by Lady's Day in March 1635 was the year's wages for her army of servants – a mere 345£ for all. (Few servants dared to be as pressing as John Porter, the steward at New Hall, who demanded his wages on time for collecting the rents and for "looking to the grounds and goods there.") A year later, the sculptors of Buckingham's monument were still waiting to be paid - 420£ for Le Sueur and 56*l.* for the lesser-known Besniers. Then there were the Duke's legacies long overdue. Although short of cash, Kate was scrupulous about paying Olive Porter's allowance and Frances Purbeck's annuity.

Kate had always been secretly sympathetic to her sister-in-law who had been so persecuted by George and his mother. Not to be missed were the remaining installments to the Earl of Pembroke, for Mall's dowry: 600£ in 1634 and 2,000£ in 1635. Apart from the dowry, the Earl held Kate's bond for 2,600£ payable August 1635. Some of her indebtedness was due to her continuing charity, for instance 270£ for land bought for the poor of Ireland.

With her father gone, Kate turned for financial advice to Sir Richard Weston, the Lord Treasurer whom the King had recently raised to the peerage as Earl of Portland. A gruff man with a prominent paunch, Portland exuded power as the official who controlled the purse strings of the realm. Kate had rented Wallingford House to him for a London residence thus he was her near neighbour. A bond between them was the fact that he was a secret Catholic. He had long been a financial advisor to the family, first to Buckingham and later to her father and herself. Although his advice was normally sound, it did not always prove profitable. In the early 1630s, King Charles decided to challenge the Dutch monopoly over fishing in the North Sea. With the approval of his Treasurer, he granted a charter to a company called the Association for the Fishery and announced that henceforth all fishing vessels would have to have a license from this company at a fee. Working capital was to come from shareholders known as "Adventurers." Endymion Porter was promoting the enterprise and quickly found investors among the courtiers. The Lord Treasurer himself ventured 1,000£, the Earl of Rutland, 500£, and on their advice Kate invested 300£. Predictably, the Dutch fishermen refused to take out the licenses and Kate and the others lost their investment. But especially after her father's death, Portland proved a valuable advisor and she leaned on him. In gratitude for overseeing her finances, she made him a gift of 1,000£.

Although Portland never had the supreme power that Buckingham had enjoyed, he was, nevertheless, Charles's first minister in the early thirties making him the most important of the privy councillors. But Portland had a dangerous rival. The prelate William Laud, not satisfied with having succeeded George Abbott as Archbishop of Canterbury, was determined to replace Portland. All at court knew his jealousy of the Lord Treasurer. In 1634 he saw an opportunity to bring down his rival. With some grounds, he accused the Lord Treasurer of cutting timber on crown lands that was reserved for the King's ships and selling it far below value and he urged King Charles to dismiss him. Charles had no intention of dismissing the man who kept him solvent without Parliament, but a charge of mismanagement of government funds coming from the Archbishop of Canterbury could not be brushed off. Portland did not underestimate his adversary. To counter Laud he needed an unimpeachable and highly-placed person to bear witness to his good character. Who better than the Duchess of Buckingham? Portland knew that the King always heard her with favour though she rarely went to court these days.

On a fine spring day in 1634, Kate was going about her daily activities as chatelaine of York House when the Earl of Portland came to call. Not as an advisor this time but as a supplicant for a favour. He informed her of

Laud's accusation and asked if she would stand up for him at a hearing before the King. Kate was a friend of his accuser as well, but seeing this proud man humbling himself before her, she agreed to his request.

On the appointed day the Duchess, flanked by the Earl of Denbigh and his son Lord Basil Feilding who was married to Portland's daughter, appeared at the hearing before the King into Archbishop Laud's charges against the Lord Treasurer. She looked pale and even plainer than many remembered her. Those present had never heard Buckingham's wife and widow utter a word in public. To their astonishment she pleaded forcefully on behalf of the Earl of Portland, saying she could attest to his financial probity from her personal knowledge. With Kate's help, Portland weathered the storm. The secretary at the Venetian embassy reported to the Doge that it was the Duchess of Buckingham, "heiress of the royal favour of her husband" who caused the King to dismiss all charges against Portland.

Laud was hurt, as he always was when trusted friends deserted him. But he had given his loyalty to Buckingham's widow and he would not withdraw it. In any event he had the satisfaction of knowing that for all practical purposes he had replaced Portland as the King's chief minister. Charles was determined to have a well-ordered established church based on bishops unalterably loyal to himself and a service book that would create uniformity of worship throughout his realm. In his eyes the Puritan brand of Protestantism could only lead to anarchy. He had given Laud the archbishopric of Canterbury because this prelate shared his views on religious conformity and had the dedication and strength of character to impose it.

Kate's feelings for the Archbishop were mixed. She appreciated his loyalty to her late lord and his concern for her and the children, but she often felt stifled by it. She sometimes thought he had adopted this paternal role more for himself than for her. His father had been a well-to-do clothier in Reading and he was deeply sensitive about his middle-class beginnings. He had once confided to Kate that a youthful marriage to a woman of the lower orders – "a very troublesome and unquiet wife," he called her - had almost ruined his career. He did not say how he had released himself from this harridan, whether by death or by an annulment obtained through his church connections. So to ally himself with the Rutland heiress and widow of the great Duke of Buckingham gave him a connection to be proud of. Despite his devotion, Kate could not regard him as a father figure. Still, she often reminded herself, he could claim a close attachment to her family. He had christened her sons, buried dear little Charles at the age of one year and four months, and was about to conduct the marriage of her daughter.

Mall was thirteen, Charles Herbert was sixteen; Kate and the Earl of Pembroke agreed that it was time for the marriage to take place. There were visits back and forth between York House and the Pembrokes' London town house so the two young people could get acquainted. As it turned out, Mall much preferred the younger brother who was better looking and livelier. She begged her mother to let her marry him instead but (as was reported by a family friend) Kate "chid her out of it." The older boy was the one who would inherit, she explained to the disappointed girl, and it was her father's and her grandfather's wish that she marry Charles, the heir.

The royal couple were so delighted with the match that the wedding was held at the palace on January 8, 1635. The marriage ceremony was performed by Archbishop Laud in the Queen's apartments. Afterwards, the King tendered a sumptuous wedding feast for the two families. Unenthused about her husband but thrilled at having been the centre of attention, the thirteen-year-old bride accompanied her mother back to York House. A month later the young groom left for the Continent with his tutor. It was the usual thing for a youth to go abroad to learn languages and to attend one of the academies that were basically riding schools. Both bride and groom would be allowed to grow up before the marriage would be consummated.

The Earl of Pembroke commissioned Van Dyck to paint a family portrait to commemorate the marriage. Mall, a luminous figure in a white satin gown, is the centre-piece of the painting with its ten larger-than-life figures. Against a rich background of tapestry displaying the Herbert coat-of-arms, the Earl makes a welcoming gesture towards the young girl. The boyish groom, standing to the left of the central figures, also extends his hand towards his bride. Cloud-borne cherubs bless the union. The magnificent painting was hung in the Herberts' London residence (later to find a permanent place at Wilton House).

PART TWO:

RANDAL

CHAPTER SEVENTEEN

With her wealth and the favour she received from the King and Queen, the Duchess of Buckingham was the most eligible widow in England. Suitors were discouraged from coming to York House but a handsome, red-haired young Irishman named Randal Macdonnell, recently back from travels on the Continent, rapidly gained entry. Kate was lonely. George had been dead for seven years. Her daughter was married and before long would be leaving home. The boys were too young to provide her with companionship. At thirty-two she was middle-aged. Above all, her bed was cold. The Venetian ambassador read her correctly when he wrote the Doge that "the Duchess of Buckingham was tired of leading a widow's life."

Randal Macdonnell, Lord Dunluce, was of the old Irish Catholic aristocracy and could trace his antecedents back to the High Kings of Ireland. His maternal grandfather was the Earl of Tyrone, the Irish chieftain who had led the rebellion against the English until 1607 when he fled the country in the famous "Flight of the Earls." Randal's father had at first joined in the rebellion but soon made his peace and henceforth co-operated with Whitehall and the English Lord Deputies in Dublin. King James made him lord lieutenant of the county of Antrim in Ulster and in 1620 created him Earl of Antrim in the Irish peerage. Historically, the Macdonnells had been the lords of Ulster in the north east of the island, and with new grants from King James the Earl had "planted" that hitherto wild region with Protestant Scots. As his elder legitimate son, Randal stood to inherit this enormous plantation. Kate had known no Irishmen before him and she was fascinated by his family history and stories about his own life. An extremely talkative man, she had no trouble drawing him out.

"I was bred," he told her, "in the old Irish way. I wore neither hat, cap, nor shoe, nor stocking till I was seven or eight years' old. Dunluce Castle where I grew up was full of children. Six sisters I had and four brothers. Of the boys, only one was born on the right side of the bedcover as I was. The others were my father's bastards, but to me they were as much my brothers as my lawful brother Alexander." His description of his father had Kate laughing.

"The old man is chieftain of the Macdonnell clan and rules like a king. He is a law unto himself. Anyone who naysays him can find himself in the stocks. I have seen my father put a bailiff in the stocks for trying to execute a warrant without his consent. He takes prisoners out of jail and thinks nought of executive writs: just tears them up if he does not like them. I recall going to the Quarter Sessions at Carrisfergus with him as a lad. Two of his servants were on trial. In he marches with me behind him like a lackey. 'Och surra,' he shouts, 'how durst ye offer to hang my men.' 'But it was you who indicted them,' says the magistrate. 'No matter,' says my father, 'unhand them.' "

"We spoke Gaelic at home," he told Kate. "Yet in my early youth he sent me to France to learn French. My father had been to Whitehall and he saw how the English lads came back from the Continent 'frenchified'. If that was what it took to be an English gentleman then off to France with me!"

On future visits Kate learned the rest of his life story. After spending three years in France he heard from his father that King Charles had ordered him to come back - not to Ireland but to the English court. With England at war with France and Spain, there was some fear at Whitehall that Irishmen travelling on the Continent were consorting with the enemy. Certainly many Irish soldiers and several chieftains were serving in the foreign armies. Swearing that his son had been sent to France solely to learn the French language, the Earl obtained the King's permission to keep his son abroad. A year later the Earl himself was making arrangements for Randal to cross the Channel in the suite of the English ambassador to Paris.

Then nineteen and proficient in French, Randal spent several months of 1627 at the English court. ("Would you recall seeing me?" he asked Kate who had to admit that she had no such recollection.) Meanwhile his father was impatiently waiting for him to come to Ireland but King Charles was loath to let him go. Secretary Conway wrote the Earl that "His Majesty having seen your noble son on his return from France is anxious to keep him at court. His Majesty is willing he should go to Ireland to present his duty to you, but wishes that, when that is done, he may return as soon as possible." After a short visit home Randal went back to England and was still there in October 1628 when once again King Charles would allow him only a brief visit to Ireland.

In a letter to Lord Deputy Falkland, Charles added the postscript that he was "permitting the son [of the Earl of Antrim] to leave court and go home for two months. I desire that afterwards he may return to court." On these terms, Randal returned to Dunluce Castle. In February 1629, the Earl of Antrim requested leave to accompany his son to court and King Charles granted it. Perhaps the Earl was hoping for an appointment for his son or himself, but it seems to have ended as nothing more than a social call. At this point Randal, on his own, left the British Isles to travel on the Continent. It was not until 1634 that he turned up again in England. In the interim, King Charles's enthusiasm for the young Irishman had clearly waned. This may have prompted Randal initially to wait upon the Duchess of Buckingham who was known to be a close friend of the King.

Kate ventured to ask why a handsome fellow of twenty-five was not betrothed or married. He smiled. "They tried to wed me to a daughter of Lord Abercorn but I went on my travels and they could not catch me."

Notwithstanding his father's accommodation with the Stuart regime, Randal was brought up strictly as a Catholic. His religion was one of his main attractions for Kate – but not the only one.

A big man, taller and broader than the slender Buckingham and with a shock of red hair, Randal looked nothing like George but he reminded Kate of her late husband in his vitality, his self-confidence, his ready laughter. From the beginning she was strongly attracted to him physically. At first she wondered if he could return her passion. After all, she was six years older and looked worn out. But Randal dispelled any worries she had about the age difference by the fond, teasing way he had of calling her "my dear old duchess." He begged her to marry him. She could not resist. Kate knew the

King was against her remarrying. If he were not, he would have arranged a marriage long before this. So the marriage arrangements would have to be conducted in secrecy. She turned to her own family connections - there were others than Uncle George she could call upon. She was already sleeping with Randal.

Reports came back from her negotiators that the Earl of Antrim approved the match and was offering to give the couple 2,000£ a year and to pay Randal's debts, at the time amounting to 3,000£. The Irish peer was gleeful that the son whom he had come to regard as a ne'er-do-well wandering purposelessly through Europe had managed to win the wealthy widow of the great Duke of Buckingham. Kate had converted and the wedding took place quietly in April 1635 in front of a priest.

The King had to be told. Kate went to the palace the next day and was received by Charles informally in his own apartments. She had barely risen from a deep curtsey when he spoke: "Have you come to ask my advice about something you wish to do or to tell me of something you have already done?" Obviously, he knew of her marriage. She was so taken aback at this sudden question that she did not know how to answer. Giving her an extremely cold, angry look and without another word, he turned away and walked out of the room. Afterwards the King told his intimate circle that the Duchess had taken an audacious step and he blamed her severely. He said he would not have the Buckingham children brought up in a Catholic home and that he would take the administration of their revenues out of her hands. In future, he did not want to see her at court.

The following day, word arrived at York House from court that the little Duke and his brother were to be placed temporarily in the care of Archbishop Laud and the Duchess was ordered to have them ready at once. On that same day, the Earl of Pembroke stormed in to tell Kate that he was taking his daughter-in-law to live with his family. Mall was not consulted and when she heard about it she became hysterical, screaming that she would not leave her mother.

In persuading her to marry him, Randal had assured Kate that she was such a favourite with King Charles that he would accept their marriage. But Kate, being the realistic person she was, knew that marrying without the King's blessing could lose her his favour, consequently she was not surprised. But she had not foreseen that her children would be taken away from her.

Meanwhile English society had not welcomed the handsome young Irishman into its ranks. Partly this was due to the fact that the Irish nobility were scorned by the English as second-rate and someone from its ranks hardly an acceptable spouse for an English duchess. But prejudice aside, the man himself was not held in high regard. A typically harsh opinion was that of Edward Hyde, a rising lawyer who years later as the historian Lord Clarendon looked back on the Duchess of Buckingham's second husband. "Handsome" he granted, but "of excessive pride and vanity and of a marvelous weak and narrow understanding." The Venetian ambassador summed up the general opinion about Kate's chosen mate: "perhaps more remarkable for his bodily than his mental qualities."

Kate's peerless reputation evaporated overnight. She found herself the object of "intense speculation and cruel gossip." Randal was portrayed as a fortune-hunter and she, a foolish victim of her own lust. Archbishop Laud shook his head and attributed her fall from grace to "the frailty of women" (although he added that in all fairness men could be equally so). Writing to Lord Wentworth in Ireland, he said that friends of the Duchess were "ill satisfied with her marriage, that it had lost her much ground with the King himself as well as all others of quality." As for himself, he felt he was more troubled by the marriage than any other friend she had. "But it was now past remedy." Despite his disappointment in her, for the sake of the late Duke, the children, and she herself he would continue all his "wonted respects unto her." He felt pledged to the Duke to look after and protect his wife and children. Knowing how the Duchess loved her children and what an excellent mother she was, the Archbishop admired the "noble" way in which she accepted the wrenching loss of having her children taken from her. Still, she had no other recourse, the King having willed it.

Frowned upon by the King, Kate found old friends forsaking her. She was bitter and saddened. Laud understood how deeply hurt she was. "The truth is," he wrote Lord Wentworth, "the good lady finding all her friends ill satisfied with her marriage, is very sensible of anything that might add to her grief." Unfortunately, one who would have stood by her was no longer living. Kate felt certain that the Earl of Portland would have defended her reputation as she had defended his. Alas, the Lord Treasurer had died a few weeks before her marriage. What had begun with a sore throat turned out to be an absess that stopped his breathing and he had choked to death after four days of illness on March 23, 1635, at the age of fifty-eight.

The Queen, who had enormous influence over the King, sent word that she was cooling him down and hoped to have him pacified in a few days. Within a week, Kate was summoned to court and found the King ready to forgive. The reconciliation was meaningless however for Charles was unshakeable in his determination to remove her children from her. He told her he would not have Steenie's children brought up in a Catholic home. He pointed out to Kate that even Henrietta Maria had ceded her right under the marriage treaty to raise their children as Catholics for the first twelve years of their life. Prince Charles's Catholic governess, Lady Roxburgh, had been replaced by the very Protestant Lady Dorset.

The next blow came when King Charles revoked Kate's wardship of her elder son and made the seven-year-old Duke of Buckingham his own ward. He immediately took steps to protect the boy's inheritance. Kate and Randal were presented with an indenture to sign on May 11, 1635, that assured the little Duke of income from "divers manors and lands in Hereford, Derby, York, Rutland, Essex and Bucks." Annexed to the indenture was an inventory of "all such Hangings of Arras Tapistry and other Hangings Plate Jewells Aggats Pictures Statues household Stuffe Goods Chattells rings and other things" that were not to be sold or given away. Charles had moved to prevent Kate and her second husband from selling off the York House collection that had meant so much to her first husband. Moreover, and of greater consequence to Kate and Randal, was that all the lands, manors and contents in the indenture were to be held in trust by the Earl of Pembroke and a Buckingham executor, Sir Robert Pye, and they would be accountable to these two. The trustees were to ensure that Randal did not get his hands on the young Duke's estate so that it would be delivered intact to him when he reached twenty-one. Adding to Kate's sense that she had been ill-used by her friend King Charles was the news that Uncle George had been made her son's official guardian.

Yet after the lonely years, Kate was finding compensation in her newfound happiness with Randal. But that comfort was temporarily interrupted. To protect his position as heir with his peppery old father, Randal felt he had to go to Ireland and the sooner the better. Knowing that Laud maintained a regular correspondence with the Lord Deputy of Ireland, Sir Thomas Wentworth, Kate appealed to him to prepare the ground for Randal. Laud had been troubled as to the attitude he should adopt towards the Duchess's new husband. After considerable prayer, he had decided that although he did not much care for this brash young man, if he was to protect and assist the Duchess, as he had promised the Duke, he must extend his care to him. He had heard that Wentworth had conceived a dislike of the young lord, so he prepared a letter for Randal to present to the Lord Deputy. In his letter he asked him to "use Lord Dunluce nobly for my sake" and out of pity for the Duchess: "I am loath," he wrote, "that any more should be added to that poor lady's affliction."

Perhaps her own fall from grace made Kate sympathize with a most unfortunate lady, and one whom she had called sister. For some time she had been besieged with letters from Viscountess Purbeck who had fled to France to avoid being promenaded through London streets in the white sheet of an adulteress. Her lover, Sir Robert Howard, had helped her escape dressed in men's clothing, but he could not accompany her abroad because there was an injunction against his leaving the country. Even on the other side of the Channel, Frances was fearful of being forcibly returned to England by bounty hunters and had taken refuge in a nunnery. Under the influence of Sir Kenelm Digby, an expatriate who took it upon himself to convert English ladies in distress, she had become a Roman Catholic. Her conversion had won her support from the Queen of France who requested her sister-in-law, the Queen of England, to procure a license for Lady Purbeck's return. Frances longed to go back to England, trusting that with protection in high places she would be safe. She had left the nunnery and was living in Paris in much distress. Her letters to Kate were heart-rending pleas to intercede on her behalf. Kate took up her cause. But she found King Charles adamantly opposed to Lady Purbeck's return and she soon found out why. The Countess of Denbigh was invoking Buckingham's memory to discourage Charles from allowing Lady Purbeck to return to England with impunity. Presuming on their long friendship, Kate went to Sue to ask her to stop inciting the King against their poor sister-in-law. But Kate found that because of her remarriage Sue had turned against her as well.

She had reason to be happier with the King's treatment of her faithful Doctor Moore. Charged with recusancy in 1626 (one of the sporadic periods of enforcement of the penal laws against Anglo-Catholics), he had made no attempt to avoid conviction by using bribery or string-pulling. He had relied on the King's assurance to the Duke that he would not be prejudiced. Now ten years later, the Commissioners for Recusants were demanding that he make a composition with them for that old conviction which would cost him a great deal of money. Moore wrote to the King, reminding him of his promise in 1626 that if he allowed himself to be convicted "he should not at all be damnified." Charles lived up to his promise. He directed the Commissioners to drop their claims and to lease back to Doctor Moore his sequestered lands at a nominal rent of three or four pounds per annum.

Charles had taken Kate's children to be brought up with his own family at the palace. Her little boys seemed completely happy in the royal nursery and Mall was thrilled living in the Queen's apartments. She began modelling herself on the queen, adopting Henrietta Maria's style of dressing her hair and taste in clothing. To her mother's amusement, she even began mangling the King's English like her royal mistress. As it happened, Kate was on the verge of starting a new family. She was several months pregnant when Randal returned in July. He was delighted and relished informing his cantankerous father who had taunted him that his great peeress was too old to breed. The couple were using the princely York House as their London residence. Right after their marriage, they had thought of living in Wallingford House and had notified Portland's widow that she and her family would have to move. But they later changed their minds, instead renting Wallingford House to the Marquis of Hamilton. The latter was reconciled to the wife he had scorned as beneath him. The Marchioness, the former Mary Feilding, was one of the most admired ladies of the court. In her goodness and quiet dignity, she was the polar opposite of the Countess of Carlisle who in her merry widowhood had a raft of male admirers.

The Duchess of Buckingham's pregnancy, which was very visible by midsummer, gave a fresh subject to the ha'penny rhymesters, who made their living by libelling or just poking fun at the aristocrats. The latest quatrain making the rounds was "A health to my Lady Duchess/ that loves redd hayr so well/ and to my Lord her husband/ that made her belly swell." When in late summer Kate had a miscarriage, she and Randal were terribly disappointed. For her convalescence Randal insisted they go to Tunbridge Wells. The waters would do her good and might help her to become pregnant again. But boredom at the spa led to much gambling. In a game of ninepins with the rakish court poet, Sir Robert Suckling, Randal lost 2,000£ of his wife's money.

Kate had married a second spendthrift. Randal's spending habits were nothing short of George's but George had spent his own money (or rather the King's money) and Randal was spending hers. His father, the Earl of Antrim, had backed down on his prenuptial promises. Unprepared for a daughter-in-law so far above him socially, Antrim had taken a dislike to Kate. Her wealth and position, originally the subject of much boasting to his cronies, now made him feel inferior and he was threatening to disinherit Randal. Archbishop Laud, in his self-appointed role as Kate's protector, advised the Lord Deputy of this development. "Now the Lady Duchess is married to his son, the Earl proves not overkind, or overfull of performance. You know my relations to that Lady," and he asked Wentworth to bring the father around. "When you see him next, put him in mind how honourable it will be for him really and fully to perform with her Grace whatever he hath promised."

In any event, Kate could not and would not deny her young husband anything. After some years of retirement from the social life at court, to please Randal Kate attended masques and boat races and all the other festivities sponsored by the pleasure-loving queen. She had to admit that court life was far from unpleasant. King Charles's sense of decorum and exquisite taste had created a court such as that envisaged by Castiglione in *Il Cortegiano* - required reading in translation for all Charles's courtiers. Like George before him, Randal had a taste for ostentation. At York House and their other residences, Kate maintained the luxurious style of living that George had insisted upon. There were no more arguments with the likes of Balthazar Gerbier over upholsteries that Kate had regarded as too expensive. Now she ordered with abandon armchairs and stools upholstered in scarlet,ue silk or silver damask, tapestries, velvet curtains trimmed with gold and silver lace, inlaid cabinets from Italy. She and Randal had the best that money could buy without paying for it; their creditors included practically every London tradesman.

Randal had wasted all the ready money that was available from Kate's estates. The situation called for desperate measures: they mortgaged Kate's lands, borrowed from the little Duke's estate, pawned Kate's jewellery, and borrowed from everyone. Still, their mounting debt had Kate begging from George's most devoted servants who, still grateful to him and revering his memory, could not say no. However, one very discontented creditor was John Ashburnham. A relative of Buckingham's, Ashburnham had been a member of the Duke's household and one of Buckingham's final acts of patronage was to install him as a Groom of the King's Bedchamber. Kate had urged the appointment on her husband and Ashburnham was grateful to her. Before her remarriage, Ashburnham had lent the Duchess 500£, and in October 1635 the loan fell due. All he got, however, were excuses either from the Duchess herself or from her secretary, Anne Smedley. Knowing that his old friend in Buckingham's service, Edward Nicholas, had ready access to the Duchess, he turned to him for help. Although Nicholas's own legacy of 500£ from their deceased master had still not been paid, he agreed to plead Ashburnham's case and henceforth all correspondence over the unrepaid loan was with him. Nicholas had no better success than Ashburnham but not for lack of trying.

The Duchess blamed the trustees of the Buckingham estate, claiming that they would not release the money for her to repay the debt. Ashburnham dismissed this excuse, telling Nicholas it was entirely her own "inclination" to be "adverse" to repaying him. At one point, her secretary hinted at payment in kind, perhaps a jewel. Six months later Ashburnham, still unpaid, wrote his friend to thank him "for his constant solicitation made to her Grace." In April 1636 a "smackering" of hope appeared in a letter from Anne Smedley saying that Her Grace had commanded her to inform Nicholas that, although unwell herself, if he would send a man to the writer's attention he should have 100£ "to begin with." Within days the Duchess herself wrote to Nicholas to say that she was "infinitely ashamed" to have to postpone even that portion. She claimed that Sir Robert Pye, one of the trustees, had broken his word to her. She entreated Nicholas's patience. She would never trouble him again in like kind. "I am more in pain for this than ever I was for anything," she wrote her devoted cavalier in what sounded like sincere regret.

CHAPTER EIGHTEEN

In January 1636 Charles Herbert died of small pox on the Continent. Mall was a widow without ever having been a wife. How unpredictable life was, Kate mused. The younger Herbert boy, whom Mall had preferred, was now the heir to the Pembroke and Montgomery titles and all the entailed property including Wilton House which had just received a handsome south front and a monumental double cube drawing room designed by Inigo Jones. As it turned out, if Mall had been allowed to choose her own husband she would have become the Countess of Pembroke and Montgomery. Sage heads had made the decision that now left her high and dry. It was the old question that Kate had mulled over many times. Should children be permitted to marry for love or only for family aggrandizement? A match with the younger son was out of the question. A new husband would have to be found. The King felt the only suitable candidate for the daughter of the great Duke of Buckingham was his own relative, the 24-year-old James Stuart, Duke of Lennox.

James Stuart had succeeded to the dukedom in 1624 at the age of twelve, receiving little interest or care from his stepmother, Kate's friend Frances. King Charles had assumed the role of parent and undertook direction of his education. After a short period of study at Cambridge, the boy was sent to the Continent where he was placed in an academy at Saumur in France. There he was trained in the manly arts of horsemanship and the handling of weapons, as well as fortification and siege warfare and their prerequisites, mathematics and geometry. To acquire languages he spent years not only in France but in Italy and Spain (where he was made a grandee), and did not return to England until he had come of age in 1633. Charles immediately began grooming him for a leading role in his government. He made him a privy councillor, a groom of the bedchamber, and bestowed the Order of the Garter upon him. The King also made him his intimate friend, bringing him into the circle of those who "discoursed with His Majesty in his bedchamber rather than at the council board." Slim and blond, Lennox had that air of superiority natural to his birth and education.

Although Mall had to be in mourning for a year, informal negotiations for the match were under way in 1636. But Mall was in a sad state. She was no longer enjoying court life and when Kate visited her she clung to her mother and begged to go home. Kate explained to her weeping daughter that as she was the King's ward her mother was powerless to take her away. Kate was not at all well; she thought she may have had an early miscarriage. Randal was insisting on taking her to New Hall where she would be able to regain her strength. Kate dreaded telling Mall she was going to the country and when she did the girl made a scene.

As a groom of the King's Bedchamber John Ashburnham often encountered Mall at court. One March day in 1636 he saw her trailing behind the Queen's ladies, looking dejected. He had known her well in the years when he was a member of Buckingham's household so he did not hesitate to ask, "What is the matter, Lady Mary?" The homesick girl broke down and told this familiar figure from her childhood all her troubles. Ashburnham reported the incident to Nicholas: "I fear the Duchess's being in the country has undone her daughter. Lady Mary does not now put such great a value upon Her Majesty's care of her, for she is resolved to fall upon her knees to the King that she may live with her mother." No servant of Buckingham's had been closer to the family than Edward Nicholas. He had been Buckingham's secretary even before his marriage in 1620, and when Buckingham became Lord Admiral he made him Secretary of the Admiralty. Nicholas remembered the Duke bringing his little daughter with him to the Admiralty, and what a happy, exuberant child she had been. Ashburnham's letter saddened him. Apparently the King refused her pleas to let her go to her mother. In April Ashburnham wrote that "Lady Mary angers me to the heart." Nicholas understood this to mean that Lady Mary was in rebellion, and surely that was not helping her to fit in at Henrietta Maria's frivolous court.

Meanwhile, Kate's influence with the King was far from what it once had been. Formerly, she had had Charles's ear on account of her first husband but on her remarriage she had lost that privileged status. In fact, observing the extravagant style of living of the Duchess and her new husband, Charles became suspicious that they were dipping into the second Duke's inheritance. The indenture of May 11, 1635, had provided for his present maintenance out of the rents from the late Duke's country manors and lands. But what of the properties that George had left to Kate? These had to be kept whole and free of liens and mortgages until the boy reached his majority when they would pass to him by the law of entail. To keep a closer eye on Kate and her new husband, in March 1636 Charles ordered the Court of Wards to make William, Earl of Newcastle, a guardian of the royal ward jointly with the Earl of Rutland, the present guardian. Newcastle was the richest peer in England and had ingratiated himself with the King by spending 20,000£ entertaining him at Welbeck Abbey, his estate in Nottinghamshire. Charles was apparently well satisfied with Newcastle's guardianship of the little Duke of Buckingham because two years later he appointed him governor of his own son and heir, the Prince of Wales.

Though Kate was out of favour with the King, she found the Queen surprisingly friendly. Henrietta Maria had stayed true to her promise to her mother to promote the Roman church in England and Charles was so fond of his wife that he looked the other way at her brazen encouragement of English Catholics. Kate and Randal could be said to be her lieutenants. At York House they had priests lodging with them openly, and the couple wined and dined the papal legates, first Gregorio Panzini and later George Con. Shortly after Con arrived in England in the autumn of 1636 he informed the Vatican that the Duchess of Buckingham was "instrumental in converting women of quality to Catholicism." Indeed, the suave Con cultivated Kate's friendship as the best way to reach the aristocracy. One of the first to succumb to their proselytizing was Olive Porter. Always impetuous, Olive threw caution to the wind and proceeded to make deathbed conversions in her immediate family, first her father and then her brother-in-law, Captain Tom Porter.

The Queen's chapel at Somerset House (formerly Denmark House) was the fulcrum of conversion activities. Built on ground that had been used for a tennis court in Queen Anne's day, the chapel was six years in construction. On the 10th of December 1636, the Queen and her court came to hear the first mass held there, conducted by the Bishop of Angouleme, the Queen's grand almoner. Once the royal party was seated, a curtain was drawn back to reveal a vista as magnificent and ingenious as any set Inigo Jones had designed for the royal masques. All eyes were raised to behold a glorious depiction of Paradise in an oval arch soaring forty feet in the air, supported by classical pillars. Through this archway the congregants saw a sequence of arches carved and painted with angels and saints, diminishing in size to create the illusion of depth.

At the end of the vista was the Holy Sacrament of the Eucharist in the pyx on a gilded stand, so dazzlingly lit by the many tapers that it appeared to be on fire. The chapel rang with the glorious sounds of the organ melding with the voices of unseen choristers. When the music subsided, the bishop emerged from the sacristy in pontifical garb, attended by acolytes and deacons. He mounted the steps of the portable altar, and with great solemnity celebrated the Mass. Queen Henrietta Maria's face was wet with tears of joy, and Kate, sitting near the Queen, felt her own eyes well up. To be able to worship openly in her dear Catholic faith was the one aspect of her second marriage that improved upon the first. Afterwards, Kate and Randal lined up to receive Holy Communion from the bishop. From that day forward, throngs of English Catholics attended mass without hindrance at the Queen's chapels at Somerset House and St. James Palace. Although Charles as head of the Church of England was unshakeable in his Anglicanism, he was tolerant of Catholics in these years when he ruled without Parliament. This was in sharp contrast to the punishing strictness with which Puritans were treated.

The priests in Henrietta Maria's chapel were Capuchins, an order of the Franciscans favoured by her mother and her brother, King Louis. After the troublesome Oratorian priests were expelled from England and with the signing of the Anglo-French peace treaty in 1630, a dozen Capuchin friars were sent on a mission to England to serve as Henrietta Maria's religious mentors. Construction of the Queen's Chapel at Somerset House began on their arrival. At first the friars appeared circumspectly in the black cassock of a secular priest, but under the Queen's protection they felt sufficiently secure to wear the habit of their order: the roughly woven brown robe and the tall pointed hood of the mendicant friar. The Capuchins were in hot rivalry with the Jesuits for the Pope's sponsorship. Kate in her childhood had known only Jesuit priests and her good Doctor Moore was a Jesuit. Nevertheless, she and Randall worshipped with the rest of the Anglo-Catholic aristocracy at the Queen's Chapel at Somerset House.

Sometime after the event (word travelled slowly by horse and sail) Randal learned that his father had died in Ireland on the very day of the opening of the Queen's chapel. He also learned to his great relief that the old Earl had not followed through on his threat to disinherit him. Randal not only inherited the title but as the second Earl of Antrim he became one of the greatest landowners in Ireland, holding hundreds of miles of territory and vast estates with several castles including Dunluce Castle, the place of his birth. Kate was now the Countess of Antrim but by choice she would continue to be known as the Duchess of Buckingham to the end of her days.

By the end of the year, the negotiations for Mall's betrothal to the Duke of Lennox were completed and in January 1637 the formal announcement was made at court. Kate regretted that her prospective son-in-law was not a Catholic, however his wider family was all of the Old Faith and he was most sympathetic to it. As with many arranged marriages, the couple barely knew each other. Although Mall had got her way and was back with her mother, York House saw little of Lennox who, it appeared, was enamoured of the widowed Countess of Carlisle, twelve years his senior. The irony of it, Kate thought, was that this woman who had so often kept her husband from her was now depriving her daughter of her intended.

At thirty-six Lucy Carlisle was still the uncontested beauty of the court and men of all ages fell victim to her charms, one elderly admirer dubbing her "the killing beauty of the world." One of her conquests was Sir Thomas Wentworth, the stern, aloof Lord Deputy of Ireland, who came over to England in July 1636 and, partly because he could not tear himself away from Lady Carlisle, did not return to Dublin until late November. Another was her cousin, the Earl of Holland, who wrote amateurish poems to her, thinking to rival court poet Thomas Carew's exquisite "Lucinda" poems. He and Wentworth were rivals over her and with young Lennox it had become a three-way contest for her favour. Some courtiers in the crush around Lady Carlisle merely gave lip service to her beauty; her real charm for them was her influence with the Queen. Aspiring for the Order of the Garter, Randal was one of those who flattered Lucy shamelessly. He joined her circle with Kate's approval, for she knew that the route to the Queen through Lady Denbigh was closed to her socially ambitious second husband.

Mall's engagement had paved the way for Kate's return to the King's good graces. Charles sent for her. He welcomed her back to court and expressed the hope that she would henceforth come regularly. The union of the Stuart and Villiers families was very near to his heart, he told her. The new Earl of Antrim was well pleased with the renewal of royal favour for his wife even though his own noble line had been ignored.

Now that she was to be a duchess and could lord it over the other ladies, Mall was ready to return to the Queen's court. Hoping to have her appointed a Lady of the Bedchamber, one day shortly after her engagement Kate had taken her daughter to the Queen's Side of the palace. Unfortunately, Henrietta Maria bore a grudge against the young girl for deserting her and would not take her back. Indeed, she gave Mall one of her famous scowls that could empty an entire room: "I looked her out," the Queen told her ladies.

While King Charles was anxious to proceed with the wedding, the groom was far from eager. As the Venetian ambassador wrote the Doge in February 1637, "the Duke's affections rather lead him towards the widowed Countess of Carlisle." Then in April the wedding was further postponed when the mother of the bride took dangerously ill.

Randal was over in Ireland seeing to his estate, and when the news reached him he rushed home. Kate appeared to be at death's door yet the medical profession was at a loss to diagnose her illness. The King's physician, Sir Thomas de Mayerne, blustered about mysterious vapours but all he could do was to fall back on his usual treatment of purging the patient. Randal was beside himself with worry over his "dear old duchess." He had more confidence in Doctor Moore, hopeful that the Jesuit would save Kate through prayer if not by medical treatment. By the end of April Laud was able to report to Wentworth that "my Lady Duchess if now recovering, God be thanked, but she hath been in great danger." By June she was no longer confined to her bed and Randal took her to New Hall. The servants were happy to see the Duchess walking in the garden, leaning on the Earl's arm. But unheard by observers, Kate was complaining to

Randal that the air was not salubrious. After all these years she suddenly found the Essex countryside unhealthy. Archbishop Laud, a constant visitor, agreed with Kate: "At this time of year Essex air is aguish."

Kate mentioned to the Archbishop that she wished to purchase a new country estate where the air was better but it would certainly have to be in no way inferior to New Hall or Burleigh-on-the-Hill. As it happened, Laud was able to put her on to a magnificent country house in Hampshire that was for sale. Bramshill had been built in the early years of James's reign to entertain the King by old Lord Zouch now deceased, and his heir had no use for the huge pile. Kate was interested, so Laud referred her to young Lord Zouch. Assured by Laud and other friends that the air of Hampshire was extremely good, she had little difficulty persuading Randal that they should buy Bramshill. Naturally the purchase was made in Randal's name though the 12,000£ came from Kate. All their acquaintance told him this was a very low price for such a mansion, and Randal basked in congratulations (particularly from the vendor) for making such a great bargain.

In his regular correspondence with Wentworth, Laud mentioned that Lord Antrim had bought the mansion Bramshill in Hampshire because his wife found the air at New Hall unhealthy. Wentworth's reply was sour, "It was not "unhealthfulness so much, as because he conceived it in diminution to himself to live in his wife's house." Laud firmly corrected the Lord Deputy's assumption. "The truth is Bramshill was purchased for the unwholesomeness of New Hall," he wrote, and described his own role in the purchase. "The Duchess of Buckingham disliking the air at New Hall (as she had reason) spake with me about Bramshill, and I referred her to young Zouch, the owner of it. So the business went on." No doubt smiling as he dictated, Laud suggested that Wentworth take Antrim's boasting about his purchase of the mansion "as but the flourish of a young man who may live to understand himself better."

The date had finally been set for Mall's wedding. Unlike her first marriage, this was to be a large affair at York House. Kate was happy to see Mall all smiles and frolicksome in her old way. It did not seem to bother her that on the odd occasion she saw Lennox he was distant and dour, reserving his caresses for the large golden dog that accompanied him everywhere. She told her mother, "Now I'll be a duchess just like you." Then taking her hands she swung her around. "But you are just an old dowager duchess. You will have to walk behind me." Kate gave her a reproving slap on her bottom.

On August 3, 1637, Archbishop Laud married Buckingham's daughter to the Duke of Lennox in his chapel at Lambeth Palace, in the presence of the King and Queen. Laud noted in his diary that it was a very rainy day. After the ceremony, the wedding party crossed the Thames to York House where a great company was waiting for them. Kate looked around her with satisfaction. There was Sue Denbigh, full of smiles and repeatedly calling Kate "sister", and among the numerous countesses was a most complimentary Lucy Carlisle. With her daughter's marriage to a close relative of the King, an alliance arranged by His Majesty personally, Kate had recovered her position of influence, a woman to be courted by all. Randal was in high spirits. He had taken over the planning of the event as Kate was still weak from her serious illness and, typically, he had spared no expense. A masque, then supper, followed by dancing was the order of the day. The King and Queen set the tone of jollity that prevailed all evening, and capped their patronage of the event by sleeping at York House.

The day after the wedding Mall, now Duchess of Lennox, was sworn in as a Lady of the Queen's Bedchamber. She would not live in the Queen's quarters at Whitehall as she had when she was a maiden. Rather she would keep a fine London town house with her new husband. It suited both mother and daughter that Kate should sell Mall "a quantity of plate and jewels" (to quote the sales document) since Kate needed the money and Mall needed the goods.

CHAPTER NINETEEN

Kate's illness had interrupted Randall's stay in Ireland leaving much unfinished business. As soon as the wedding was over she urged him to go back, assuring him that she was on the mend, but it was several weeks before he would leave her. On the 28th of August Laud informed Wentworth that "my Lord Antrim went hence almost as soon as my Lady Duchess was perfectly recovered and will not come from thence until he hath settled his business." Knowing the couple as well as he did, he feared that without the Duchess's guiding hand, the young earl would be a prey to experienced predators, "projectors and greedy courtiers." There was plenty of the sort too among Irish officials who grabbed land away from the true owners by claiming some error in the title. In fact, Antrim's inheritance was under this very threat. Even in his father's day, there had been claims against the Macdonnell land holdings in Ulster on the ground of defective title. Before his death the first Earl had petitioned the Council in Dublin to issue him a new patent to secure his vast holdings in the northeast of the island. To obtain this patent was the business that brought Randal to Ireland.

Laud urged Wentworth to keep a watchful eye on the new Earl of Antrim's affairs, to ward off predators and to facilitate passage of the patent so long as there was no conflict with the King's interests. It was not for the

Earl himself that he was begging the Lord Deputy's favour but for his wife's sake: "You know my obligations to the House he married into because you know my relations to that family." Indeed, the prelate and the lord deputy had an unspoken mutual arrangement: "You look after my friend in Ireland and I will look after yours here."

Unfortunately, Lord Wentworth's dislike of Antrim was growing on further acquaintance. He regarded him as a spendthrift and a braggard. On Antrim's previous trip to Ireland he had promised the Lord Deputy to economize in return for his help, so when Wentworth heard of his purchase of the Bramshill estate he was disgusted. Taxed with this, Randal said truthfully that his wife had persuaded him to purchase it. Despite the Archbishop's corroboration, Lord Wentworth was skeptical. Such decisions were always made by the man in the family, he thought. From his inquiries, Wentworth estimated the couple's debts at around 30,000£ with the foolish purchase of Bramshill. When Antrim was in Ireland in April, Wentworth had suggested that he and the Duchess move to Ireland to save money. The Earl had not dismissed the idea. When Laud heard of it he commended it as good advice but thought it would not be taken. "I do not know how my Lady Duchess would brook going out of England," he wrote Wentworth. In any event, the matter could not be raised while her lord was out of the country and she herself was ill. In his considered opinion, she would never consent to living in Ireland.

Moreover, Wentworth believed (as he wrote Secretary Coke) that Antrim was doing things in Ireland "seemingly to procure the rights of the Duke of Buckingham, now in ward, when as indeed it tends only to get a present profit to the Earl of Antrim." This had to do with an estate Buckingham had granted or sold to the Lord President of Munster, Sir William St. Leger, in 1625 for twenty-one years. Antrim claimed that St. Leger owed money to the Buckingham estate from which the Duchess would derive 200£ in dower rights per annum. The garrulous Earl was spreading it all over Dublin that St. Leger was defrauding his stepson and his wife, the Duchess of Buckingham. Wentworth was incensed at what he called their "molesting" of St. Leger. The Lord Deputy asserted that, in any event, money recovered from the President of Munster while the Duke was in wardship would have to be repaid when he came of age.

The Archbishop agreed with the Lord Deputy that Antrim "would get little honour" out of prosecuting the Lord President of Munster. He said he would try to discuss the matter with the Duchess although his intervention might be "unwelcome." As it turned out, Kate was very civil but it was clear to Laud that she, not Randal, was behind the Munster business. It seemed she had been moved by the sad plight of a widow of one of Buckingham's sea captains. The story as she told it to the Archbishop was that a certain Captain Gosnall stood to get a little money if the Lord President of Munster paid what he owed to the Buckingham estate. The captain had died but the money would go to his needy widow.

Certain that it would have been Buckingham's wish she pursued the matter, Kate had requested the Lord President of Munster to show the widow some kindness but he had "roughly refused." Laud wrote Wentworth that this rebuff was "not the least motive why the Duchess was so earnest in this case." Wentworth scoffed at this portrayal of the duchess as an angel of mercy. He knew St. Leger, and he refused to believe that the stout soldier would deprive a captain of the royal navy of his due. Oblivious to the fact that the Duchess was renowned for her compassion for the underdog, particularly where servants or clients of the late Duke were concerned, Wentworth was convinced that she was bringing suit against the Lord President of Munster simply to get some money out of him because she and her husband were so heavily in debt. He sent off a damaging report to the King, claiming that the second Duke would ultimately have to repay anything taken out of the Munster estate at present. The King asked the executors of the late Duke's estate for their opinion on the Lord Deputy's report.

While the Munster affair was brewing, Kate was deeply involved in proselytizing activity in London with George Con, the papal legate, and Olive Porter, who had become almost a zealot. Kate was most anxious for Buckingham's niece, Mary Hamilton, to become a Roman Catholic. The young Marchioness was unwell. She was expecting her third child but her persistent cough and fragility indicated that she was ailing from more than just her pregnancy. Kate was dreadfully worried that this young woman whom she had loved since her childhood would die a heretic and suffer torment in the afterlife. Though her methods were gentler than Olive's, who painted lurid pictures of hell fire, Kate was no less determined. Still, Mary sweetly but firmly resisted her well-meaning aunt-by-marriage. She admitted to leaning in Rome's direction but would not convert because it would embarrass her husband: the Marquis of Hamilton was the King's closest adviser and friend and she would not give the Puritans reason to attack him and through him King Charles. Olive had better fortune with one of her own relatives, her youngest sister Anne, Countess of Newport. This was to blow up into a scandal that touched Kate as well.

Anne, Countess of Newport, had made an advantageous marriage to a half-brother of the Earl of Holland and the couple aspired to the very highest circles at court. No one enjoyed social life more than Lady Newport. Such was her reputation that one of the popular libels making the rounds began with "A health to my Lady Newport/ that loves to play and dance." Still, she was a regular communicant of the Anglican Church and had tried her best to thwart Olive's forced conversion of their father. This did not stop Olive in her zeal. Accompanied by the Duchess of Buckingham, she played upon her sister's weakness for social success. The two women regaled her with the papal legate's comings and goings. Indeed, Monsignor Con's velvety manner acquired at the papal court in Rome made him a sought-after guest at all the best tables. A typical bit of gossip designed to impress the impressionable Lady Newport was that the fashionable Countess of Carlisle had brought Con to dine with her sister the Countess of Leicester at the latter's new town house. Flattered by the Duchess of Buckingham's attentions, Anne listened to the sirens' call.

Anne loved the theatre, so there was nothing unusual about her attending a performance of a new comedy with Olive. However, it was to be a very different evening from others. Afterwards Olive took her by coach to the Queen's Chapel at Somerset House where a Capuchin friar was waiting to welcome her ladyship into the Roman Catholic church.

The Countess of Newport's conversion caused a "horrible noise" because of her husband's position at court. Newport was furious. He rushed over to Lambeth Palace to complain to Archbishop Laud who was already deeply concerned over the society conversions. The Earl was so "fierce" about the "perverting" of his wife that the matter was debated at the Privy Council the next day. The Earl blamed the converts Wat Montagu and Tobie Mathew; others held the Capuchins to blame. When he rose to speak, Laud's small frame was shaking with anger and he was red in the face as he condemned the increasing influence of the "Romish party" and the proselytizing by the Capuchins at Somerset House. He stated that the Queen's Chapel should be closed to English Catholics. Afterwards, he took coach for Whitehall palace. Getting down on his knees, he begged King

Charles to allow him to try Sir Tobie Mathew at the High Commission and to banish Montagu from court. But Newport and the Archbishop were putting blame on the wrong shoulders. Lord Wentworth in Ireland was informed by a person who should know that "the truth is that neither Montagu nor Mathew had a hand in it. My Lady Duchess of Buckingham, her sister Porter, and Con were the chief agents in her conversion though it is wholly laid on the Capuchins." This was the general view when the dust of scandal had settled. The King did nothing of substance about Lady Newport's sensational conversion and the hornet's nest it stirred up. The Queen rewarded Lady Newport by openly arranging for her to celebrate Christmas mass at Somerset House. "The Queen is very displeased with me," Laud wrote Wentworth.

The Munster case was dragging on, favouring first one side then the other. Not long after the Newport scandal involving the Duchess, Laud was stopped at Whitehall by the Earl of Antrim who had just returned from Ireland. "My Lord showed me a paper," Laud wrote Wentworth, "in which it was affirmed by the officers and council of my Lord Duke that nothing but justice was demanded of the Lord President, and that nothing could be demanded back from the young Duke. I am not lawyer enough to judge of these things, but it seems upon your Lordship's letter to the King the officers were commanded to set down the whole case for his Majesty's view, out of his royal care that the young Duke might not suffer by it. And a copy of this paper was sent to me upon this speech which I had with my Lord Antrim. And whether any copy be sent to your Lordship by the King's command I know not." Wentworth, for his part, obtained a contrary opinion from Irish judges. Kate would bring the case to the Court of Wards in Dublin where ultimately the Lord President of Munster would triumph.

As usual, Antrim had a favour to ask of Laud. He had received word that the new patent that would secure his land holdings had been passed but since he would not be in Dublin would Laud have his good friend the Lord Deputy wind up the matter for him? For the Duchess's sake, Laud obliged. An exasperated Wentworth found himself deputizing for Antrim. Laud thanked him for taking care of Lord Antrim's patents, though actually the renewed patent ran counter to both Laud's and Wentworth's overall objective. Anxious to put royal finances on a sound basis – much of Ireland had been granted away recklessly in King James's time - both men wanted all leases to be returned to the Crown with no possibility of alienating crown lands in future. The King would then reap substantial rents from hand-picked English landlords. Protestants of course!

With his patent secured, Antrim had a big land scheme in mind. A huge plantation in Londonderry in Northern Ireland held by the city of London had been so poorly and corruptly administered that it had been forfeited and was now available to speculators. Antrim had become noticeably friendly with the Marquis of Hamilton and it came out that the two lords were planning to put in an offer for the Londonderry plantation. Wentworth thought this ridiculous considering Antrim's indebtedness but he did not underestimate Hamilton's influence with the King. In this matter, he had no intention of obliging his friend the Archbishop by assisting Antrim.

At the same time, Wentworth was having a dispute with Kate. Buckingham had parcelled out the customs for goods passing through Londonderry port and removing this from private hands was one of Wentworth's objectives. All the customers had been willing to sell their grants back to the King at Wentworth's request. Only the Duchess of Buckingham was holding out. It took a firm order from the King before she unwillingly yielded up her patent. This incident did not endear her to the Lord Deputy.

Meanwhile Kate was very occupied with dear Mary, Hamilton's wife. Since the birth of a baby girl early in the new year, the Marchioness was obviously dying. Kate hardly missed a day at Wallingford House. With the best of motives, together with Con and Olive Porter she attempted a deathbed conversion. But Lady Mary continued to resist them. Watching her waste away, and certain of the Purgatory awaiting her, Kate grieved for Mary and for her parents, the Denbighs. The Marquis too was miserable. As proud as ever, he had nevertheless come to appreciate the angelic qualities of his wife. Though Charles had ordered him to go to Scotland, he would not leave while his wife lingered. On May 8, 1638, the beloved Marchioness of Hamilton died of consumption, steadfast until death in the Anglican faith.

Kate was confronted by change on all sides. Reality had at last penetrated the exquisite hermetic life at court. Hitherto, Puritan opposition to Laud's High Church ways had been effectively put down by draconian measures. In June 1637 Dr. John Bastwick. a physician, Henry Burton, a Bachelor of Divinity, and William Prynne, a barrister, were charged with libelling the church hierarchy. Their cases were heard in the Star Chamber with Laud presiding. The three were found guilty and sentenced to have their ears cut off. Prynne had lost his ears a few years earlier for a tract denouncing masques and other frivolities that was taken as a personal attack on the Queen. What was left of his ears was now lopped off with the ears of the others. This barbarity, though not an uncommon punishment, had led to the posting of libels against the Archbishop of Canterbury in public places.

Charles was sluggish in recognizing opposition at home to his church policies but he could not ignore the protests in Presbyterian Scotland. Hundreds and thousands of Scots were signing the Solemn League and Covenant by which they swore to defend the Presbyterian kirk and never to accept the Anglican prayer book. For Charles this was out and out treason and it was to put down the incipient rebellion that Hamilton, his Scottish lieutenant, had been ordered to Scotland.

On a personal level, Kate's life was about to change radically. In the summer of 1638 what had seemed impossible to her a year earlier was now a live possibility. She and Randal were swimming in debt. The pension she had enjoyed since Buckingham's day had been cut off. Faced with the rebellion in Scotland, the King had stopped all pensions and the loss of 6,000£ a year was a serious blow to Kate and Randal. They mortgaged York House and other properties, they borrowed from the second Duke's estate, they pawned some magnificent pearls that the Queen had given Kate. But none of this even began to cover their debts. Randal had been trying to persuade Kate that they should move to Ireland to save money. Finally Kate gave in. They rented York House to the Earl of Northumberland and made plans to leave.

As it happened, Randal was going over to Ireland with a secret assignment from the King. It was obvious that Charles was favourably inclined to both Kate and Randal. He was even taking their side in the Munster dispute. In discussing Irish affairs with Laud one day, Charles said, "My lord, you must write plainly to the Deputy about the business concerning my Lord Antrim and his lady, for I protest their cause is very fair."

In advance of their arrival, Laud advised Wentworth that the Earl was high in the King's approval and to bear this in mind even when the young man aggravated him. Laud had long been puzzled by his friend's animosity towards Antrim and not for the first time he inquired the reason. If he knew, he could talk to Antrim and hopefully resolve their differences. "He knows he has gone back in your opinion and professes much sorrow for it." Moreover, and this was what troubled Laud, it put the Duchess "under a cloud for his sake." Wentworth offered no explanation and Laud continued to advocate for Antrim, saying that he could not "but wish heartily to them, in remembrance of my Lord Duke that is gone."

By the end of August Kate and Randal were ready to depart. "He desires one of your whelps for the safe conveyance of his lady," Laud wrote Wentworth. However Randal had already arranged for transportation with the Lord Deputy. The whelp was a small ship and certainly not good enough for his Duchess. Writing from York House on July 17 he issued a virtual order to Wentworth: "I desire this courtesy to accommodate my good woman with one of the King's ships to meet us at Liverpool." He would have a great ship rather than a pinnace because the latter had just one small cabin. "Do us the greater courtesy to provide us with the bigger ship at Liverpool by the 25th or 31st of August," he wrote, and looked for an answer from the Lord Deputy by the first packet. The commanding tone enraged Wentworth. But forewarned by Laud that Antrim enjoyed King Charles's favour, he despatched a big ship to Chester to transport the Earl and the Duchess across the Irish Sea. Randal carried a letter from Laud for Wentworth in which the Archbishop expressed the wish that their stay in Ireland "would be so discreetly managed by them as that they may get out of debt and live the rest of their life the freer, and with the more honour. So I leave them to God's blessed protection, and all the help and assistance your lordship can give them."

CHAPTER TWENTY

Kate's first sight of Dunluce Castle left her terrified. Perched atop a rocky outcrop anchored to a headland at its base and by a bridge 150 feet above sea level, the tall, towered castle appeared about to topple into the churning waters. Randal laughed at her fears. The castle had been standing for hundreds of years, he said, and would be standing for centuries to come. Reluctantly, she crossed the drawbridge to the castle enclosure. Observing her disconsolate expression as she looked at the forbidding pile that was to be her home, Randal hugged her and said he would build her a house with gables and bay windows just like an English manor. And he showed her the location, reassuringly away from the sheer cliff side.

In the castle the family was waiting to greet her. Numerous women, sisters and half sisters, made deep curtseys to her. The men doffed their hats with a respectful flourish. A long line of servants stood at the back of the hall. Randal was bursting with pride to present his duchess-wife to his people. Then began the introductions to his sisters, brothers and cousins. Kate was warmed by her reception, her initial feelings of desolation vanished, and she decided she was going to like her new family though she would never like this castle.

Kate did not meet her mother-in-law on this occasion. The Antrim lands were comprised of four baronies and by the charter the first Earl was required to have a castle in each. Dunluce was the most ancient and the grandest but there was also Ballycastle, Glenarm, and Kilconway. Shortly before his death, the old Earl had rebuilt Ballycastle for his wife as a fitting dower house for her imminent widowhood.

Thus Randal's mother, Lady Alice or Ellis as the name was spelled at that time, lived miles away at Ballycastle. In due course Kate was taken in a bone-shaking cart to be introduced to her mother-in-law. The dowager Countess of Antrim, born an O'Neill, surprised Kate. Having expected her to be as rough an individual as Randal's father, she was taken aback to see a beautifully gowned woman with a stately bearing and exquisite manners who would have cut a fine figure at King Charles's court. How could Lady Alice have presided over Randal's childhood home with its barefoot servants and rustic Gaelic ways? Afterwards Kate raised this question as tactfully as she could with Randal. 'Why, she seldom lived with us," he said. "She did not fancy bringing up father's bastards." As well as Ballycastle, his father had provided for her generously. In his will he left her "all Ballycastle's household stuff, his linens, and half of his silver plate" which after her death was to go to my brother Alexander and not to me as it should have, said Randal. Worse than that Alexander inherited Glenarm Castle. Kate chided him for selfishness. He should understand how unfair the law of entail was. He was just lucky to have been the first-born legitimate son.

After her visit to her mother-in-law's well-stocked castle, Kate understood why Dunluce was so poorly provided for in household goods. Happily, the cartloads of furnishings Kate had brought with her helped to make Dunluce Castle less inhospitable. Upholstered armchairs and stools, all with cushions, provided comfort, velvet curtains kept out the winds that seeped through the windows. Persian rugs - "Turkey carpets" - were laid down on the cold floors, tapestries brightened the grey stone walls. Heaps of damask tablecloths and bed linen kept the washerwomen busy every day of the week. And Randal immediately had a large kitchen built for Kate. At the foot of the headland was a little town established by the first Earl of Antrim to service the everyday needs of the castle. But Kate and Randal soon fell into their old ways of extravagant purchases of luxury goods, much to the delight (at first) of the Dublin merchants.

Although the Macdonnells of Antrim were Old Irish, descendants of the Celtic tribes that had crossed over from the Highlands and the Western

Isles long ago in the mists of time, Randal had kinship through marriages with the Old English whose forefathers were the Vikings and Norman knights who invaded Ireland. Both the Old Irish and the Old English were Catholics, but like his father, Randal with his vast plantations also had an identity of interest with the New English, Protestant landowners who were colonizing Ireland with English and Scottish settlers.

Kate was happy to go along with Randal's wishes to keep house in the traditional Irish manner as in the days of his father and his grandfather, Sorley Boy Macdonnell. It was Sorley Boy who had captured the castle for his family in the time of Queen Elizabeth. The servants all wore Irish clothing (however Kate insisted they put on shoes) and Randal hired a harper to play the wailing, strangely-shaped Irish harp as well as a bard to beguile visitors with tales of ancient times. Kate loved to hear the bard sing of the High Kings of yore and the gathering of the clans at the seasonal festivals when the great chariot races were held with the warriors and charioteers as naked as the horses. After dinner the host would hold forth on any subject that took his fancy. He was witty and charming, above all voluble. Unlike their life in England where he was only "the husband of the Duchess of Buckingham," here Randal was looked up to as the local magnate. Besides he was a generous host. Kate took great pride in his new importance. She laughed with the Irish guests when Randal made sport of the English Lord Deputy. But she had some misgivings when he unabashedly boasted about the large assignment King Charles had given him for the King's now unavoidable war with Scotland.

Before leaving for Ireland Antrim had gone to Charles with an offer to take his clansmen across the narrow channel separating Ulster from the western coast of Scotland and conduct raids against the rebellious "Covenanter" Scots. It would not cost the King a penny. He himself would pay for it out of his rents. He explained to the King that the battleground would be the Kintyre peninsula then under the control of the Earl of Argyle, chieftain of the Campbell clan. Kintyre, he told the King, had traditionally belonged to the Macdonalds in Scotland who were the same clan as the Macdonnells in Ireland. Not only could he claim his hereditary right but his father had repurchased Kintyre for a goodly sum from the Argyles. So in return for fighting the Covenanters Randal wanted the King to renew his rights as chief of the Macdonnells to the lands occupied by the Campbells. Charles agreed. As it happened he was angry with the Earl of

Argyle who had offered him the unwelcome advice to stop his attempt to impose episcopal church government on the Presbyterian kirk in Scotland that had abolished bishops that November. As a preliminary, Antrim had sent his servant Archibald Stewart to Scotland to sound out the Scottish cousins and they were enthusiastically in favour of an invasion from Ireland to recover their lands from the Campbells.

Shortly after the turn of the year, Wentworth received a letter from the King ordering him "to furnish the Earl of Antrim with arms, though he be a Roman Catholic." His commission was to be kept secret, and Wentworth was to reply directly to the King rather than to one of the secretaries of state. Shortly afterwards, Wentworth received a letter from Antrim setting out what he called his "Propositions." This was in fact a peremptory order for Wentworth to supply what the Earl felt he would need to command his army:

Grant me a commission under the Great Seal to levy three regiments of 1600 foot, 200 light horse, and power to make officers. Send letters to my friends to have their men ready. Send 100 of the fittest soldiers from the Irish army to train my companies. For shot, all muskets; pike with headpieces and corselets. Tangents for defence against arrows if a pike breaks - the arrow is much in use with Scots. For light horsemen, carabines, pistols, swords. Buff coats (defensive against arrows), powder and lead. Long bows with four strings with 24 arrows for Highlanders who will fight for the King. 200 cars or sledges to carry victuals and munition. Two ships and 2 pinnaces with arms before April 5 under my command. All this was to be charged to His Majesty. To maintain an army for three months he wanted a loan from His Majesty of 20,000£.

Wentworth had only contempt for Antrim and great suspicion of his motives. In his opinion, the Earl did not want to fight the Covenanters, rather he intended to use the army paid for by the King to recover land from the Campbells that had once belonged to his own clan. Moreover, he saw it as sheer folly to put weapons in the hands of the wild Irish clansmen. It ran counter to his policy as Lord Deputy of diminishing Catholic influence in Ireland. He would not put it past Antrim to take up the rebellion his grandfather Tyrone had started. After all, Antrim's own mother was the daughter of the rebel chieftain. He vented his anger in a letter to Laud. "He is a papist of the race of O'Neil and upon my knowledge the great admirer of his grandfather Tyrone,"

In his reply, Laud revealed his true opinion of Antrim. "If Lord Antrim was a man of great brains, or great courage, or any way able to go on with a business where Tyrone left it, I should think somebody stark mad to leave or put any power in such hands. But sure I think there can be no fear from thence." Yet Laud acknowledged the danger that such a man could find able supporters, "men of brains, and courage, and malice to set them both on work," especially as in Antrim's case "where great means and great alliances are found to support other defects." So, on reflection, if he were the Lord Deputy he would not rely on Antrim's stupidity. If the King furnished Antrim with arms, "the world will have cause to wonder, and I to despair."

In spite of his opinion of Antrim, Laud implored his friend to be kind to him for the Duchess's sake. He had no interest in the Earl; "tis only his wife that I look upon, and should be glad should prosper, and for her sake is all that I have done, or shall do." But the fact was that "now she cannot be happy unless her husband be so too."

Laud was quite right. Randal was a very loving husband, and Kate was happy with him in a way she had never been with George. She had idolized the magnificent Buckingham. Had she not given up the true Catholic religion for him? He was twelve years older and she was only a girl when they married. Although their marriage had been a happy one, indeed sometimes rapturously so, at least once Buckingham had driven her to wishing herself dead. She had had no influence over him. He had made life-altering decisions without consulting her; even over her strong opposition he had undertaken the godforsaken Ile de Rhe expedition. And then there were his women. His long affair with Lucy Carlisle still hurt her. With Randal it was different. She was sure he was absolutely faithful. Moreover, he looked up to her as the more experienced and influential partner and showed her deference. As Laud had observed, she was the one behind the Munster business. Indeed Kate recognized that there was a maternal element in her protective love for Randal. Did this have something to do with the fact that her own sons had been taken from her, she wondered. In March 1639 Kate knew she was pregnant and she and Randal were delighted. In May Randal informed the Lord Deputy, and for a change Wentworth was most gracious. "I am right glad to hear my Lady Duchess is with child. God grant her a happy delivery and every contentment your own heart can wish," he wrote the Earl.

At this very time, King Charles was moving north with an army to subdue his Scottish subjects. The Marquis of Hamilton was to land troops from the sea and Antrim was to attack Scotland from northern Ireland. He would have to set up camp at Knockfergus on the coast, he told Kate. Kate wanted to go with him but Randal would not allow it in her condition, it was too dangerous. Knockfergus was the embarkation point for the King's ships and as such was open to attack from the Earl of Argyle's longboats. Argyle had signed the Solemn League and Covenant and was fighting on the Covenanters' side. Already he and his red-trousered Campbells were driving the Macdonalds off their lands.

Randal kept Kate posted almost daily and what he had to report was very discouraging. Wentworth was using his high position to work against him. Early in March Randal had gone to Dublin to meet with the Lord Deputy about his mission from the King. The meeting had heightened the animosity between the two. Randal insisted he had immediate need of the magazine of munitions he had listed in his Propositions, and the armed ships before April 5 as well as the 20,000£ loan from the Crown without delay.

When Wentworth pointedly inquired where his clansmen were assembled, Randal made a vague reply. Now, from Knockfergus, Randal besieged Wentworth with complaints and demands. On April 12, Good Friday, he wrote: "I hear from a gentleman just returned from Kintyre that Archibald Macdonald and his son have been taken prisoner." The same had befallen two spies he had sent over. "Send relief or all the Macdonalds will be cut off. For the love of God, let us sleep no longer. Give me leave to revenge my friends, and especially the King's quarrel." In May, three hundred Macdonalds, fleeing from Argyle's Campbells, descended upon him with their servants. This was very "chargeable" to him, he complained to Wentworth, especially with the drought that had cut his rents in half; he suggested that the "Covenanter" Scottish settlers in Ulster adjacent to his own plantations in County Antrim be dispossessed and their lands and goods be given to "us." Wentworth replied that the three hundred clansmen "may in no wise be imposed upon the country, as you propose. It would be a public scandal." You will have to bear the cost, he told Antrim. This searing response took Randal by surprise. What was so different about his proposal from the Lord Deputy's declared intention of seizing their lands and banishing all Scottish Ulstermen who would not swear under oath to renounce the Covenant? Indeed, all Randal's demands met with the same hostile intransigence from the Lord Deputy.

Thus Antrim had reason to complain that he did not receive the necessary help to fight the Scottish Covenanters. As for Wentworth, he was disgusted with Antrim who had boasted at court that he would fight the Covenanters at his own cost and then had shifted the charge upon the King. Wentworth did not bother to conceal his contempt. When an emissary from Charles passed through Dublin on his way to the Earl of Antrim at Knockfergus, Wentworth wrote the King that "he will not find amongst all that Earl employs one that doth therein understand anything at all. We hear now and then that they mean to beat, to bang, to conquer; but the way how, the means whereby they should make themselves good as their words, as yet appears not to the Ministers of this State."

Growing increasingly impatient, Antrim complained to Wentworth that none of the royal ships had arrived to transport his men, he even suggested that the masts from his own longboats had been removed by Wentworth's men. The Lord Deputy replied that there was no lack of His Majesty's ships, that one whelp was already there and three more were coming, "bringing the masts for your boats to get them fit for service." The truth was that Wentworth had no intention of placing royal troops and ships under Antrim's command. On May 13, he wrote the King that he had ordered horse and foot regiments to rendezvous at Knockfergus and had given the command over land and sea forces to the Master of the Ordinance. This official happened to be St.Leger, Lord President of Munster, whom Kate so disliked for failing to respond to her request to help the sea captain's widow. This sturdy Protestant, St. Leger, would give the Earl of Argyle more to think of, Wentworth wrote King Charles, "than the raising of a company of naked and inexperienced Irishmen by my Lord of Antrim."

The power struggle between Antrim and Wentworth was brought to an end when Charles made a truce with the Scots in June. As everyone on both sides of the border knew, the Pacification of Berwick was recognition that the King could not take on the Scots at this time. He had to retreat and plan to fight another day. Charles's courtier generals had proven themselves cowards and fools. He'd shown the same lack of judgment in appointing commanders in the war with Scotland as he had in appointing Antrim who wasn't up to the task of dealing with the Covenanter Scots.

Randal wrote letters to influential people in England blaming Lord Wentworth's obstructionism for the failure of his planned invasion. Wentworth countered with letters to friends at court, highly critical of Antrim. Well-meaning friends, or troublemakers, sent copies of Wentworth's letters to Kate. Controlling her anger, she sent the letters to the Lord Deputy: "I had hoped your displeasure against my lord was passed, but these letters from England show that you are still disgusted with him." This "troubled her greatly," she said. In this letter Kate was very explicit about her devotion to her husband. "I must be included in your anger for any misfortune to my Lord must be mine, and it will prove a great misfortune for me to live here under your frowns. Do not make me a sufferer undeserved from you." Unmoved by this wifely appeal, Wentworth gave his side of the quarrel. "Untruths regularly come out of England to my prejudice," he wrote Kate. These were spread by Lord Antrim and his servant, Archibald Stewart, who put the blame on him for the failure of an impossible scheme to excuse themselves. "You ask me to deal clearly. You might advise your husband to do the same."

Shortly after Antrim returned to Dunluce from Knockfergus Kate suffered a miscarriage. She had so desired to give Randal an heir. She was now thirty-six and soon her child-bearing years would be over. However, she had problems that left little time for such thoughts. Their credit had dried up with the Dublin merchants and Kate decided they must economize. As a first step, some of the servants at Dunluce were dismissed; Wentworth told Laud that these were all Protestants. She and Randal began to take stock seriously of their financial situation. They put Bramshill up for sale and reluctantly Kate decided she would have to sell her jewels. In late September she travelled to England with their trusted servant, Archibald Stewart. While Kate was offering the jewels in a genteel way to her rich friends and relatives, Stewart was spending his time at Goldsmiths' Row on Cheapside, driving hard bargains with the proprietors. On this flying visit, Kate of course saw Mall and the boys. Only she knew how the brief reunion tore at her heart.

She visited court and paid her respects to the King and Queen. She explained that Lord Wentworth had obstructed Randal's plans to invade Scotland by denying him the agreed-upon ships and supplies. Nevertheless, her husband authorized her to guarantee that he would provide 8,000 clansmen for an invasion at a signal from King Charles. She left the royal presence satisfied she had erased any bad impression Charles might have formed of Randal because his army had in fact never left Ireland that year.

It was clear to Kate that in the one year she had been away from England, the conflict between the Puritans and the royal government had increased noticeably. The Covenanters' rejection of the English prayer book in Scotland had unleashed the hitherto underground opposition in England to Archbishop Laud and his Arminian church. Kate remembered Laud oft times saying "there was no question that there was a great concurrence between the tumults in Scotland and the Puritans in England." He had been right. Archibald Stewart told her that libels against the Archbishop were posted on Cheapside Cross and on the doors of St. Paul's Cathedral. These accused him of introducing "Popish, idolatrous innovations" into the Church of England and some were actual threats on his life. Kate felt sorry for her friend and protector. To incur the hatred of the people was a torment; she remembered how much it had made Buckingham suffer. Moreover the popular campaign against the Established Church did not augur well for the King's hopes for sufficient money votes from the Puritan Parliament he was said to be calling.

While Kate was in London, Lord Wentworth arrived. He had been sent for by the King although he was ordered to pretend that he had come over on personal business. Charles had to raise money for a renewed attack on the Covenanters and he needed an efficient, trustworthy counsellor. Holland, Hamilton, Lennox and the other royal favourites had proven worthless. Now Wentworth, backed up by Laud, counselled Charles to send out the writs for a parliamentary session to get money grants. It would be the first Parliament in eleven years.

With the money realized from the sale of the jewels, Kate and Randal resumed their lordly entertaining. One evening during a fierce autumn storm, the hosts and their guests were lounging at table after a filling repast, trying to listen to the bard's recital over the wind that wailed like a banshee, when they heard a thunderous crack and the very walls of the hall seemed to shudder. Randal started up, ran out of the hall, and returned ashen-faced. The new kitchen had collapsed, carrying into the sea the cooks and apprentices who had been working there. None could have survived, he announced with evident emotion; they would have been dashed on the rocks or drowned. Kate rose. "My lords and ladies, please follow me," and she led them to a withdrawing room on the far side of the castle. The harper played dirges while the company sat in stunned silence.

After this disaster, Kate informed Randal she would not stay in the castle any longer. The manor house that Randal was building for her was not yet ready so they moved inland to a manor house nearby. For a short time, they considered building a house in Coleraine on land the King had just granted to Randal. (It was like to prove the last of royal patronage, Kate thought, with war looming and the King's finances as bad as their own on a mammoth scale.) But after much discussion, they decided to move to Dublin, hopeful that the King's business would keep their enemy, Lord Wentworth, in London.

Despite the fact that Antrim's army had not materialized and the planned attack on Argyle had not taken place, Charles continued to show him favour. He appointed the Earl one of two Royal Commissioners.

CHAPTER TWENTY-ONE

The summer of 1640 found Kate and Randal in a rented house in Dublin and Randal took his seat in the Irish House of Lords. Ireland's capital under English rule was enjoying prosperity as witnessed by well-dressed people on the streets and many new buildings. Court life was even more magnificent here than at Whitehall. Indeed, a well-travelled Englishman said the court kept at Dublin Castle was so splendid that "except for that of the viceroy at Naples he had not seen the like in Christendom." But this was so only when the Lord Deputy was in residence, and, happily for the Antrims, Wentworth was in England for they would not have enjoyed his patronage.

Although he had never taken to Wentworth, King Charles had at last given the man his due. During this visit to England Wentworth was created Earl of Strafford and it was understood he would remain by the King's side. His title was also dignified to Lord Lieutenant of Ireland. Although the acting Lord Lieutenant was Sir Christopher Wandesford, a close friend of Strafford's, Kate and Randal found his real successor was James Butler, the Earl of Ormond. Ormond was the only Protestant member of an illustrious Irish Catholic family. Left an orphan early, he had become a ward of King Charles who had placed the boy with a Protestant family. This quirk of fate now made him eligible for appointment as General of the King's forces in

Ireland. Even Ormond's worst enemies (and Dublin was a place where everyone had enemies) could not deny the man's high character and ability. Wentworth had early recommended him to Charles as "a staid head" in contrast to Antrim.

Anxious to curry favour with Ormond, Randal joined him in a scheme to help the King in his upcoming struggle against the English Parliament. It came to nothing but served Randal to establish an alliance with Charles's appointee in Ireland.

Meanwhile, Kate was finding their Dublin house well beneath her station in life. What she wanted was the now-uninhabited palatial residence Strafford had built at Naas in County Kildare not far from Dublin. On a visit to Naas Kate had been impressed with the state rooms and magnificent furnishings and thought what a contrast it made with the shabby Dublin Castle now fallen into disrepair. Paid for out of his own purse, Strafford had intended his palace to function as a fitting vice-regal mansion to receive important visitors – hopefully, the King himself. Kate now set about getting Randal named "housekeeper" of Strafford's impressive palace. Keepership of a castle or palace in the royal gift was a common perquisite for courtiers; it carried with it the use of the place and a maintenance allowance. To obtain what Kate wanted, Randal turned to the Marquis of Hamilton whom he regarded as a close friend. In a letter dated June 16, 1641, he told Hamilton that the Duchess "had set her heart" on Strafford's palace at Naas, and he begged his influential friend to press the King to make him keeper. Hamilton had a good opportunity to oblige his friend since he was to accompany the King to Scotland, but it is doubtful he even mentioned it. With revolt boiling up in Scotland, the King and his Scottish lieutenant had far more serious matters to discuss.

Though balked of her desire, the always practical Kate had settled down to life in Dublin when two unprecedented events changed everything.

The disagreements between King and Parliament had escalated into serious conflict. Indeed, England was heading into civil war. Religious differences between the official English church and the Puritans were at the heart of it but there were other causes arising from Charles's authoritarian personal rule of the past eleven years. Opposition to taxes imposed without the approval of Parliament now found its voice as did complaints of the continuing abuses of monopolies and patents. The tyranny of the High Commission and the Star Chamber came under fire. The House of

Commons was virtually to a man opposed to the Laudian Church and was determined on reform. The Upper House also had its Puritan lords, however many liked the old ways and some were even grateful to the King. Families were split. Kate heard that there was much tension between the Earl and Countess of Denbigh and their son Basil Lord Fielding who had declared for Parliament. In vain, Sue reminded her son that they owed everything to the King and Queen. Kate was grateful that her own sons were too young to be drawn into what was certain to become an armed struggle. As for Mall, she was devoted to her royal mistress and her husband the Duke of Richmond swore loyalty to the King unto death.

The first casualties of the conflict between the King and Parliament were the Earl of Strafford and Archbishop Laud both of whom were impeached by the House of Commons and imprisoned in the Tower. Over in Ireland Kate could hardly believe what was happening in England. She had no sympathy for Tom Wentworth. He had worked against her darling Randal at every turn. But she was sincerely saddened by Laud's fall. She now recognized that the "little bishop" had been her family's best friend. She remembered how he had tried to smooth the way for Randal with the now fallen Lord Lieutenant.

The second earth-shaking event was a rebellion in Ireland. With the breakdown of unity in England the native Irish saw an opportunity to recover what they had lost under English rule. And also to get some recompense for their suffering. Not only had their ancestral lands been taken from them and given to English and Scottish planters, but they had suffered torture and death at the hands of their oppressors. One of the worst had been St. Leger, Lord President of Munster. His murderous treatment of Catholics had horrified Kate but it was no surprise, considering his hard-hearted response to her request to aid a naval widow.

One day in the summer of 1641 Randal brought home some extraordinary news. A plot was afoot to seize Dublin Castle, the seat of English rule. Rory O'More and Sir Phelim O'Neill were the leaders, he told Kate. Both men were well known to her (Phelim was a cousin of Randal's) and had often been guests in their home. Kate thought Phelim an opiniated, stubborn ass though she did not doubt his passion for the Irish cause. Rory, handsome and courtly, was far more congenial, yet Kate sensed that his charming manner masked great cunning. He too came from the Old Irish nobility but from the lesser ranks. Both had spouted revolutionary talk and she had listened sympathetically when they ranted against the English for their attempt to root out Catholicism in Ireland. For his part, Randal hoped the plot against Dublin Castle would succeed as he felt he had been badly treated by the English establishment under Wentworth. However, there was nothing more to fear from the latter. On the 12th of May 1641 Thomas Wentworth, Earl of Strafford, was executed on Tower Hill by order of the English Parliament, allegedly for planning to bring over a Catholic army from Ireland to fight for the King against English Protestants. The Irish Parliament, predominantly Protestant New English, had slipped from Strafford's iron grip and was clearly on the side of the English Parliament in opposition to the King.

Meanwhile an open revolt against the English broke out in Ulster. All the Irish rose with their chiefs. Led by Sir Phelim O'Neill it began simply with Irish bands chasing English Protestant planters off their farms and plundering the larger estates, but the stored-up anger of the dispossessed Catholics soon escalated into destruction of property and mass murder of Protestants. Randal received cries for help from his Protestant tenants in County Antrim. Many made their way as refugees to the safety of Dublin. Good-hearted Kate suffered anguish at the reports of rape and the slaughter of innocent children. Never had she expected to hear of such things in the British Isles. She had heard of atrocities occurring on the Continent during the present war but it was unthinkable here at home. She got Randal to shelter as many of these unfortunate Protestant victims of Catholic rage as could be accommodated at houses he owned in County Kildare and County Meath out of the range of the furious attacks.

At the same time she understood the anger of the native Irish who had had their ancestral lands confiscated by the English government. She herself was a beneficiary of the rape of Ireland by King James and Buckingham. At the time she had gratefully accepted the land grants George had put in trust for her. She had never questioned his activities in Ireland. But living here she had come to understand the injustice of the English government's land grab.

While all hell was breaking loose in the north east of the island, the assault on Dublin Castle failed to take place. Loose talk had revealed it to the authorities who promptly put it down. Meanwhile Randal was under suspicion. As the friend of Phelim O'Neil and grandson of the Earl of Tyrone, father of the great Catholic rebellion at the turn of the century, he was suspected of aiding the rebels. And the Duchess who was reputed to dominate her husband had openly criticized the Protestant administration at the Castle so that people assumed she was supporting the rising.

Actually the Antrims had intended to stay out of the conflict until word reached them from Queen Henrietta Maria that she viewed the Irish rising of October 1641 as an opportunity to return Ireland to the native Irish and hence to Catholicism. The King too had reason to support the rebels. The Irish Parliament was on the side of his parliamentary enemies in England. Moreover, Charles would need an Irish army to fight the English Parliament: he looked to Randal to rouse his clansmen or to regroup Strafford's disbanded troops. In the meantime, he enlisted Randal to negotiate a peace with the rebels on his behalf. Neither Randal nor Kate could imagine a time when royal patronage would not be the source of all rewards (and punishments) so he answered the call. As a result, Randal and Kate were seen consorting with Irish Catholic leaders. This of course fueled rumours already rampant that Randal was a leader of the rebels. Kate found herself deemed a traitor by the English Protestant Establishment in Dublin. Charles brushed aside reports of the Antrims' disloyalty but typically did not say that they were acting on his orders. Thus Charles used the Antrims but did nothing to quell the rumours swirling around English circles in Dublin that they were turncoats. Kate felt hostility whenever she ventured out in Dublin. While she had never stood on ceremony before, now feeling under siege both by society and by her creditors she acted the imperious duchess. In Dublin they spoke of her as a domineering battle-axe.

The rebellion intensified in 1642, spreading throughout the island under a new commander Owen Roe O'Neil, a seasoned general who had been called back from the continental wars. His swift military successes in Ireland decided the Catholic Old English, Irish chieftains, and Catholic clergy to form an association for the purpose of unifying their disparate forces. Calling the new body the Confederacy, they established headquarters at Kilkenny in Munster and declared for King Charles on his promise to accord Catholics full rights in Ireland. The body was formalized into an Irish Catholic assembly, a two-chamber shadow parliament to parallel the English Protestant Parliament in Dublin.

In early spring of 1642, Randal accompanied by Kate set forth for northern Ireland on his secret mission to negotiate with the rebels to bring them over to the King's side. As well, he was ordered to mediate a peace with the Covenanter forces that had arrived from Scotland to quell the Irish rebellion. However, the commander of the Scottish troops, General Monro, took his commission and pay from the English parliamentarians and was not likely to change his colours. Randal was acting under orders from the King and Queen, but also out of self-interest. Since the rebellion began, he had not received a penny in rents from his plantations in County Antrim. Now the planters' farms were occupied by Monro's soldiers and he hoped to retrieve them through an alliance with the Scottish general.

The Antrims first stop north was at the castle of Randal's eldest sister, Anne, and her husband, Baron Slane. They made their stay there very short because the Baron was an open supporter of the rebellion and Randal was doing his utmost to avoid identification with the rebels. From there they went on to Maddenstown, south of Kildare, the estate of James Touchet, Earl of Castlehaven. Although this young noble was a Catholic supporter of the King, he was happy to allow the Antrims to make use of his castle as a haven for their distressed Protestant tenants, victims of the bloody rebellion. Kate had them fed and clothed before sending them on to Dublin. During the Antrims' stay that lengthened into several months their thirty-year-old host conceived a respectful attachment to Kate. For her part she liked James's company very well especially as Randal was occupied with his plans. They walked in the spacious park and gradually James told this sympathetic older woman the story of the family scandal that had shocked the British Isles and spread a dark cloud over his life. When he was fourteen his father had been convicted of rape and sodomy by a jury of his peers and given the death penalty - and it had been *his* doing, he told Kate.

"A few years after my mother died, my father married again," he began. "My new stepmother, a daughter of the Earl of Derby, had been married before and she brought her young daughter to live with us too. Soon after their marriage I would hear my stepmother screaming at night and there would be a lot of scurrying in the halls. It upset me but I was only a lad and I thought I could not interfere with the affairs of a married couple. Besides I was afraid of getting a thrashing. Then I began to hear the voices of my father's favourite servants mixed in with my stepmother's screams. I had known for years that my father took these thugs into his bed. I had discussed it with some older relatives who told me this was common in the great houses and even in the late king's castle." Here he stopped and looked embarrassed, having remembered that the Duke of

Buckingham was the greatest of King James's catamites. When Kate did not take umbrage he continued. "And so I kept silent." On a later stroll he continued with his story. "Not long after my father's second marriage, I was told that I was to be married to my new stepsister. My father said this would be most beneficial for our family. It would cement the alliance with the Derby family that he had initiated with his own marriage and he spoke of the estates that would come to us as a result. I raised no objection to this marriage. I liked Elizabeth well enough and since she was but twelve and I myself hardly a year older, my father assured me we would continue as sister and brother rather than man and wife."

So life went on as before. Except that his stepmother's screaming became even worse and some nights he thought he heard Elizabeth crying too. Meanwhile the thugs his father employed as bedmates were becoming ever more insufferable, bossing the rest of the servants and even taking a high tone with him. Noticing that Elizabeth had become pale and wan and hardly ate, he asked her if it had anything to do with their marriage. She said not at all so he did not trouble his mind about her any more. Then one night she came to his room in a hysterical state. "Your father forces himself upon me in my bed and my mother cannot stop him." She was weeping. "And now he says I'm to have his brutish men in my bed just as he makes my mother do while he sits in the bed chamber and watches."

"Enough was enough," the young Earl told Kate. "Although hitherto an obedient son, I knew I would have to act. I rode over to a neighbour's estate, an older man I had known all my life, and told him the whole story. He did not question the horrible things I related, and, in fact, said he had suspected my father of sexual improprieties even in my mother's time, which made me weep. This neighbour went to London and laid my story before influential members of the House of Lords and in a short time my father was prosecuted before a jury of his peers, Lord Coventry in the judge's seat, and myself as chief witness against my father. The peers unanimously found him guilty of raping Lady Anne, his wife, and Elizabeth, his stepdaughter, while a majority found him guilty of sodomy with his servants." At this point he broke down and Kate held him in her arms and wept with him. It was as a mother comforting a son. Kate knew the rest of the story. The Earl of Castlehaven had been beheaded. The trial and conviction had been the talk of the court in 1631. And she remembered with some shame that gossip about the trial had beguiled her in the dark hours of her widowhood.

After the sensational trial, James told Kate, he had gone abroad and served with various commanders in the wars, not caring if he was fighting with the French or the Spanish. When the first war with the Scots began, King Charles commanded him to come home. After the truce he returned to Europe but was back in Ireland when the Irish Rebellion broke out. It was then he met Randal. He would not pretend with her, he told Kate. Like Randal and herself he supported the rebels secretly while pretending to oppose them in order to preserve his estate.

Meanwhile in accordance with his plan, Randal had extended an invitation to General Monro to stay at Dunluce. Now word came back from the Covenanter general accepting "his lordship's hospitality" and setting a date for his visit in the near future. So he would have to leave at once, Randal told Kate. Furthermore he was to meet Phelim O'Neill en route and travel northward to Ulster with him – in disguise, he added. Randal was adamant that Kate could not go with him. It was too dangerous for her to be at Dunluce with the fighting going on. At the same time it was too dangerous for a Roman Catholic to stay where she was. Her good works with the Protestant refugees from Ulster would not protect her from the wrath of the Protestant majority in this region. Therefore she was to return to England as soon as possible. "I'm leaving my good woman in your hands," he said to their host. The Earl of Castlehaven fell over himself to assure Randal that it would be his highest honour to protect the Duchess. The safest place for her, Randal suggested, was to take her to his mother's castle. He would arrange with General Monro to leave Ballycastle untouched.

After Randal departed Kate and James started out on horseback, staying at friendly houses on the way. At Ballycastle Kate found Randal's half-sisters and brothers, all of whom had taken refuge with the Dowager Countess. They painted a dreadful picture of General Monro's brutality in Ulster, ousting Catholics from their homes and killing entire families. They themselves had got out of Dunluce just hours before he arrived with his troops. They expressed much doubt when Kate told them Randal would make a deal with Monro not to attack Ballycastle. Well might they doubt, as it happened.

Randal arrived at Dunluce Castle where he hoped to win over Monro with Irish hospitality. Instead he found himself taken prisoner by his ungrateful guest who charged him with supporting the rebels and simply laughed in his face when Randal claimed he had come north to negotiate a peace with him. The Scottish general brought him in irons to his headquarters at Carrisfergus, locked him up, and announced he was now going to capture Ballycastle where "the dowager duchess and the Earl's bastard brothers and sisters" were in hiding. But they had received a warning, and before the Covenanters arrived the Earl of Castlehaven had assisted Kate and the others to escape across the River Bann. From there he brought Kate safely back to Dublin. For his own safety he departed without delay, Dublin being too dangerous for him as the Lord Justices had indicted him for treason in 1642.

CHAPTER TWENTY-TWO

Not knowing which way to turn, Kate decided to follow Randal's advice and go to the King at York. After a failed coup against the parliamentary leaders, Charles had fled London with the Queen and the children. He was now at York where he was joined by many courtiers and officials. Kate had hoped for a reunion with Mall but the Duchess of Richmond as she was now styled had accompanied her mistress to Holland. Henrietta Maria had escorted her nine-year-old daughter Mary to live with the child's in-laws, the family of the Prince of Orange. But the Queen's real purpose in going to Holland was to sell the Crown jewels to raise money for her husband's army. Kate was dreadfully disappointed. Mall had converted to Catholicism and what a joyous reunion mother and daughter would have had at York.

Kate had expected that as the King's wards her sons would be at York. They were, but the poor mother was extremely distressed to find the thirteen and fourteen-year olds drinking, gambling and, she suspected, wenching. The King was recruiting an army and her boys were picking up all the vices a garrison town had to offer. They wouldn't listen to her admonitions, in fact they boldly retorted that she was no example as she was known to be engaged with the Irish rebels.

Above all, Kate was frantic with worry about Randal. It was only at

York that she learned of his capture and imprisonment at Carrickfergus. They said he was to be taken to England to be tried for high treason by Parliament. Kate was sick with fear that the parliamentarians would execute him as they had Strafford. She went down on her knees to the King. Charles agreed to demand his release but he explained to Kate that he had no influence either with General Monro or with the Irish Parliament, both being in the English Parliament's camp. Her next best hope was Marquis Hamilton, the King's Scottish lieutenant. She hounded him to use his connections to free his friend and sometime business partner. He refused to get involved, saying he would have nothing to do with a friend of the Irish rebels. Kate answered hotly that Randal was no rebel. He was just carrying out the King's assignment. But the stubborn Scot could not be convinced and the King said nothing. She soon realized that she could expect no help from the court. Everyone from the King down was interested only in self-preservation. She wanted to share Randal's imprisonment but was told that was impossible. When Hamilton was sent back to Scotland in July to try to keep the Scots out of the coming civil war, she decided to go to Leicestershire and wait for Randal there. On July 11, 1642, her old friend, Edward Nicholas, now Secretary of State in the disordered royal government, wrote to the Earl of Ormond in Dublin that "my Lady Duchess was here with the King about ten days and is now gone to her house in Leicestershire."

From there Kate took her worries about her sons and her husband to Queen Henrietta Maria in Holland who immediately wrote her husband:

The Duchess of Buckingham has begged me to write to you that you would order Secretary Nicholas to write on your behalf to her children to obey her, or else they will be lost for they have no one near them to take care of them, and they are becoming debauched. As to their concerns she will not meddle with them in any fashion in the world, only let them believe what she says to them that they may not be lost in this world. It would be very small honour for you to see them ill brought up, after you have taken them under your care.

In a second letter to Henrietta Maria, Kate set out her worries about Randal's imprisonment and her fears for his life. Once again the Queen acted. She urged her brother Gaston, Duc d'Orleans, to use his influence to have the Earl of Antrim freed though it seems nothing came of it. Kate continued to press for Randal's release, using her connections to the full, but Randal required no help from abroad. In the end he escaped from the Carrisfergus prison with the help of one of Monro's senior officers. It so happened that Randal's youngest sister Rose had married Colonel Lord George Gordon, brother of the Duke of Sutherland, shortly after he had come to Ireland with General Monro. Billeted at Carrisfergus Castle, Lord Gordon took it upon himself to prepare an escape route for his new brother-in-law. Disguising himself as a beggarly cripple, Randal made his way to the coast, subsisting on handouts of food and sleeping rough. After a harrowing time evading discovery, Randal arrived at Newcastle in Yorkshire. As it happened, Kate was there with other Royalists. Approached by a disgusting specimen in rags dragging his foot wrapped in dirty bandages she doesn't recognize her husband. Randal enjoying his joke, does not reveal himself for a good half hour. Only then, throwing off his filthy cap, did Kate recognize the mop of red hair of her beloved husband.

The reunited couple made their way to the King's wartime court at York. It joyed Kate's heart to see the welcome her darling Randal received.

Her worries about her sons continued however. Charles had raised his standard at Nottingham Castle in 1642 and England was now formally engaged in a civil war between Royalists and the men of the Parliament. Kate's young sons had joined up with the Royalists and she was desperately concerned about their safety. When she heard that they had participated in the storming of a heavily armed nest of enemy soldiers in Lichfield led by the daredevil Prince Rupert, the King's nephew, she was furious. She wrote an angry note to the officer she held responsible, Lord Gerard: "Why did you tempt my sons into such danger?" She could not sleep for thinking of her young boys in the field in a shooting war. The Royalist troops were meeting with initial success; Charles himself rode into battle at the head of his troops and spirits at York were high. Still hoping to bring Basil over to the King, Sue Denbigh wrote her son that the Royalists were certain of victory.

In February 1643 the Queen returned from Holland laden with arms and money. For some time she had been corresponding with Kate and Randal about a plan to bring an Irish army over to England to fight for the King. Receiving authorization and arms from the Queen to try again to negotiate with the rebels Randal set off for Ireland. Alas, General Monro was waiting for him. Randal's ship, its hold filled with arms and ammunition, was captured off the coast of County Down and he was again imprisoned at Carrisfergus Castle. His and Kate's secret correspondence with Henrietta Maria was found on his person and printed by Parliament to further compromise the Queen. The so-called "Popish Plot" was the talk of London and all over the country. The revelation of the letters moved Parliament to declare the Earl of Antrim "a notorious rebel." Pro-Parliament pamphlets and newssheets spread the message far and wide. "The Earl," wrote one, "was a rebel not worth the naming, nor that precious piece of iron-work, his duchess; yet I must needs say she was a lady rarely marked out for two eminent husbands, the beds of Buckingham and Antrim; this latter more pernicious than a bed of scorpions." Kate was now suspected by Royalists to be working hand-in-glove with the Irish rebels. A reputation she would never shake off as the royal couple never openly owned up to their attempts to bring over Irish troops to fight the English.

To Kate's joy the resourceful Randal escaped his captors at Carrisfergus castle, reappearing at York to a hero's welcome, but he was soon off again with secret instructions from the King and Queen. He was to go to Ulster and make peace with the Irish rebels and in conjunction with the Confederacy's troops use his clansmen to fight the Scottish invaders in Ulster. The reinforced Irish army would then cross over to Scotland to fight the Earl of Argyle's Covenanting army, and if all went well moving south into England. This scheme like the earlier one came to nought. The truth was that Randal was regarded as unreliable and out for himself. Much of this distrust can be attributed to the fact that he was operating under secret instructions from the King and Queen. Nor did he get recognition from the Irish rebels. In the end it was the Earl of Castlehaven, Kate's chivalrous knight, who was appointed Commander of the Confederate Forces to drive Monro and his Covenanter army out of Ulster. But Castlehaven was undermined by Owen Roe O'Neill who (like Randal) had expected to be given the supreme command himself. It was this kind of rivalry and factionalism that doomed the Irish rising to failure.

Kate, meanwhile, was trying to save some of their valuable furniture and household goods. She arranged for storage in Chester but most of her beautiful things at Dunluce Castle were looted by Monro. What he left, his troops destroyed out of ignorance of their value. For these luxury goods, they had beggared themselves Kate had to admit to herself, and now these had disappeared into thin air.

Her mother-in-law, the stately Lady Alice, had suffered similar losses. After driving her out of Ballycastle in 1641, Monro had seized the castle and forced her tenants to pay the rents to himself, thus leaving her with nothing. Kate learned from a doctor friend of the Countess that "reduced to great difficulties, she had pawned her rings, a cross, and a jewel of gold inlaid with rubies and diamonds." Her sons, Randal and Alexander, could give her nothing because they too were ruined.

In 1643 Charles established permanent headquarters at Oxford and Kate and Randal joined other courtiers there. The university town had been transformed. The colleges had been taken over and used as arsenals to house muskets and the six-foot tall pikes along with cannons, ammunition and powder. The King had made Christ Church College his headquarters. The Queen held court with great ceremony at Merton College as if she was still at Whitehall. As with all garrison towns, hordes of camp followers appeared. But it was not only the prostitutes. The great court ladies, wives and daughters of the nobility were acting like sluts in Kate's opinion. Straitlaced as she was, their behaviour offended her high moral standards. She despised the air of easy virtue that infected the once dignified university town. One thing that made her very happy was that Randal did not even glance at these women who brazenly put themselves forward to attract her handsome husband. Kate thought how different it would have been with her first husband. Compared with Randal's devotion and loyalty, Buckingham's lechery now seemed more harmful to her than it had at the time.

At Oxford, the Duchess of Buckingham was known to have great influence with the King and Queen. Randal never stopped boasting of it. Even the Earl of Ormond, newly appointed Lord Lieutenant of Ireland, worried that he might have fallen out of favour with her. "I hope to be restored to her favour," he told a friend. If he was sincere, he missed a number of opportunities to ingratiate himself with the Duchess.

Kate was determined to use her influence to have Randal raised to the rank of marquis and she importuned the King ceaselessly. Charles put her off. Kate took this to mean that Randal would have to prove himself. His attempts to bring over an army of his clansmen to fight for the King either in Scotland or England had so far come to nothing. Randal had to stop talking and act. A new opportunity presented itself when the Marquis of Montrose arrived from Scotland. This military leader, chief of Clan

Graham, had changed his allegiance from the Covenanters to the Royalists and had come to the King to ask for additional troops. Charles queried the Earl of Antrim. Randal insisted he could furnish as many experienced infantrymen as Montrose desired. Royalist fortunes had turned sour after an unsuccessful siege of Gloucester, and Kate boldly told the King that her husband was offering him "most hopes to bring Your Majesty with honour out of your misfortunes."

Kate was aware that Randal had a strong personal motive for sending his clansmen into Scotland. He had told her many times that as chieftain of the Macdonnell clan in Ireland he had a right to Kintyre in the Scottish Highlands. Conquering the "Covenanter" Campbells would give him the opportunity to retake Kintyre, the Scottish lands rightfully belonging to his Scottish cousins the Macdonalds. King Charles had agreed that he could claim these lands if he could conquer them for the Crown. Kate was encouraging him, agreeing that his claim was legitimate, and he sailed to Ireland with her blessing.

In Ireland Randal enlisted the King's representative in his plan to fight the Covenanters and receiving Ormond's full cooperation, mustered his clansmen and dispatched several thousand of them under a kinsman, Alastair McColla, known as Colkitto, to Scotland to join Montrose's army. In due course Randal went over and led them into battle himself. The Confederacy bore the cost of his army. To acquire this support he had to sign the Confederacy's Oath of Association to promote Catholicism in Ireland. He did so with King Charles's secret approval but it only confirmed the general opinion that he was a rebel. Antrim's Irish troops known as "redshanks" because they fought bare-legged were a significant factor in Montrose's victories over Argyle and his Covenanters. At last Randal had made good his promises to the King.

Kate was at loose ends with Randal away. As she had done in Buckingham's absences, she busied herself with an attempt to improve the family's finances. Randal's brother-in-law, Baron Slane, had died leaving his eldest son a minor. This placed the lad in the clutches of the Court of Wards. His inherited lands and any other assets would be at the disposal of the person who purchased his wardship, and who in turn would pay dearly for it to the grasping officials of the Court. The King through the agency of the Lord Lieutenant in Ireland got his share so everyone but the bereaved family profited. Kate wrote an appeal to an influential courtier turned

Royalist general, Sir George Digby. Digby was the son of the Earl of Bristol, Buckingham's sworn enemy from the days of the Spanish Match. That was long water under the bridge and she had no fear that he harboured any ill will towards her. She asked Digby to approach the Earl of Ormond who would have the final say to request the wardship either for Randal, the boy's uncle, or for his mother, Baroness Slane. In conveying the Duchess's message Digby requested the Lord Lieutenant to either "oblige her or else direct me to persuade her from her pretension." Ormonde's reply was superbly respectful of Kate but unhelpful. Prefacing his refusal with kind words regarding his infinite obligation to my lady Duchess, he said that if he granted the wardship to the Catholic Lord Antrim or to his sister it would cause a scandal in Dublin. Kate's surprising response was to agree with him. Since it would cause scandal to give the wardship to a Catholic, she said, she now requested it for one Pearce Moore, an Irish Protestant – no doubt a Slane family flunky. Kate had cornered him. Ormonde would be hard pressed to refuse this surrogate for Lord Antrim and his sister.

Randal and his clansmen fighting with the Montrose forces were enjoying successive victories. Meanwhile Kate desperately wanted to return to Ireland so that she and Randal could be together at least between his military engagements. Despite the dangers in Ireland she would leave England in a minute if she had somewhere to stay. All Randal's castles and manors were occupied by Monro's Scots and nothing was to be had in Dublin, filled to bursting with Protestant refugees. From the battlefield Randal turned to Ormond, supposedly his friend and ally. "Would your lordship do my good woman the favour to let her have your house at Carrick if she chance to come hither; which I shortly expect?" Ormond's response was an exquisitely polite refusal. He would be glad (he wrote Randal) "that my Lady Duchess would make use of my house at Carrick if it were in my absolute power. As it were, I can but profess that I should receive great satisfaction that anything that ought to be mine may serve her." In a later letter to Randal after Kate had found a place, he wrote smoothly as if he had in fact offered the house at Carrick, "which I shall think very happy to receive your lady to whom I have great obligations and desire to be serviceable."

While waiting for a suitable house in Ireland, Kate passed the time at Pendennis, a watering place near Falmouth. By August 1644 she was so impatient that she impulsively crossed over to Dublin. Knowing that Randal was being balked of his desire to head the Confederacy's forces, she quickly took in the situation. In a letter to Ormond she complained that Randal was distrusted by the Irish bishops on the supreme council of the Confederacy for being too Royalist and not Catholic enough. (This was her subtle way of winning over the Lord Lieutenant – a Protestant and a royal appointee - to support Randal's ambitions.)

In November Kate and Randal returned to England at the King's request. It was a harrowing trip. Their frigate was chased by a parliamentary warship. Once back in Oxford, King Charles rewarded Randal with the marquisate Kate had begged for him for his successful forays into Scotland.

At Oxford Kate was saddened to hear that Parliament was proceeding with the impeachment of her old friend Archbishop Laud. A finding of guilt was a foregone conclusion. Laud's archenemy, William Prynne, made the case against him with documents he had found in Laud's chamber in the Tower. Unforgiving of the Archbishop for the loss of his ears and the years in prison, Prynne had tampered with the evidence. Kate herself was not immune from his revenge. Prynne produced a pamphlet he claimed to have found in Laud's cell entitled "Rome's Masterpiece or the Grand Conspiracy of the Pope and his Jesuited Instruments to Exterpate the Protestant Religion and Reestablish Popery". The pamphlet implicated the Duchess of Buckingham in a conspiracy behind the rebellion in Ireland. At Laud's trial Prynne read from this pamphlet that "the rebellion was part of the plot confederating with the Duchess of Buckingham and withal they procured the Queen by the Earl of Antrim and the Duchess of Buckingham's mediation and to attempt to raise an insurrection in Scotland too."

Kate could not deny that she was the conduit between the English queen and the Irish rebels. At this time she was even keener than Randal in supporting the Irish rebellion. Like her royal mistress her heart's desire was to see Ireland return to a Catholic state. Randal though nominally a Royalist was essentially self-seeking. His objective was to preserve his plantations in Ulster, indeed, at the beginning of the rebellion he had despatched Archibald Stewart to raise a force among his tenants to fight the rebels. Similarly, his multiple plans to invade Scotland were motivated more by his desire to recover Kintyre that had once belonged to the Scottish branch of his clan than to fight the Covenanters for King Charles. Actually, he had more than ancient custom to back up his right to the Kintyre lands. In the 1620s his father had purchased them in his son's name for 1,500£ from Argyle's brother but Argyle refused to honour the transaction. The lands would have to be won by the sword.

On January 10, 1645 Laud was beheaded on Tower Hill. His will showed his enduring friendship for the Buckingham family. He left Kate a hundred pounds and to the second Duke " my chalice and patens of gold" as well as a gold cup with a cover. Nor did he forget Mall, "Mary, Lady Duchess of Richmond, daughter".

CHAPTER TWENTY-THREE

Marquis of Antrim he might be but Randal's penury made a mockery of his new title. His Irish lands were occupied by the Covenanters. He could no longer borrow from his stepson's estate. Indeed, friends of young Buckingham were trying to salvage what they could for him by secretly bringing the famous York House art collection to the Continent for sale. Kate still had her inherited English properties but they yielded little or nothing in the war-torn country. All Randal had was his army of clansmen, and their numbers had been decimated at the battle of Philiphaugh that ended Montrose's winning streak in Scotland. So he decided to sell the remaining battle-hardened Ulstermen as mercenaries to serve in the continental war between Spain and France and their respective allies. He chose to do business with the Spanish side that was still at war with the Dutch. This suggested to the Spanish envoy in Brussels the couple's dire need for money. In his dispatch to the King of Spain, the envoy wrote that "Antrim's wife, being a confidante of the Queen of England, and so much a friend of France and enemy of Spain, would not let him do it if it were not for the extreme shortage they have of money."

As usual, Randal's activities were a mixture of the political and the personal. On the one hand he expected to profit personally by selling his clansmen to the Spanish. But at the same time he had obtained King Charles's approval of his mission to Brussels by promising that any payment forthcoming from the Spaniards for the Irish mercenaries would be used to purchase arms and ammunition for the now virtually hopeless Royalist cause. In January 1644 the Scottish army had entered England as allies of Parliament. In return, the parliamentarians signed a Covenant abolishing the English Church and introducing Presbyterianism. Then on June 14, 1645, Charles lost the decisive battle of the war at Naseby.

Thus when Randal and Kate travelled to Brussels in the spring of 1645 they went for personal benefit. Certainly this was the view of the Spanish envoy at Brussels. Their advent created considerable excitement, not on account of Randal but because of his wife, "Antrim is married to the widow of Buckingham" King Philip of Spain was informed. The general opinion in the capital of the Spanish Netherlands was that Antrim allowed himself to be much influenced by his wife, the Duchess of Buckingham. They were entertained lavishly by the Spanish court and at the start Brussels provided a nostalgic, fleeting return to the elegant life at Charles' court in the thirties. A deal was reached. The Spaniards would provide two frigates in return for a negotiated number of Antrim's battle-seasoned clansmen. However, Randal soon departed for Ireland, leaving Kate to tie up the loose ends.

The reason for Randal's sudden flight may have been word of the arrival of a papal nuncio in Ireland. Archbishop Rinuccini, nephew of a cardinal, had been sent by Pope Innocent X to work with the Confederates at Kilkenny to secure the victory of Catholicism in Ireland. He had come over laden with money and arms as well as prestige and the Pope himself could not have received a more rapturous reception from the Irish Catholics. It was this splendid personage with whom Randal hoped to ally.

Kate's husband had ambitions to play a leading role in the Confederacy but he knew he was not trusted by the Confederates. Kate laid this distrust at the feet of the Irish Catholic bishops who were very influential on the supreme council of the Confederacy. In their view, Randal was too closely linked with the Protestant Royalists whose primary aim was an Ireland controlled by King Charles, with some religious privileges for the Irish population: this was the position of the Lord Lieutenant, the Marquis of Ormond. For their part, the bishops wished only to see a Catholic Ireland free of England. Before departing for Brussels Kate had remarked to the Royalist Ormond "My lord is believed so much the King's creature as I was told by good hands that was the reason they would not trust him." Allying with the papal nuncio could buttress Randal's position at Kilkenny. The Irish bishops would take their lead from the nuncio.

The Confederates were split into two factions. On the one hand, were those, mainly the Catholic Old English, who wanted to sign on to Ormond's plan to make peace with the Royalists even though the latter offered little for the Catholic religion. On the other hand, the new nuncio challenged Royalist policies claiming they were not in Ireland's best interests. The Irish clergy and the Old Irish families followed the nuncio in demanding an Irish Catholic state. Randal had turned against Ormond as a false friend and threw in his lot with the nuncio. From Kilkenny he instructed Kate not to send her letters through Ormond's hands: "Ormond and I be not upon good terms."

Meanwhile Kate, left alone in Brussels, was living in virtual poverty. She was reduced to pleading for a pension or a loan from the Flemish and Spanish officials in Brussels who were deaf to her pleas, suspecting her of being a spy for France. Brussels and Antwerp were filled with English Royalists in exile and, impelled literally by hunger, the proud Duchess went cap in hand to these as a last resort. Like herself they were reduced to penury having left all their worldly wealth behind when they fled the new powers in England. Moreover, her reputation as a friend of the Irish rebels precluded even a dinner invitation. Kate did not blame Randal. Their plight was a tragedy of civil war and revolution that had turned their lives upside down.

Randal, now leading his troops in Scotland, apologized abjectly for his inability to send her money. He sent plenty of sincere affection, however: "I am only yours or God forsake me, your own Randal." He begged her "to be cheerful though I grieve for us both." As he had throughout their marriage, he turned to Kate for advice. "I will follow your advice concerning the nuncio," Randal wrote on the tenth of January 1646. This was a bitter letter from one who felt he had sacrificed much in the royal cause all for nothing. Henceforth, he would just look after their own interests not those of the King, he told Kate. The Royalist cause was lost so they must make peace with Parliament "as other of the King's friends have done." The King must make peace upon any terms, and he asked Kate to be sure to make "our peace with the Parliament." Having great faith in her influence, he asked her to see they were "not forgot" in the peace. In short, this letter informed

Kate that they were abandoning the lost royal cause. In May 1646 King Charles surrendered to the Scottish army, the ally of his enemies, and was a prisoner in their camp in the north of England.

Although King Charles was defeated and she no longer had a commission, Kate proceeded to close the deal with the Spaniards: in return for the two frigates she undertook to send 1200 soldiers from the Antrim estates. Meanwhile, her financial situation was desperate. Salvation came through her religion. Taking her dire plight to the Bishop of Ghent, that kind cleric arranged for her to take refuge in the English Benedictine convent in Ghent.

For fifteen months she lived as a lady pensioner at the convent. She was not an enclosed nun, she could come and go if she wished but, as it happened, she relished the cloistered life. After a lifetime of extraordinary wealth and privilege she seemed to have found deep contentment in humility and self-abnegation. Observing her piety, the nuns said among themselves that this great lady would join them if she did not have the obligations of a married woman. Moved by religious fervour, Kate occupied herself by writing Meditations, six in all. These prayers represent a complete repudiation of her life as a duchess and heiress. In the first Meditation she laments that "living in the world" hindered her from "the practice of mental prayer and vocal, filling my thoughts full of distractions." In the second, she castigates herself for over-valuing "human praise." Henceforth she would "make fierce war against myself ... endeavouring to be pleased when anything is spocken to my prejudis," adding parenthetically ("though not true"). In clear reference to the years with Buckingham when she repudiated Catholicism she resolved to speak out boldly for her religion whomever it may displease. In the third Meditation she proposed to live simply when she left the convent, "although my condition should be in as great plenty as ever it was." Indeed, she had lived in the lap of luxury and in the end all had vanished. Henceforth she would live as the Saviour had done:

> "I will be less curious in my meat, furnuture of howses, and attendance, being confident this brings a habit of pride in my hart which maks it uncapable toreceve my Saviour, who contemned these worldly greatnesses as vaine, idele, and unfit for his servants, being erringes to a soule that desiers to goe forward in the practis of vertu & never to runne in deat [=debt] for anything which is a convenience."

The fourth and fifth Meditations are intended to remove the fault of pride, something "I more than any stand in need of." Following Christ's example of washing the feet of Judas, she promises to perform acts of humility, she will "bear disrespects even from servants." She resolves never to expect to be treated according to her quality. Clearly the lack of respect she has endured in recent years has hurt her deeply - she uses a symbol to indicate from whence this disrespect has come without naming it - and she begs God to fortify her in this resolve "or all this will prove nothing."

After this purpos I found myself as mery and cheerfull as ever I was in my life, being before sad at my ill treatment."

This Meditation is personally revealing. It shows the Duchess's bitterness at the "ill usage and disrespect" (her own words) that she had received after a lifetime of privilege and honour and her "sadness at such ill treatment." She claims to be the victim of an unnamed "enemy faction" for whom she uses a symbol. Who were these enemies? Certainly Randal had not received the honour he was entitled to in her view and as she had said to Wentworth those who injure him injure her. The unidentified enemy was probably the now Duke of Ormonde, Randal's former ally, who had let down her darling and consequently herself. As Lord Lieutenant of Ireland Ormonde had teemed up with the Protestant Royalists and sought a peace with the Irish Catholic Confederates by offering some religious concessions. For his part, Randal had lined up with the Papal Nuncio in opposing any settlement less than complete autonomy for a Catholic Ireland and was, consequently, in the enemy's camp. Kate had been shunned by the officialdom in Dublin. Moreover, her wealth had melted in the heat of civil war in England and revolution in Ireland to say nothing of her own extravagance, thus the world being what it was even those who were not her political enemies no longer bent the knee to her. Kate had come to the realization that wealth and position was a poor foundation to build a life on. Nevertheless she underestimates or even ignores the charity she had unfailingly dispensed throughout her changing circumstances.

She concludes her meditations with a simple vow never to despise the poor because God chose for Jesus's mother and foster father two poor people who had to live by their labours.

Kate's soul-satisfying interlude in the convent came to an end when Randal prevailed upon Rinuccini to send the money for her passage to Ireland. In his battle for the heart of the Irish Catholics the papal nuncio felt obliged to satisfy this important follower. Once again Kate was reunited with her beloved Randal. But his desperate activities kept them separated more often than together. Much of his time was spent on battlefields in Scotland or at Kilkenny where he opposed a treaty with the Royalists.

Nevertheless, in March 1648 the Confederacy named him with two other delegates to go to Henrietta Maria's court of exiles in Paris to find a protector for the Irish Catholics; one idea was to have the Queen enlist the Pope. Randal seems to have stolen a march on the other two, going ahead in the company of a Cistercian monk named Patrick Crelly. Crelly was one of those men of mystery who acted as spies under cover of religion. His business with Antrim was to keep him from lending his fading power to Ormond's Royalists – no danger of that with Randal's jealousy of Ormond. Randal wrote Kate asking her to accept the monk as a reliable ally. Crelly showered Kate with letters to some of which she responded. While in France Randal had a nervous breakdown, the result of his frantic attempts to stay on top of the chaotic events of his time. Kate on the other hand was a tower of strength, bearing up even when she learned that her beautiful son Francis had perished in the civil war over in England.

CHAPTER TWENTY-FOUR

When Randal returned to Ireland in July 1648 he joined Kate at Wexford on the Irish coast where the couple now made their home. It was the two frigates traded by the Spaniards in payment for the Irish mercenaries that was providing their living. Privateering was rampant up and down the coast and Randal had decided to use the frigates to go into that profitable business. Shortly he was able to add four more vessels to his fleet. Although money from the sale of goods taken from the prize ships was supposed to go into the coffers of the Confederacy, Randal ordered his captains to hand it over to the Duchess during his frequent long absences. Kate, in fact, administered "the most profitable and largest privateering operation during the later 1640s." Unfortunately for the Antrims, a parliamentary blockade put an end to the privateering.

Unlike those Royalists who remained loyal and were already planning to renew the lost civil war, Randal was filled with rancour against Charles because he had thwarted his ambitions. Encouraged by Kate, he had nurtured the hope of becoming Lord Lieutenant of Ireland and when Charles from his captivity reappointed the now Duke of Ormonde, Randal turned against the King with finality. In late 1648 he launched a rebellion of his clansmen against the Lord Lieutenant of Ireland. His declared reason was that Ormonde had surrendered Dublin to the Protestant English Parliament to the ruin of Irish hopes. Thus he claimed to be leading a Catholic crusade but in reality his revolt against Ormonde was for little other reason than jealousy. "Ormonde is no friend to me," he reminded Kate bitterly.

After the predictable failure of his rebellion Randal went into hiding. Kate was left alone, unwell at Wexford. It was the common opinion that considering her long recognized influence over her husband she had been responsible for the unfortunate event. "I be sorry for the poor lady," a neighbouring Irish noble wrote the Lord Lieutenant, "though she be guilty of his late folly." Her own son, the young Duke in exile in France, apologized to Lord Ormonde for "her follies which no man censures more than I." It would seem from such first-hand testimony that Kate was the moving force behind Randal's rebellion. There can be no doubt that she bore a strong grudge against Ormonde just as she had against his predecessor Wentworth. Neither had been friends to Randal, blocking him at every turn. Given her protective love for Randal, she regarded them, not without reason, as enemies to herself as well. This leaves little doubt that the unidentified person or persons indicated by a symbol in her Fifth Meditation who showed her such painful disrespect was Lord Ormonde and his circle. Clearly, the good intentions in her Meditations, to be humble, to love her enemies, etc. had evaporated once she left the convent.

On the other hand, the Christian virtue of caritas remained her guiding light. The charitableness that was second nature to her made Kate find the money to ransom two Irish lairds who had fought in Randal's misguided rebellion.

After his defeat, Randal made his way back to Wexford, eluding his foes. He found Kate very ill, emaciated and unable to rise from her bed. She did her best to rouse herself but languor overpowered her. She saw well enough, however, that Randal was a shattered, almost broken man. Gone was the bravado with which he had started out. He was suffering pangs of remorse for what he had done to his clansmen endlessly repeating that he had called them out, that he had not had the guns to arm them but nevertheless they had gone into battle with swords bravely roaring the age old war cries and were mowed down by Ormonde's musketeers and cavalry. Did he recognize Kate's dire influence (so obvious to others) in such self-reproach? The dreadful self-inflicted tragedy had aged him. The red hair was threaded with grey. Unable to express herself in words, Kate squeezed his hand in sympathy - and perhaps in apology.

Seeing how ill Kate was, Randal wrote a letter to Ormonde begging his erstwhile enemy to send a renowned Dublin doctor to her. "I beg this favour upon my knees," he wrote, and he asked the Lord Lieutenant to do it not for his sake but for her son's sake, "which will be of much more force than argument by your excellence's humble servant."

At the beginning of 1649 news arrived from England that King Charles had been beheaded by the all-powerful army as an enemy of the state. England had become a republic under the strong man Oliver Cromwell. Kate in her sickbed was horrified. Her mind returned to the glory days when "Steenie" and "Baby Charles" had been closer than brothers. Scene after scene passed before her eyes. She hoped that the two inseparable friends would meet in Heaven but, alas, she believed there could be no Heaven for Protestants. As for herself she had no fear of the after life. Indeed, Catholicism was her comfort. "I would pour out my life in defence of it," she once told Rinuccini. And perhaps she had.

Randal's next appeal for money to the Lord Lieutenant was even more desperate. The triumphant English general, Oliver Cromwell, had invaded Ireland with a large force of his Roundheads, determined to put down the rebellious Irish once and for all. He attacked the port of Drogheda, laying waste the town and butchering the inhabitants. He made no secret that Wexford was next. Randal hurriedly moved Kate to Waterford, but with no certainty that town would be safe from attack he wrote to Ormonde pleading for money. His "good woman" he said, "must be forced for security to move further and if the danger increases she must part this kingdom." Her son George had offered her a home with him in France, and she was planning to go when death claimed the Duchess. Her fatal illness was diagnosed as "the flux" – most likely dysentery.

Randal was devastated. The only thing he could do for his "dear old duchess" now was to give her a decent burial. Forlornly, he again begged Ormonde for money so he could "perform the last office I owe unto a friend so dear unto me."

Before she died did Kate know that Randal had contacted Cromwell, seeking to win the favour of the new power in the three kingdoms of England, Scotland and Ireland? Would she have approved? It may well be that in her dying days she returned in spirit to the unworldly Flemish convent and banished all thought of the vicious politics that plagued her own life and times.

Kate was not to be laid to rest beside her first husband, the Great Duke of Buckingham, under the magnificent monument she had built for him in Westminster Abbey though her effigy lies beside him for all to see. Nor would she lie beside her second husband, the Marquis of Antrim. After her death Randal was to marry a daughter of his kinfolk the O'Neills, but on his death in 1683 he would be buried alone in the Macdonnell family vault his father had built in the church at Bonamargy.

Katherine Manners, a duchess and once the richest heiress in England, was buried modestly outside the walls of Waterford.

About the Author

Lita-Rose Betcherman received her doctorate in 17thC British history from the University of Toronto. She has published extensively in academic journals, and University of Toronto Press has published her notable works on Canadian social history and biography.

Other books by Lita-Rose Betcherman:

Court Lady and Country Wife: Two Noble Sisters in 17th Century England (HarperCollins)

Buckingham's Man: Balthazar Gerbier (Bev Editions)

The Riviera Set: From Queen Victoria to Princess Grace (Bev Editions)

Reds Under the Bed: How Communists Frightened the Canadian Establishment, 1928-32 (Bev Editions)

The Swastika and the Maple Leaf (Bev Editions)

Thank you for reading The Richest Girl in England.

If you enjoyed this book, tell us what you think! Leave a review at your favourite ebook retailer, tweet us @beveditions, or tell us on facebook. If you want to read more ebooks by Lita-Rose, head to our website beveditions.com

Printed in Great Britain
by Amazon